Covenant, Community, and the Common Good

D0022211

COVENANT, COMMUNITY, AND THE COMMON GOOD

An Interpretation of Christian Ethics

Eric Mount Jr.

The Pilgrim Press
Cleveland, Ohio

BJ
1251
.M665
1999

The Pilgrim Press, Cleveland, Ohio 44115
© 1999 by Eric Mount Jr.

Excerpted from Eric Mount Jr., "The Currency of Covenant," in *The Annual of the Society of Christian Ethics, 1996*. Reprinted by permission. • Excerpted from Eric Mount Jr., "Homing In on Family Values: The Family, Religion, and Culture Series," *Theology Today* 55, no. 1 (April 1998): 77–89. Reprinted by permission. • Adapted from Eric Mount Jr., "European Community and Global Community," *Soundings* 79, nos. 3–4 (fall/winter 1996): 365–83. Reprinted by permission. • Excerpt from Wendell Berry's 1978 commencement address at Centre College reprinted by permission of the author.

Biblical quotations are from the New Revised Standard Version of the Bible, © 1989 by the Division of Christian Education of the National Council of Churches of Christ in the U.S.A., and are used by permission. Adaptations have been made for inclusivity.

All rights reserved. Published 1999

Printed in the United States of America on acid-free paper

04 03 02 01 00 99   5 4 3 2 1

Library of Congress Cataloging-in-Publication Data

Mount, Eric.
    Covenant, community, and the common good : an interpretation of Christian ethics / Eric Mount, Jr.
        p. cm.
    Includes bibliographical references and index.
    ISBN 0-8298-1355-1 (pbk. : alk. paper)
    1. Christian ethics.   2. Covenants—Religious aspects—Christianity.
    3. Community—Religious aspects—Christianity.   4. Common good—Religious aspects—Christianity.   I. Title.
    BJ1251.M665   1999
    241—dc21   99-34475
                                                                      CIP

JESUIT - KRAUSS - McCORMICK - LIBRARY
1100 EAST 55th STREET
CHICAGO, ILLINOIS 60615

Dedicated to our grandchildren and their generation's future:

William Mount Nisbet
Matthew Lander Nisbet
Sarah Truly Nisbet
Benjamin Mount Grimes
Ellis Truly Grimes
Eric Evans Grimes
and any others to come

CONTENTS

ACKNOWLEDGMENTS

Once again, and perhaps more than ever, a book of mine is a gift as much as it is an accomplishment. The prominence of covenant as a theme in my last book, *Professional Ethics in Context: Institutions, Images, and Empathy*, could prompt me to begin by thanking the people who made that contribution possible and accorded it an affirmative reception. Instead, I begin with 1992–93, the year that my French-teaching wife, Truly, and I spent directing Centre-in-Europe in Strasbourg, France. That experience, made possible by Centre College's generosity and tolerance, led to a paper and then to an article in *Soundings* entitled "European Community and Global Community: A View from Alsace and Beyond," which bears marked resemblance to the fifth chapter of this book. Centre College, the people who selected papers for the 1995 annual meeting of the Society of Christian Ethics, and Ralph Norman, the editor of *Soundings*, are therefore important and appreciated contributors to this project.

At that same meeting of the Society of Christian Ethics, Douglas Ottati and Douglas Schuurman, the conveners of the Covenant Ethics Group, asked me to write one of the four articles for the "Professional Resources" section of the 1996 *Annual* of the Society dealing with our group's theme. My task was to survey recent and current Christian ethics literature on covenant, and that endeavor was what ultimately led to this book. My sabbatical leave at Vanderbilt (winter–spring 1996) gave me the opportunity and the resources to complete that assignment. Centre College (again), Richard Zaner, director of Vanderbilt's Center for Clinical and Research Ethics, and Joseph Hough, dean of the Vanderbilt Divinity School, deserve particular thanks for affording me that opportunity. Joe also read a draft of what became "The Currency of Covenant" in the *Annual* and made useful suggestions, and such other colleagues in the Society of Christian Ethics as William Everett and Max Stackhouse provided helpful bibliographical tips before the writing began. It was also because of the Vanderbilt sabbatical

x   Acknowledgments

that I developed greater knowledge of Edward Farley's work, which in turn influenced the book as it developed later.

The chance to develop and air my covenantal explorations with a live audience appeared due to the invitation to be one of three lecturers at the Interpreting the Faith conference at Union Theological Seminary in Virginia in the summer of 1996. Douglas Ottati and Charles Swezey were, I am confident, instrumental in my receiving that invitation. I entitled those lectures "Covenant Ethics," and with them the general contours of this book began to emerge. I am therefore indebted not only to the friends that got me invited, but also to my fellow lecturers, Rebecca Chopp and Dean McBride, and the hardy souls who listened to the three of us all day long for a week. Rebecca set something in motion there in Richmond that she may now have cause to regret. It was she who commented privately to me that what I was presenting was going to make "such a good book." You do not forget encouragement like that from someone of her stature and accomplishments, and the book idea was born.

The common good side of the project got its boost when a paper proposal of mine was accepted for a section of the southeast regional meeting of the American Academy of Religion in March 1997. Pilgrim Press editor Timothy Staveteig asked to see a copy. After he assessed the way I linked covenant and common good in that paper and the other work I was doing on covenant, he expressed interest in my developing a book. Had he not taken that initiative and offered that encouragement, I doubt that this book would exist, as least not yet. He deserves the largest measure of credit for the book's being completed as soon as it has been, although he bears no responsibility for its deficiencies.

Although I did not realize it immediately, another boost came from Patrick Miller, co-editor of *Theology Today*. If an old friend had not asked me to write a review article on eight of the volumes in the Religion, Family, and Culture Series, edited by Don Browning and Ian Evison, I would have declined the request because of the time commitment involved. It turned out, however, that reading those volumes was a further stimulus to the project rather than another diversion. Both the content of the series and the response of the authors to my review were assets in the evolution of the manuscript.

As the actual writing of the book unfolded, several of my Centre faculty colleague-friends provided me with helpful leads and materials—notably Rick Axtell, my fellow ethicist in the religion program, Brian Cooney in philosophy, Nayef Samhat in government and international relations, and Milton Scarborough in philosophy and religion. When I had a draft to review, my wife, Truly, our third daughter, Marcia Mount Shoop, in the midst of her doctoral studies in theology and ethics at Emory, and Rick read it all under tight time constraints and provided invaluable observations, questions, and encouragement. My student assistant, Kerry Rhoads, did patient and painstaking work on the notes. Our divisional faculty secretaries, Patsy McAfee and Barbara Ludack, and our director of communications, Mike Norris, made sure that no technological troubles daunted the conversion and delivery of the disks. Recent Centre graduate Sarah Cantrell assisted with proofreading and indexing, and Barbara Ludack typed the index at crunch time. Discretionary funds from the Rodes Professorship in Religion that I currently hold have covered any expenses that the project has entailed. Kelley Baker and Ed Huddleston of The Pilgrim Press were most efficient and genial facilitators of the venture at numerous junctures.

All of these people and institutions and others have provided me not only the opportunity, but also the encouragement and support required to write this book. Each contribution that I have mentioned was an occasion for gratitude at the time, but as I look back at the number and importance of these gifts, I am even more grateful and even more cognizant of my indebtedness than before. In the end, my greatest indebtedness is to my family—wife, four daughters, four sons-in-law, and six grandchildren. I have already referred to some specific instances of assistance, and readers will find other references in the chapters that follow, but there is more to be said. In a manner that goes beyond specific acts of assistance or specific citations as examples, these people have been sources of stimulation and insight that have shaped the contents of the book, and sources of loving confidence that has fostered the completion of the book.

In a sense, I wrote this book for them, but in a more painful sense I did this book to them. They were the ones from whom the time was taken to get this job done. Above all, it was my beloved partner of forty years, Truly, who both shared and suffered the work in progress. It is she and our Boykin spaniel, Mattie, who are happiest to see the project completed and most responsible for whatever measure of sanity I maintained during the crunch of meeting the deadlines.

That the people whom I have mentioned cared enough to make this book possible matters more to me than the book's publication. At a time in my career when no one was suggesting that I needed to write another book to please my institution or anyone else, colleagues, friends, and loved ones have given me an opportunity that I could hardly refuse, and one that makes the sacrifice exacted by this venture worth the trouble.

Introduction

Covenant, community, and common good have not suddenly become important context-setting and normative concepts for ethical discourse. These terms are all carriers of substantial and lengthy traditions. Covenant is a distinctively, though not exclusively, Hebraic metaphor and model that locates the relational self in a community of identity, promise, and obligation with God and neighbor. It is distinguishable from both the individualistic and the organic trajectories of Greek thought in the West in that the first makes the self atomistic and the second makes the self incidental, not essential to the whole. In Christian ethics, covenant has figured most prominently in Protestant ethics, especially in the Reformed tradition, but it has assumed growing importance in Roman Catholic ethics in recent decades.[1] Chapter 1 is devoted to this tradition.

The end or norm of the common good has roots in Plato, Aristotle, and Cicero. Because of the influence of Aristotle, it is not surprising that Thomas Aquinas assigns considerable importance and broader political implications to it, and the concept assumes prominence in the papal encyclicals and speeches of Pius XI, Leo XIII, John XXIII, and John Paul II. Thus it is primarily a Catholic legacy that now has numerous Protestant proponents.[2] Chapter 2 discusses this tradition.

Like the covenant tradition but more organic in its understanding of community, the norm of the common good limits individual pursuit of private happiness by setting the self in a corporate body whose well-being takes precedence over that of any single member. Once again the self is communal. Use of one's property is subject to the constraints of the common good; each person should be enabled and obliged to contribute to the common good; and public authority has both the role of defining it and the responsibility of promoting it.

Both traditions then affirm the centrality of community and resist the extremes and neglects of Western individualism with its suspicion of any effort to advance a common good because of plural versions of the good and its tendency to make all associations voluntary and contractual. Users of covenant language express varied levels of comfort with the Enlightenment tradition of liberal individualism. All of these endorse liberalism's insistence on the dignity and worth of the individual and yet believe that the language of individual rights should at least be balanced by the obligations and responsibilities of life in community. Some remain liberals in making the individual the starting point of ethics, while others prefer to call themselves communitarians because they oppose elevating the individual over the good of the social group or community.

After communitarians begin with concern for the kind of community that we want to be, the question of which community we mean and how it relates to the larger civil society makes for great variations. Sectarian communitarians such as Alasdair MacIntyre and Stanley Hauerwas set themselves most adamantly against liberalism and focus on the tradition, identity, and shared values found in smaller communities, religious and otherwise, that stand in contrast to the isolated self in pursuit of self-interest that epitomizes classical liberalism. They do not try to address the common good of society in general or explore a consensus among the various communities within society.[3]

Against both classical liberalism and this sectarian communitarianism, Ronald Thiemann and others set revisionist liberalism. Liberalism as they conceive it can be made compatible with "a socially constituted self, a community-based notion of virtue, and a conception of the good adequate to a pluralist society."[4] Liberalism for them is not a comprehensive philosophical doctrine, but a way of designating a set of practices that justify the core values of liberty, equality, and toleration or mutual respect that the American founders upheld. Sectarian communitarians, according to liberals, risk junking the liberal tradition but providing nothing to replace it that overcomes the communitarian tendencies toward elitist communities and cohesion around a common enemy as the reason for surrendering individual interests.[5] As Thiemann explains, these revisionists are "seeking a middle way," "a dialectical balance between individual liberty and communal solidarity."[6] Neither classical liberalism nor sectarian communitarianism provides such a balance by itself.

There are also what we might call societal communitarians who are seeking this balance. Giving priority to communal solidarity based on a shared heritage and shared values, they focus on the kind of society we want to have as a nation or even as a world. Without trying to nail down what the common good is, they argue for the necessity of shared values (such as the liberty, equality, and toleration of which liberals speak) and a shared language that make possible a continuing conversation about the common good as a work in progress. Amitai Etzioni, Michael Sandel, Douglas Sturm, Gary Dorrien, and Robert Bellah and his coauthors of *Habits of the Heart* and *The Good Society* are examples of this kind of communitarian. Some are hard to categorize. For example, Charles Taylor of the liberal revisionists is sometimes linked with societal communitarianism of this sort, and Michael Walzer has been placed in both groups.[7]

Classical liberals may speak of the utility or greatest total economic benefit that results from free trade in the global market, but the common good goes otherwise undefined and really should not be further defined in their view. Proponents of some other definition of the common good could all be labeled communitarians although they vary greatly. They all put shared values and achievement of a good society or community at the center. Their variations emerge over the means of its determination and its tolerance for difference. Some ethicists shy away from combining the languages of covenant and common good because they fear that elevating the common good could involve a sacrifice of individual rights and respect for difference. These very concerns have also occasioned criticisms of the covenant tradition, as we shall see.

The liberal–communitarian debate is by now a staple item in social ethics. It seems less important to choose a label than to find a balance between individual liberty and communal solidarity. Why then say more when so much has already been said and when individualism has a strong contingent of detractors from both revisionist liberals and communitarians? One reason is that the individual pursuit of self-interest still seems largely unchallenged and even resurgent as the driving force of morality in much of our society. Instant individual gratification, individual self-help, and individual success have lost none of their luster as American preoccupations. Nine of ten Americans will marry, and four of five single adults say that they want to be married, but four million Americans are living together instead of tying the knot, and 40 percent of our first marriages end in divorce.[8] We like to be part of a team, but we also like free agency. We want to belong, but we like freedom of movement.[9] Personal self-fulfillment is often seen in tension with community identification and obligation instead of in tandem with them. Making and keeping covenants and promoting the common good may be household words for some, but these same people might not want to take those words out in public.

The covenant tradition and the common-good tradition are not only less than uppermost in the popular mind, but are also under critical scrutiny in the academy from postmodern, feminist, and other liberation perspectives, to name a few. As chapters 1 and 2 elaborate, they are under suspicion as having perpetrated and perpetuated various forms of exclusion, domination, and suppression of difference. The questions cannot be ignored; they must be addressed. Some deconstruction and reconstruction are necessary if the traditions are to remain viable for growing numbers of people.

Perhaps even more unsettling to these traditions is the shaky status now being attributed to all "deep symbols" in our culture, to use Edward Farley's term. Community, identity, purpose, and principle are all at issue when these values are in trouble.[10] Not just the covenant tradition but tradition as such, not just covenantal obligation but the very idea of obligation, not just the common good, but the very idea of the good now require defense. What kind of theological or ethical truth claims are allowable and even thinkable? Can our public discourse be about truth or reality, or can it deal only with competing interests and preferences, polls and market trends?

Our public discourse is also poisoned by the venom of the "family values" conflict that marks our culture wars. Nostalgia may be recalling the family of the past in roseate hues, but there is a widespread sense of loss. Our families seem diminished, if not to have disappeared. They don't eat together. They don't stay together. They can't find time for each other. The supper table has been superseded by the TV, the microwave, the computer, and fast food to go. The search for common ground has at least prompted people of very diverse political persuasions to register themselves as champions of "the family"—acknowledging its importance and promoting its welfare. The debate still rages, however, about what a family is and what true family values are, and the gulf has not closed appreciably on such litmus tests as abortion and same-sex marriage. Covenant, community, and common good are crucial considerations in this values conflict, and chapter 3 makes this connection.

Related to the family values discussion in several ways are issues of work and welfare that are addressed in chapter 4. At the very least, the list would include the friendliness of the workplace to families, the combination of family and work in one's sense of vocation, the weighing and balancing of the competing claims of family and work, and the impact of poverty, unemployment, and the welfare system on the family. The increased pressure to work imposed by welfare reform and the need for two full incomes to maintain a family's standard of living reshape the question about what constitutes good work. These issues in turn connect to covenant, community, and the common good. Can the employer–employee relationship be a covenant instead of a contract in today's downsizing and relocating environment? Are employers' covenants co-option with a velvet glove? Who gets to the table where the real decisions are made? Is the common good even a factor for consideration in the global market, or must it be left to flow inevitably from market forces? Can the workplace be a true community, and how does that community relate to the common good? Should a government have a covenant with all of its citizens to assure the necessary levels of food, shelter, health care, education, and employment or income required for full participation in the economy and the polity, or is the whole notion of a national community a fated fiction? Is there any sense in which we are a national family in which everyone should have a place at the table?

Still another reason to concentrate on covenant, community, and the common good surfaces from the recent attention to civil society in America in both political and academic discussion.[11] Chapter 4 also treats this topic. Conservatives and liberals alike have been decrying the apparent vacuum between the state and the market on the one hand and the individual on the other. Voluntary associations, service clubs, churches, bowling leagues, unions, PTAs, neighborhoods, networks, and political parties that constitute people's communities of conversation and the cells of democratic citizenship have gotten squeezed out by the demands of work and the claims of family. We are consumers of religion, recreation, and politics in search of an immediate individual payoff.[12] Where does the table talk occur that trains us for citizenship and embodies our belonging?

The enemy in this discussion is alternately, and sometimes simultaneously, identified as the government or the state, the market, or feminism. The government is depicted as intervening increasingly in our lives and ignoring or even usurping the role of family, neighborhood, church, and other voluntary associations. The market is depicted as destroying workplace community through downsizing and relocation, eroding the family, and swallowing the small, intimate centers of commerce with megabanks, Wal-Marts, and multinational corporations. Feminism is depicted as emptying the home and the voluntary associations of the women who "manned" them. The language about what we have lost and the civic virtue we need— trust, reciprocity, mutual obligation, responsibility, fraternity, solidarity, and love—sounds very covenantal. And the laments about a "decivilized" America suggest a concern about the future of the common good if we forget how to be a democracy because we don't go to practice anymore.

On the global scene, which is the focus of chapter 5, we are likewise plagued by questions about the nature of the communities we inhabit and seek. Clashes among narrow nationalistic communitarian expressions, integration in regional economic "communities" in a global market of former enemies and fierce competitors, and efforts to recognize and/or promote global community create divided loyalties. With the vaunted end of East–West confrontation, North–South tensions and inequalities have assumed center stage. Are our economic agreements and communities, such as the European Union, the General Agreement on Tariffs and Trade, and the North American Free Trade Agreement, harbingers of a true global community or hazards to the common good of the whole human and nonhuman membership in the family of beings? How can the welfare of particular communities and of the global community of communities both get their due? Is there or can there be a universal covenant and a universal common good? Are the traces of a global civil society signs of a new kind of international conference table where global community is fostered?

In light of these current realities, this book is an effort to explore the continuing importance of covenant, community, and common good as relational and conceptual framers of moral discourse. The discussion is not offered merely as a public service, however. I have a personal stake in the importance of covenant, community, and common good. That tiny band of souls that has followed my scholarly work will know that the themes of intersubjective or relational selfhood, covenant advocacy, institutional well-being, and feminist critiques of both covenant and common good have occupied my serious if divided attention. I care professionally about being involved in both the deconstruction and the reconstruction of these important concepts. I see the traditions in question as continuing conversations, not as fixed deposits.

An even more intimate personal investment also warms me to the task at hand. Covenant, community, and common good describe a way of life that is more inclusive than professional interest. When I look at the legacy of family, church, education, and community involvement that I inherited and absorbed, I see these themes embedded there. The forty years of marriage that my spouse and I have shared, the nearly forty years that we have shared as parents and now grandparents, the more than thirty years that we have invested in one college (my grandfather's college), the generations of Presbyterian ministers and elders behind the two of us, and the untold hours of involvement in community service of various kinds define us as people of covenant and community who care about the common good. What I understand about human love, religious faith, moral responsibility, vocational commitment, and civic virtue is connected to covenants. The enduring and joyful faithfulness to the people we love, the work we do, the larger community we inhabit, and, yes, the God whose common grace and special grace make all of these fidelities responses to gift—these are what give life meaning and melody. We are known by the covenants that we keep—and break. The explorations of this book may appear to be a scholarly exercise, but they emanate from personal experience and constitute a personal testimony. Covenants are our schools of faithfulness, communities our laboratories of love and justice, conversations about the common good our practices of hope, as chapter 6 elaborates in discussing schools of virtue.

We find ourselves in nonchosen associations that shape us profoundly. These communities or groupings in which we are set place us familially, religiously, economically, educationally, politically, racially, ethnically, and sexually in connections that we may sometimes escape or reject but not instigate. People mired in poverty or plagued with disabilities rightly remind us how limited choices may be. We cannot shed our skins, for example, although we may change racial identification culturally. We can move out of many of our affiliations, but we do not start from scratch. The identities shaped by these connections in turn dispose us toward other associations that we may embrace or resist. We are carriers of a communal past with conditioned freedom to shed excess baggage and take on new burdens of identification and responsibility. Our covenants are given and chosen. Our community membership is unavoidable but escapable. Our connection to the common good is undeniable but continually redefinable. Our freedom is real, but it has to start somewhere.

These pages ask us to take stock of where we are and what we want to become as persons in community. How do we find that dialectical balance between commonality and difference, between community and freedom? At issue is not simply the location of a comfortable philosophical or political niche. We are dealing rather with our very humanity, with reality, with the health of our communities. The traditions captured in the language of covenant and common good are gifts that we cannot any longer take for granted. They are also resources that we ignore to our impoverishment and even to our peril. At their worst, they do serious damage. At their best, they designate an ongoing conversation by communities about identity, participation, responsibility, and respect for individual uniqueness. This "table talk" is made possible by covenants, and the talk itself is a common good that attends to table size and shape, to table fare, and to table manners.

I

The Currency of Covenant

Words of power, that is, deep and enduring symbols that shape the values of a society and guide the life of faith, morality, and action, are subject to powerful forces of discreditation and even disenchantment. This thesis applies not only to certain selected deep symbols but to the very idea of deep symbols. If this is so, we must either find ways to recover their power or live without them. But are the deep symbols of the past recoverable? Are they like an endangered species that has passed the point of no return: Have they simply disappeared with the village blacksmith and cobblestone streets? Or do they offer themselves for reenchantment? The answer is not a trivial one.[1]

—Edward Farley, *Deep Symbols: Their Postmodern Effacement and Reclamation*

If there are reasons to believe that all deep symbols are shaky these days, there is no reason to think that *covenant* enjoys an exemption. In fact, it may not only have shared jeopardy with certain other words of power; it may have special problems of its own. What is more, it just may be that some of its problems lie at the root of the general disenchantment and that a reenchantment could work wonders for the words that Farley treats in his discussion—namely, tradition, obligation, reality, law, and hope.

Covenant as Common Currency in American Culture

Any roll call of deep symbols or words of power in our culture's past would have to include *covenant*. Farley calls it a "primary term," as distinguished from a deep symbol that is connected to a variety of terms, but it is clear that there is a cluster of other terms that express values and virtues related to covenant.[2] *Obligation, commitment, promise, responsibility, fidelity*, and *vocation* would be strong candidates for the short list and for further mention in these explorations. The point now, however, is to explore the judgment that *covenant* merits a place of equal importance on the deep symbols list and the endangered species list.

Covenant as a Deep Symbol

Choosing to flag covenant's power in the American past does not mean, as Farley explains, that it is being called an archetype from the collective unconscious after the manner of Carl Jung. Nor is it being offered as a cross-cultural image reflecting common social experience. Deep symbols are more community-specific than that. They arise out of a particular community's history. Make no mistake, there is something virtually universal about human experience that is expressed in covenant making and breaking. As H. Richard Niebuhr has observed, "The fidelity which is trusted is that peculiar element in personality without which selves—though feeling, knowing and desiring subjects—are not selves. It is the mode of self-existence which comes to appearance in the making, keeping and breaking of promises, in the acts of loyalty and treason of which selves are capable and in which they exist."[3] What is more, one can cite, as Daniel Elazar has, examples of other contractual and constitutional societies with covenant flavor outside of the biblical tradition and the American experience. He gives the examples of covenant-style oath societies in ancient Norway and Ireland that were destroyed by Christianization and of what can be discovered about Cheyenne society through the filter of missionary renditions.

Despite such examples, Elazar still finds no "developed covenantal tradition that is not derived from the Bible," which is the source of American covenantalism.[4] For our present purposes, all we need is an admission that any semi-sensitive journey down the American memory lane would find covenant not merely among the landmarks but among the hallmarks of this national experiment. If deep symbols are the shared values of a community that provide identity, purpose, and moral guidance, covenant has clearly qualified in the past.

A classic placement of covenant where it belonged in our nation's foundational centuries was provided by H. Richard Niebuhr in his 1953 presentation to the American Historical Association, "The Idea of Covenant and American Democracy."[5] He noted the close correspondence and dialectical relationship among people's views of themselves, their society, and the cosmos—in other words, among their ethics, their politics, and their religion, or among their psychology, their sociology, and their metaphysics. For example, organic models likened the human body, the body politic, and the cosmic whole. Selves belonged to organic wholes of kinship and geographical location by birth rather than choice. Nature, human nature, and divine nature mirrored each other's fertility, vitality, and order. Medieval society saw everything in hierarchies; it was pecking orders all the way down to the composition of the self. The seventeenth century brought the mechanical model into a dominant position; Newtonian physics seeped into everything. The reigning image at the time Niebuhr was writing was that of a field of forces. From Freudian psychology to realpolitik, conflict was the norm.

It was not so in America's most formative years. Writes Niebuhr, "A *fundamental* pattern in American minds in the seventeenth, eighteenth and early nineteenth centuries was the covenant idea, competing with the mechanical pattern and displacing the organic and hierarchical ideas."[6] The sources of what surfaces on these shores primarily as a Puritan idea can be traced to Calvin and other Reformed sources and to the development of contract law and commercial companies, but the Bible was the primary point of origin, and the pervasive knowledge of the Bible in early American society stamped the American character. Associations based on nature (marriage and family) or on contractual merging of interests were alike transformed by the addition of covenant or promise. In Niebuhr's words,

> The question was not whether society has a natural or a contract origin but to what extent every society becomes truly human and truly a society within the cosmic society by having the moral dimension, or the covenant character added to it. . . .
>
> Covenant meant that political society was neither purely natural nor merely contractual, based on common interest. Covenant was the binding together in one body politic of persons who assumed through unlimited promise responsibility to and for each other and for the common laws, under God. It was government of the people, for the people and by the people but always under God, and it was not natural birth into natural society that made one a complete member of the people but always the moral act of taking upon oneself, through promise, the responsibilities of a citizenship that bound itself in the very exercise of its freedom.[7]

The promise was not minimal but unlimited, and the bond was located under God, not merely among contracting citizens.

Niebuhr refrained from judging the extent to which covenant formed the unconscious background of democracy in the mid-twentieth century, and he acknowledged that the unlimited commitment and transcendent cause of covenant tend to degenerate to the limited commitment and mutual advantage of contract, from which it was partly derived. He was certain, however, that a democracy of limited contract was clearly quite different from a covenantal one, and the comparative strength of the two was obvious to him.

Covenant as a Symbol in Peril

Two decades later, Robert Bellah was convinced that the American covenant was broken, perhaps irreparably. There were, he believed, two Americas from the start. People came to these shores seeking both wealth and salvation. Coexisting in the souls of most Americans were a drive toward personal success and a zeal for the public good. The pursuit of happiness and the quest for social justice balanced each other when civil religion served its prophetic function as a national corrective rather than its perverse function as a sanctimonious cloak for narrow national interest.[8]

When the cancerous form of individualism that he and his coauthors diagnosed in *Habits of the Heart* took over, the health of the body politic was imperiled. Discourse about the common good and about social justice became at best a second language and at worst a foreign language. For both the biblical individualism of John Winthrop and the civic individualism of Thomas Jefferson, personal identity and fulfillment were inseparable from community membership and responsibility. For the utilitarian individualism of Benjamin Franklin and the expressive individualism of Walt Whitman, the common good could be left to work itself out automatically while people pursued their own economic interests or to be ignored as unimportant while people negotiated acceptable emotional benefits packages in their several associations, relationships, and affiliations. The Bellah team lamented that the latter two individualisms had overwhelmed the former two. In *The Good Society*, Bellah and his coauthors further claim that American society goes begging when individuals fail to pay attention to the institutions in which they unavoidably reside.

Mourning the triumph of contract over covenant and the demise of republican virtue or zeal for the public good in our time should not be interpreted as a naïve and even ominous veneration of a national past littered with the massacres and removal of Native Americans, the offenses of Manifest Destiny, the tortures and torments of slavery, the lynchings and discriminations of Jim Crow, the subordination and oppression of women, and the stigmas, insults, and persecutions of anti-Semitism, nativism, and other ethnic and religious prejudices in our land. If the deep symbol of covenant has played a central role in the American drama, it will have to face blame as well as take credit.

Writing in *Gaia and God*, Rosemary Ruether captures the ambiguity of the covenant legacy: "These biblical and Puritan roots of American national identity are a source of much of the best and the worst in American culture; both notions of America as Elect Nation, especially favored by God to impose its will as divine law upon others, and also movements of prophetic self-criticism and national reform of social evils."[9] These historical realities must be kept in mind in any assessment of the covenant tradition and inform the questions raised about it. Without trying to determine how many of the before-mentioned atrocities and monstrosities and animosities happened because or in spite of the fact that America was covenantal, we are initially observing that the deep symbol of covenant, that biblically rooted word of power, has had an influence and importance in our society in the past that it seems now to have lost. Both Catholic and Protestant church documents still invoke it, some very able ethicists still feature it, President Clinton attempted to revive it, religious marriage services often still implore it, and corporations seem at times to claim it, but covenant language is not the undisputed coin of the realm. When people use it, there seems to be a widespread inclination to bite it to see whether we are dealing with something of real value or a bogus effort to pass off as a viable medium of exchange something that has had its day and been replaced by a different currency.

Edward Farley spells out four features of deep symbols: normativity (expression of transcendent values that direct and correct a community); enchantment (participation in sacred power by pointing to the mystery of all things and of human beings); fallibility (partiality and relativity due to the changes of history and the corruptions of absolutism or idolatry); and location in a master narrative.[10] In view of these dimensions, it just may be that covenant is in trouble across the board. It may be accorded both little or no significance or authority by some and absolute authority in a questionable form by others. In her book *Personal Commitments: Beginning, Keeping, and Changing*, Margaret Farley cautions:

> It seems an obvious thing to do—to focus on the Covenant tradition in an exploration of commitment. Yet serious problems, even enormous pitfalls, beset such a move. The long history of the Covenant tradition's emergence and reapplication has been marked by countless contradictions, and any brief treatment of it today risks not only confusion but damage to individuals and groups.[11]

With the help of such warnings, we need now to undertake some risk assessment and get some estimates on the costs of damage control.

Covenant as a Devalued Currency

Covenant has a venerable history as a deep symbol and a common currency, but it is also a devalued currency. It is often connected to hierarchies, exclusivity, and propensity for uniformity—all social ills rather than goods.

Up and Down—the Issue of Hierarchy

One attack point in the covenant tradition is its connection with hierarchy. Niebuhr's treatment of covenant in American democracy distinguished it from a hierarchical model, but covenants come in more than one kind, and one aspect of the biblical covenant tradition is the emphasis on the inequality between God and the covenant people of Israel. Following George Mendenhall's *Law and Covenant in Israel and the Ancient Near East*, biblical scholars have emphasized the parallels between the suzerainty treaties of the ancient Near East and Yahweh's lord–vassal relationship to Israel.[12] The covenant writers in the court of the Davidic monarchy and in the priestly establishment after the exile had their hierarchical interests, and a long history of patriarchy, monarchy, and oligarchy has found justification in that model.

If divine sovereignty is understood as domination or control, and all covenantal relations must mirror the treaty between nonequals, there is a human penchant for according divine status to the powerful. If God is understood predominantly as a king, then not only is God assumed to exercise power as earthly kings commonly do, but earthly kings can justify exercising their power in such fashion with heavenly legitimation. History is replete with people in positions of power who suffer from cases of mistaken identity (divine identity, that is). France's Louis XIV comes to mind. He, after all, was the one who spluttered after a military defeat, "God seems to have forgotten all I have done for him."[13] Rulers of nations, masters of slaves, bosses of employees, religious authorities of the faithful, husbands of wives, and parents of children can then accord an appropriately dominant role to themselves while claiming divine sanction.

Although ours is an era of flattened pyramids and nurturing networks, at least in the lip service of most sectors of society, hierarchy has many more than nine lives, even as its reputation has taken a beating. The vigor and scope of the repudiation is, nonetheless, notable. Even calling God a king has become problematic in many settings. Ada María Isasi-Díaz substitutes "kin-dom" for kingdom of God, and Walter Wink uses "the reigning of God" or "God's Domination-Free Order."[14] Carol Robb and process theologians call for a reinterpretation of sovereignty that exchanges domination and control for shared power.[15] Rebecca Chopp cites a feminist understanding of God's relationship to the world as being that of a friend rather than a sovereign.[16] Margaret Farley argues for either the rejection or the reinterpretation of the hierarchical dimension of the covenant tradition in favor of equality in mutuality.[17] Faith as subservient obedience, love as sacrificial surrender, and sin as uppityness have been effectively challenged.

What is more, the covenant tradition can contribute significantly to the repudiation of hierarchy and the elevation of mutuality and equal partnerships. One does not have to make people into gods to make covenant a dialogue between partners rather than the monologue of a potentate. William Everett, for instance, distinguishes between monarchical and confederal covenants, and Charles McCoy between suzerainty and friendship covenants in the tradition. In both cases there is an egalitarian model to counteract or balance a hierarchical one.[18] Daniel Elazar distinguishes between an equal partnership and a partnership of equals. Israel's covenant with God was the former, not the latter, because God incurred the limits involved in a covenant relationship. The Israelites' multiple covenants with each other were partnerships of equals.[19] Women and eunuchs did not qualify, however, as equal partners.

Some recent biblical scholarship has traced the origins of Israel's covenant tradition in the family and depicted it as a continuing threat and corrective to the dominance of the covenant tradition by the monarchy and the priestly establishment. Leo Perdue, for example, explains that Israel was first of all a community of clans and households (extended or compound-dwelling families) and that the household provided both the social ground of Israel's theology and "the primary social lens through which to view the character and activity of God, the identity and self-understanding of Israel in its relationship to God, the value and meaning of the land as the *nahalah* [inheritance] God gives to Israel and Israel's relationship to the nations."[20] That social reality had already provided the key metaphors of Israelite religion (such as covenant) before there was a monarchy that provided the second social lens and that would always remain in tension with the traditions of the family (household), clan, and tribe. Understandings of God as parent (both father and mother) and redeemer, for example, have their roots in that household reality. The monarchy as social lens was represented by the priesthood and the Temple and was often advanced as the official lens for theological perception. One thinks too of the prophetic tension with the monarchy over the conditional Mosaic covenant and the unconditional promise to the Davidic monarchy. The Hebrew prophets waged an ongoing struggle against the idea that the covenant with the house of David was an unconditional promise and insisted that there were no guarantees. In the Mosaic covenant, breach of promise brought dire consequences. In that vision, no monarchy was assured a future.

Questioning the necessary linkage between covenant and monarchy does not of course take care of patriarchy. Patriarchy is surely a pitfall for any efforts to salvage covenant. The feminist critique of Israelite culture must not be ignored. Even here, however, we need more recognition of the diversity within the tradition. As a result of her archeological investigation of early Israel's farm families, Carol Meyers questions whether *patriarchy* is the appropriate term for those families in light of the managerial role of senior females in the household, a role with broad responsibilities.[21] We do not have to make the Israelite family normative to grant that some blanket stereotypes are too simple.

In and Out—the Issue of Exclusiveness

A second bone of contention is the way in which covenant can set some people aside in the process of setting some others apart. Covenantal circles of belonging are often exclusive. Elizabeth Bounds has written in response to Michael Walzer's emphasis on the given nature of Israel's chosen status, "To understand one's community as a people chosen by God is a two-edged sword, and which edge is utilized depends on the status or power of people who consider themselves chosen. Membership in a community is based as much on *exclusion* of the 'unlike' as it is on inclusion."[22] A covenant creates a community identity, and some boundaries go along with that sense of identity. If forging a strong sense of identity reaches the extreme of rigidity, then the stranger is totally excluded. Those different from insiders are outsiders and, quite possibly, enemies.

Serious problems ensue when one people's promised land is another's ancestral homeland. One people's manifest destiny is another's imminent destruction. The bonds of community can be the barriers of marginality. Major Jones could use the election theme positively for African Americans to underline the special responsibility of his people as chosen to fulfill a "larger ethical mandate," but Bounds, Margaret Farley, and Tyler Roberts fear that a sense of election more often marginalizes and deprives the excluded. Outsiders experience others' covenants as enclaves of the powerful and privileged and as stultifiers of the difference and creativity found in the covenants of other communities.[23]

Ethicists who have been trying to reappropriate the covenant tradition have shown that there is a usable past to be found in this regard as well as the previous one. Joseph Allen and Margaret Farley give priority to the inclusive or universal covenant that reaches to all. Paula Cooey interprets creation of male and female in the image of God to mean that difference is the prerequisite of covenant just as surely as kinship is. Without difference there would be no covenant. Thomas Ogletree and Darrell Fasching highlight "hospitality to the stranger" as the essence of Israel's covenant.[24] In the New Testament, it is important to cite the table sharing of Jesus with those regarded as outsiders and sinners as the epitome of his inclusiveness.

The tensions within the tradition are well illustrated in the book of Deuteronomy. In his analysis of the covenant polity found there, Dean McBride writes, "The consistent witness throughout is that each member of the larger community—whether male or female, child or adult, native born or sojourner, culprit or law-abiding citizen, land owner, laborer, or refugee slave—must be treated with the dignity due someone whose life is infinitely precious."[25] This summary certainly pushes toward inclusion. However, there is another impetus in contention with inclusion. The same Deuteronomy stresses the need for a holy people to be set apart and avoid the pollution of pagan neighbors and even supports the holy war practices of killing everything that breathes. Writes Michael Walzer, "Holy community and holy war are related ideas—not necessarily because holiness makes for hostility toward foreign nations, more likely because community does. . . . The stronger the union, the greater the enmity."[26]

A religious expression of the exclusivity problem is the ongoing argument about whether the Christian church has superseded Israel as God's people. Arrayed against the supersessionists, whose position has lent itself to anti-Semitism and helped inflame the Holocaust, are those (such as Paul van Buren and Monika Hellwig) who argue for a single covenant of which both Jews and Christian are a part, those who support two equally valid covenants for Jews and Christians (Clark Williamson and Gregory Baum), and those (such as Rosemary Ruether) who take a multicovenant position, lest only Jews and Christians be included.[27] There are then various ways in which a covenant model can both respect difference and promote inclusion, but bringing off the combination has not been easy.

Thick and Thin—the Issue of Pluralism

Another critical issue has to do with narrativity and pluralism. As Edward Farley indicates, deep symbols such as covenant are invariably located in a master narrative.

Postmodernism has at least two problems with master narratives. One is the likelihood of their continued existence. Jean François Lyotard denies that European peoples any longer have master narratives or grand paradigms in our epoch.[28] The other is their acceptability. Master narratives, if people any longer assert that they exist, are inevitably imperialistic in postmodern eyes. The colonizers try to impose their symbolic universes on the colonized, the powerful on the powerless. Pluralism then is stifled and driven underground. All master narratives are the narratives of masters only. Let the mastered or the masterable beware.

Narrativity also raises the issue of pluralism in a different way in Michael Walzer's distinction between "thick and thin." "Thick" refers to rich stories of particular communities, and "thin" to efforts at articulating universal norms that apply to everyone. The postmodern complaint is that master narratives tend to become impositions. Narrative theorists such as Alasdair MacIntyre complain that norms are always rooted in the stories of particular communities and that efforts at universal moral claims are useless and meaningless abstractions.[29] Covenant language then would be meaningful only within communities shaped and sustained by the biblical tradition, and not in a pluralistic society lacking a common story. Does a communitarian approach then lead necessarily to particularism, and thus to tribal relativism if it clings to or retrieves covenant as a deep symbol?

Walzer, whom Thiemann calls a revisionist liberal and Michael Novak calls a communitarian on the left, straddles the thick and thin issue this way. He insists that moral communities are "necessarily particular" and that humanity in general has no history, culture, festivals, or shared understandings of the social good. Still, he believes that different societies "can acknowledge each other's different ways, respond to each other's cries for help, learn from each other, and march (sometimes) in each other's parades." In light of such statements, Glen Stassen finds in Walzer a "reiterative universalism" that keeps him from being locked in particularism. Instead of espousing "covering law" universalism (which claims one universal truth for everyone—one justice, one covenant, one Exodus story in which one has to live to get the message), he holds out the parade possibility. This claim posits many stories of deliverance and many covenants in various communities and assumes that these covenants will have overlapping and reinforcing features as well as disparate ones.[30] The biblical covenant tradition (which itself has diverse expressions) has a certain particularity because of its embeddedness in a particular narrative and community, but if human relations and community structures are characterized by promises, commitments, and obligations rooted in shared history, it could well be that using covenant language would not be received as speaking a foreign tongue even though the persons in dialogue came from different thick identifications. Covenant language does not have to be limited to thick, sectarian expression.

Although he sets his position in contrast to Walzer's perceived particularism, Fasching also argues for a convergence of traditions that still protects their diversity. He writes, "In response to this demonic narrative [the technological mythos that emerged out of Auschwitz and Hiroshima], I propose a cross-cultural coalition for an ethic of human dignity, human rights, and human liberation at the intersection of those holy communities whose narrative traditions emphasize the importance of welcoming the stranger." For him human rights is "the name for a new covenant" with the whole of humanity, a renewal of the covenant with Noah. Although consensus on human rights will remain elusive, there is a growing convergence on respect for human dignity, which is, says Fasching, "the only one basic human right." David Hollenbach and Glen Stassen suggest that human rights can have a "trilingual basis" (Stassen's term). Judaism, Islam, and

Christianity can approach human rights from their distinctive stories and traditions and arrive at significant points of convergence.[31] We pursue this possibility further in chapter 5.

Center and Margin—the Issue of Social Criticism

Still another issue surrounds Walzer's use of covenant in his book *Interpretation and Social Criticism.*[32] Walzer bases social criticism on the core values within a society, after the mode of the Hebrew prophets as covenant advocates and social critics. From Amos to Martin Luther King Jr., the social critic is most effective when calling people to task for betrayal of the core values of their own society, when reinterpreting what they already supposedly know and accept. Explosive rhetoric and riotous acts lobbed in from the outside meet a level of resistance and rejection that insider admonitions to return to a society's roots are less apt to encounter. Jerusalem killed the prophets, and Memphis got King, but the prophets made it into the canon and King changed a nation by reminding people of what they were founded to be and even claimed to be.

A more cynical reading will recall that it took being crushed by other nations to convince Israel and Judah that the nay-saying prophets were right rather than the declarers of peace when there was none. Such an interpretation might also point out that the separatism and violence of other protesters in the King period made his brand of revolution seem attractive by contrast. Nevertheless, Walzer is saying that ordinarily people cannot or will not hear what they do not somehow already know. There may be moralities of discovery when Plato's philosopher-king disseminates wisdom or Moses receives revelation or Bentham introduces the utilitarian calculus or Marx unearths his historical dialectic. There may also be moralities of invention when people contract together to develop and observe rules of the game that serve their common interests. Walzer is convinced, however, that moralities of interpretation are the order in most communities. In this model, social critics do well to speak out of the common memory of the community on behalf of the founding values that constitute its normative core.

On this issue, Bounds and Roberts see problems with an underlying assumption in Walzer of a homogeneous society based on covenant religion. Core values, they argue, can be instruments of domination. Those values can squelch diversity as well as encourage it; they can silence criticism as well as level it; they can subvert change as well as trigger it. What place, they wonder, do homogeneous societies allow for the creative role of social conflict to effect a new consensus or a salutary compromise or a needed corrective? How does liberation from oppression occur if one relies solely on the corrective of core values in the very societies that are doing the oppressing?[33] Carol Robb and Carl Casebolt ask further whether a rendition of covenant that offers unconditional grace instead of the conditional promise of Sinai makes social criticism seem unimportant and social change unnecessary.[34] Margaret Farley challenges the covenant tradition to assume responsibility to change the world, to side with the disadvantaged and the outcast.[35]

Concerns about the inherent conservatism of the covenant tradition force its advocates to discern what features of it ensure the continued creation of new Jeremiahs and Martin Luther Kings and what expressions of it produce domesticated chaplains of the status quo. Any retrieval of covenant as a deep symbol for our time will need to insist that it foster and even foment self-criticism by its inclusion of disparate voices along with its endorsement of traditional norms.

Our Kind and Other Kinds—the Issue of Anthropocentrism

Another criticism of the covenant tradition comes from those who feel that the Western covenant model has often been conceived anthropocentrically. God's people are the partners, and the hierarchical rendition of covenant has made humans rulers, or at best stewards, of the rest of creation instead of fellow members of a covenant community that includes the ecosystem. Weren't the biblical covenants with people? Covenant seems like a political reality requiring the willing participation of the partners. Where does that understanding leave "other kinds" of life that can neither choose membership nor assume responsibilities?

Instead of debunking covenant as the source of the problem, a swelling band of theologians and ethicists has reappropriated the covenant metaphor to enable seeing the rest of creation in a more ecologically responsible way.[36] George Kehm, James Nash, and others return to the covenant with Noah to underline the inclusion of every animal species. William Everett calls attention to Israel's relationship to the land as a party to the covenant. Jürgen Moltmann and Rosemary Ruether underline the import of the Sabbath, the sabbatical year, and the jubilee year for letting nature rest and to the lack of a society–nature split in the Hebraic worldview. James Nash bases environmental rights on God's universal cosmic covenant of justice, on valuing what God values. Carol Robb urges that the earth needs a new covenant in which stake holding is extended to include other-kind species "because other-kind is the family to whom we belong." Based on this earth swell, it seems that covenant language is retrievable as linguistic currency as we assess our relationship to the rest of the ecosystem.

Lame, Lamb, and Lamp—the Issue of Civic Virtue

Covenant and *contract* are closely related terms, and the social contract tradition has some commonality with the covenant tradition to the extent that John Locke retained vestiges of his Calvinist background. We have, however, already referred to the critical distinction between contract and covenant. A contract constitutes an alliance of individuals for the satisfaction or guarantee of mutual interests; a covenant unites people with common allegiance to shared values or norms in a commitment to the long-term well-being of the community members. Contracts tend to be minimal, short term, and presumptive of little or no community bonding. Covenants presuppose community, lasting commitment to the other's total well-being, and the assumption of obligations to each other and to shared values that change one's life.

Liberalism, as we have seen, has traditionally been contractarian. The claim is that people enter political arrangements to protect their private interests. Liberal societies then are held together by mutual self-interest and not by common allegiance to shared values or versions of the good. Thiemann identifies as revisionist liberals or maybe communitarians those who support liberal democracy as more than a protector of negative freedom from infringement on personal pursuit of interest. Charles Taylor, for example, distinguishes "civic freedom" from liberal freedom because it emphasizes shared values and practices and not just pooled interests and minimal connections.[37]

In a similar vein, Timothy Jackson delineates "lame," "lamb," and "lamp" brands of liberalism.[38] All liberals, according to him, give ethical priority to the individual rather than the community although they acknowledge that individuals come from and exist in communities. Communitarians, by contrast, assign priority to the community.

In Jackson's categories, the "lame" type designates "liberalism-as-morally-empty." Richard Rorty and Judith Shklar, for examples, eschew ascribing moral content to a society because there is no way to ground moral claims in the midst of the diversity and pluralism of today's societies. The best we can do by way of articulating societal values is a set of pragmatic protections of our individual persons and interests against those who think that they can ground their moral claims and might be desirous of imposing their morality on others.

The "lamb" type is "liberalism-as-morally-basic." Contractarian John Rawls fits here. Rational beings can agree on certain minimal conditions for life together that constitute a definition of justice that all can accept. This justice includes equal liberty (bounded by others' liberty) and justification of inequalities of wealth and power by their contribution to the good of all, especially the least advantaged, with the added insistence on equality of opportunity to occupy privileged positions regardless of one's sex, race, creed, or class.

The "lamp" type is designated by William Galston as "morally perfectionist liberalism" and includes Amy Gutman and Charles Taylor as well as Galston. This liberalism stresses the social nature of the individual more than Rawls does but still seeks to avoid the sacrifice of the individual for the whole. It propounds a thicker view of civic virtue that goes beyond procedural justice or contracted equal opportunity to personal care as an overarching value that includes and orders political, economic, and moral-cultural life.

In covenant language, which Jackson uses for his own advocacy of "civic agapism" as a shade of lamp liberalism, we might say that the lame position wants protection from restrictive covenants, the lambs have reduced the public covenant to contract, and the lamplighters see hope for civic virtue in a public covenant. In other words, the possibility of introducing some argument based on religious conviction into public discourse is more acceptable here, and varied religious traditions might find consensus concerning civic virtue.

Whether the language is used or not, covenantal considerations are relevant for this debate within liberalism and for communitarian and liberation reactions to it. How social the self is and how far a society can go in espousing shared values or a civil religion and in advocating a particular brand of virtue are matters of moment to both the covenant tradition and to the contemporary discussion. Since one discovers that some liberals, communitarians, and liberationists can talk covenant talk and that others of all three persuasions do not use it, one can wonder what difference it makes.

Still, this discussion suggests both liabilities and possibilities in retrieval of the covenant tradition.

Yes and No—the Issue of the Techno-Scientific Paradigm of Knowledge

As Edward Farley indicates in discussing deep symbols or Philip Rieff's "god-terms," these terms are the "no-sayings" of a culture. They call a culture to account and usually connect to the sacred. "Thou shalt not kill" is such a saying, and it is not a statement of custom or consensus but an invocation of authority. It speaks truth. What happens then if all deep symbols or god-terms are suspect? And what makes them suspect? Farley judges that the "prevailing paradigm of reality and knowledge" is the reason that all deep symbols, such as covenant, are now questionable.[39] This paradigm he calls the "techno-scientific paradigm." It pervades our society's economic, governmental, military, and educational institutions, and to the extent that it becomes the sole arbiter of the real and true, it reduces obligations to customs and human interactions to negotiations. In this environment, covenant would qualify as a quaint archaism. Covenant is not alone in having a problem in this milieu; the whole family of deep symbols of which it is a venerable member has a huge problem. By the same token, if efforts at validating other paradigms of knowledge prevail and deep symbols can with that validation recover from the malaise of disenchantment, covenant's promise for retrieval takes an upsurge.

Me and Us—the Issue of Individualism

Our final source of suspicion of covenant as a deep symbol is not the scholarship of social theorists, theologians, political philosophers, feminists, or environmentalists but the individualism of our culture, mentioned earlier. Individualism is central to America's myth. Horatio Alger, the American Dream, the self-made person, Walden Pond, the lonesome cowboy, the private detective, the long-distance runner, and a cluster of other images have reinforced a vision of self-reliance, independence, self-sufficiency, and personal success that is almost stereotypically American. Cooperation, teamwork, joining groups, and being a good neighbor are also powerful images in the American story, but somehow the drive to personal fulfillment and financial success seems to accentuate our individualism if not eliminate our community spirit. How viable then is a deep symbol that highlights the givenness of our community membership and the obligations of our relational ties and the priority of long-standing loyalties over instant gratification?

Covenant as Residual Currency

Surely we have already seen enough to know that part of the covenant tradition is dated. At the very least reinterpretation will be necessary. Surely we have also seen enough to expose absolutizing covenant for the idolatry that it is. After all, the Ku Klux Klan is probably highly covenantal, and many of us can remember the neighborhood covenants established to keep blacks, Jews, or both out of particular residential areas. Because of covenant's sacred associations, the lean toward idolatry is exacerbated, not abated. Perhaps we have also already seen enough to know that the covenant tradition is not monolithic but pluralistic. If the tradition is a candidate for retrieval in the minds of some of us, what are the primary features of the retrievable tradition or the recoverable deep symbol, and where are there signs of its continuing viability despite the currency crisis indicated by the suspicions we have surveyed?

The Gift of the Tradition

William F. May has devoted much of his career in ethics to advancing or recovering covenant as a guiding image in professional, institutional, and public policy ethics. The great covenant tradition of the Bible, he posits, has four elements—a gift, an exchange of promises, the shaping of life in response to the gift and the promises, and the ritual reenactment of the foundational events of the covenant.[40] For Israel, the central gift was deliverance from bondage and being constituted as a people with a land. The exchange of promises was occasioned by the gift. In the case of Abraham and Sarah, the promise of land, seed, and blessing to others through their descendants was the occasion for an obligation or promise of faithfulness on their part. The law or instruction spread in the Torah was the institutionalization of the obligations to God and to each other that flowed from the gracious gift and the mutual promises. The Sabbath, dietary observances, and Passover and other holidays were the ritual means of recollection and renewal. These elements together distinguish a covenant from a contract, which presupposes no gift, imposes only minimal, temporary obligations, occasions no transformation of the selves involved, and elevates no sacred values other than mutual self-interest. May believes that such language is still viable in medical and corporate ethics, for instance, even without reference to the religious base that he himself acknowledges.

The Face of the Other

Another way of getting at what is retrievable in the covenant tradition takes us to the interpersonal philosophies of Jewish philosophers Martin Buber and Immanuel Levinas. These writers are steeped in the covenant tradition and its concern for the vulnerable other—the stranger, the fatherless, the poor, and the widow. As illuminated by these thinkers and such recent interpreters as Edward Farley, Thomas Ogletree, and Wendy Farley, the beginning of moral existence comes with the claim that the irreducible, inaccessible, and vulnerable other makes on me.[41] "The face" (Levinas's term), or the subjectivity of the other, makes me aware of an experience of the world that is not the same as mine, that is vulnerable to my efforts to interpret it and have it on my terms, and that is accessible only to the extent that genuine dialogue occurs. This other is not with me, in the sense of being the same as I am, or against me, in the sense of being defined in opposition to me. It confronts me in its separateness and requires a response. This experience of the "interhuman" (Buber) is, according to Edward Farley, both a given and a task. Its summons to moral existence is a call to compassion that suffers with the other and to obligation that suffers for the other by assuming responsibility. The face of the vulnerable other takes me out of myself and necessitates dialogue if we are to discover any shared meaning.[42] The other is not to be reduced to an object of my knowledge; the "face" must reveal itself through discourse.

Still another continuation of the Hebraic covenant tradition, albeit one marked by discontinuity as much as continuity, is the deconstructionism of Jacques Derrida. John Caputo calls him "Jewish without being Jewish" and speaks of his "reinvention of deconstruction as quasi-Judaism" and his widely acknowledged indebtedness to Levinas concerning the other and justice. On the one hand, Derrida is wary of the word *community* and of identification with any community because of its associations with keeping the stranger out. Part of *communio* is *munis*, which refers to a defensive wall of protection. On the other hand, *munus* refers to a gift or a public service performed beyond the demands of duty. So community can have the sense of exchanged gifts, of extravagance. For Derrida, the community identity of the communitarians is too tight, and the subjectivism of liberalism is pre-occupied with the rights of the autonomous individual and lacks any identity at all. Community and identity are both in need of deconstruction, yet they cannot be abandoned. Appropriately, Caputo heads parts of his commentary with the titles "community without community" and "identity without identity."

In distinction from both communitarianism and liberalism, deconstructionism focuses on "responsibility to the other." It is hospitality to the stranger, both personally and politically. There are tensions in hospitality as long as one remains the host, receiving the other with gifts on the host's turf. True hospitality does the impossible; it goes beyond hospitality to make the host's home the stranger's home. This hospitality to the other is what democracy should be, what it can only seek to be because the other is beyond our reach, as the face of the vulnerable other is for Levinas. In his mystifying way, Derrida represents both a critique of covenantal identity and community and an intriguing extension of a covenantal tradition that accentuates gift and gratitude as well as hospitality and responsibility toward the other.[43]

To return to explicitly covenantal language, we can say that the difference of the other makes covenant possible. To the extent that it elicits compassion and obligation, it makes covenant necessary. It is a gift that breaks through our self-enclosed existence. It is also a choice and an obligation not to violate the vulnerability of the other that draws my gaze. The covenant tradition, then, remains viable to the extent that it points us to the unavoidable sphere of the interhuman and the need for mutuality, empathy, and dialogue. The language of difference and openness to the other as irreducibly different is clearly still part of our linguistic currency in intellectual circles. Feminists, womanists, deconstructionists, and discourse ethicists, for example, keep before us the diverse worlds we inhabit or construe. *Valuing diversity*, *respecting difference*, and *openness to the other* are bywords in some political, business, and academic circles. It may be that a reconstructed covenant tradition can connect and even educate, despite the disuse into which the word has fallen in most secular and many religious circles.

Pockets of Promise

In some of my personal and professional experience, I find evidence that even explicit covenant language still has some resonance as a deep symbol for thoroughly modern (or postmodern) Americans. There are pockets of promise into which the old currency still fits. On occasion I perform marriages. The couples who come to me are usually my students or former students, or one of them is. They want a religious ceremony, and for a variety of reasons they no longer or do not yet have a pastor. Perhaps they come from diverse religious backgrounds and either want me there along with a hometown member of the clergy or see me as a compromise between the perceived distances separating their traditions. As we discuss marriage together, I find that the idea of covenant is something they can understand and appreciate. They sense that they have received a gift that they did not earn, that something wonderful has happened in their lives that has made everything different. They believe that true love, out of gratitude and devotion, wants to make promises and that these promises are not just mutual agreements but vows before God and people whom they care about and who care about them. They acknowledge that love incurs obligations, that their lives are not simply their own because of the bond between them. They see the need to recall what brought them together, to feel the support of others who were part of the past that made them the people they are, and to revisit their covenant as they attend other weddings, reread or review their service, and renew their giving of themselves to each other with each occasion of sharing, whether it be sexual intimacy, meals, walks with talks, times with children, or other shared testimony to their union. They know that a marriage thus perceived as a covenant is different from one that is only a contract. They value both the security and the challenge that come with knowing that they have chosen to make a total commitment for the rest of their lives.

In some cases, I know that their long participation in the biblical tradition and their exposure to marriages steeped in that tradition have prepared them to regard their unions as covenants. In others their relationship has opened them to an appreciation of covenant that their religious backgrounds (or the lack thereof) have seemingly done little to instill.

I also find that students respond positively to the covenant symbol in courses that deal with the ethics of medicine, health care, and business. Many students appreciate the difference it makes if a doctor considers herself or himself to be responding to a gift rather than merely marketing acquired skills. As William May explains to them in *The Physician's Covenant*, doctors are the recipients of a rich legacy of scientific and medical knowledge from their teachers and those who preceded them. They are likewise indebted to the patients who have let them practice on them during their training (and beyond it) and who cooperate by revealing what the doctor needs to know to be effective, to the government for grants and to other financial underwriters of their education, to colleagues and other health professionals.[44] Whether they see an Ultimate Giver behind it all or not, students see that the sense of obligation is more encompassing of the total well-being of the patient and family for the long term if one thinks covenantally rather than merely contractually.

In similar fashion, our joint endeavors as teachers and students in a college or university can be approached on covenantal terms. Such language emphasizes the legacy to which we are heirs in our college. It invokes the promises that we should make to each other to be true to our calling as bearers of that legacy and the obligations that we assume to each other in our common endeavor. It receives periodic ritual reinforcement at important college events. The reach of such understanding is not limited to people with explicit religious commitments, although it is no doubt enhanced for some by such commitments.

To cite one more example, one of my former students, who carries a self-designation as an agnostic, has founded and manages a thriving corporation. This friend is convinced that his corporation is being managed as a family with a covenantal relationship. The fringe benefits, the work environment, the opportunity for participation in decision making, the longevity of many employees' relationship to the company, the way in which customers are treated, and the sharing in the business's profits with employees are presented as evidences of a corporate culture that is far more than merely contractual. This former student even claims that some of my writing has shaped his vision of corporate leadership. Covenant is not a god-term for him, but it functions like a god-term or deep symbol in his business life.

Covenantal sightings get fewer as one moves from marriages to the marketplace, from a health care vocation to systemic health care, from a small college community to a megaversity, and from a workforce that is like one CEO's family to the bureaucracy of a multinational megalith. The same health care professionals who see themselves in a covenant with their patients may be less convinced about a national covenant of universal health care. The move from the interpersonal to the institutional may be their dividing line. The challenge covenant advocates face in our time is how to keep the covenant-crushing waves of social systems, institutions, and intellectual paradigms from submerging the remaining islands of intimacy and even to reclaim covenantal terrain in social institutions from the whelming flood.

As we have seen, covenant advocates have mined aspects of the tradition that can correct or counterbalance the failings cited by critics. To the credit of the tradition, its best advocates have often been its toughest critics. Its fallibility has been exposed; any pretensions to idolatry have been attacked. Now can its normativity and even enchantment be salvaged or rediscovered? Even when its detractors have had their say, the symbol carries potential that warrants such an effort.

2

The Commonality of the Common Good

For even if the good of the community coincides with that of the individual, it is clearly a greater and more perfect thing to achieve and
preserve that of a community; for while it is desirable to secure what
is good in the case of an individual, to do so in the case of a people
or state is something finer and more sublime.[1]

—Aristotle, *Ethics*

Without the organic the covenantal becomes contractual, just as
without the covenantal the organic becomes tyrannical.[2]

— James B. Nelson, *Moral Nexus*

A well-known story can still bring a smile: The teacher had all of her
third-grade class drawing pictures of anything they wanted to draw. As she
made the rounds of the desks, she could tell what everyone was drawing,
with one exception. When she inquired, she was told that the student was
drawing God. When the teacher pointed out that people really don't know
what God looks like, the pupil replied, "They will when I get through."

Such confident words from an older and more powerful source could
occasion a big chill of the hearer's blood. T. V. Smith, in his *The Ethics of
Compromise and the Art of Containment*, warns of "a little totalitarian operating in the bosom of every conscientious man, especially if he is a
middle man operating in the name of God." That same person can have
more than a few sure ideas about the common good.[3] As Karen Lebacqz
observed in 1995 as part of a panel on health care and the common good at
the annual Society of Christian Ethics meeting, "How difficult and elusive
is the common good!" It is difficult, and it is elusive; we worry about people who are too sure about what it is and how it should be advanced.

As the opening quotation indicates, Aristotle considered it a greater thing to promote the good of the whole than to secure one's individual good. The ideal or norm of the common good perhaps occupies in the Greek legacy a place comparable to that of covenant in the Judaic and Christian legacies (and Confucianism, Hinduism, and Islam have their own common-good traditions as well). As Aristotle states, the common good calls people beyond private interest to the well-being of entire communities. Elevation of the good of the Greek *polis* was reflected in the attention lavished on public buildings and the public space in contrast to the modest attention accorded private spaces and structures.

Remembering the lament of the Bellah team about our loss of a first language with which to join in discourse on the public good, we can say that the idea of the common good was a first language in elite Greek society in the same way that covenant obligation was the mother tongue of Israel and of the Christian community. Both kept prompting the conscience to make the well-being of all of one's neighbors the central ethical issue rather than reduce the moral life to an individualistic pursuit of self-fulfillment.

At first blush, it might even appear that the common good avoids some of the liabilities that critics have flagged in the covenant tradition. The common good need not entail hierarchy or exclusion or inseparability from a particular religious tradition. On second look, however, some of the very reservations that we cited about covenant reappear about the common good, and it has a few other problems of its own.

Suspicions about the Common Good

Suspicions about the common good begin with who defines it and whose voices are not heard in the process of definition. Wariness can then move from the process of definition to the possibilities of imposition. What means are used to communicate, to inculcate, to convince, and even to compel conformity once the pursuit of some vision of the common good becomes a community's purpose? Issues of scope and difference likewise invite criticism of a society's efforts to deliver its goods. How inclusive of other affected communities and ultimately of global community is the vision of the common good? How respectful and even encouraging of difference is the community that holds goods in common? If even defenses of slavery, tyranny, and ethnic cleansing can march behind the banner of the common good, one cannot be too careful.

Power and Participation

Susan Moller Okin has dissected the elitism in Aristotle that relegated farmers, merchants, artisans, and women to subservient status while the elite male citizenry contemplated the common good,[4] and there is nothing about the concept that protects it from being defined by self-appointed or god-appointed authorities on behalf of the rest of the people. If we adopt the kind of organic model used by deep ecologists, as opposed to the social organic model that Sallie McFague advocates instead, we end up with the earth as the single subject whose good guarantees no respect for various individual subjects.[5] These are but two examples of ways in which the rights and welfare of minorities or individuals can be submerged in a commitment to the common good. Assigning priority to the good of an organic or collective whole can bring tyrannical and even totalitarian results.

When the powerful define the common good, the powerless are subjected to it. If men are the dominant definers of the good, for example, women may be relegated to spheres, roles, inequalities, and subordinations that constrict their opportunities and compromise their fulfillment. If the powers that be believe that a certain level of unemployment is needed to make the economy run well for everyone's benefit, how does that definition of the common good benefit the poor and the unemployed? If hosting the Olympic Games is good for a particular nation, for a particular region, and for a particular city, how does the perceived need to displace some people's neighborhoods or individual dwellings constitute a common good that includes them? If expansion of a corporation's facilities in a city is fully endorsed by city government as a means of keeping a vital industry from moving and therefore ceasing to stimulate the local economy, where does that good leave the particular good of the people whose neighborhood has to go? Political choices about toxic waste sites raise a similar problem. Whose voice is muffled when the majority decides?

Commonality and Difference

If we make sure that everyone has a voice in determining the common good and promise that we shall all accept the outcome, even if we get outvoted, our pluralism enters in. How much agreement can we reach given the differences among us? Are there not competing goods in which people have a common interest, such as food and shelter, health and health care, a livable environment, education, economic opportunity, and public safety, to name a few? If some make an unpolluted environment a common interest, others may tout economic growth more. If some nominate public safety, others may ask how much personal freedom will have to be sacrificed. How does a society assign priorities to these when there is great disparity among the rankings of different individuals and groups?

It is no wonder that John Rawls calls the common good "certain general conditions that are in an appropriate sense equally to everyone's advantage."[6] In the liberal vision, the common good is the common interest, but who defines the common interest? And how many conditions are equally to everyone's advantage? Preference utilitarians, for example, despair of our ever arriving at the common understanding of the good that some other utilitarians envision. They, therefore, search for an alternative that satisfies everyone's diverse preferences best. Libertarians frown on any prescription of social goods, such as access to health care for everyone, if any diminution of individual freedom is involved in the guarantee. How can we affirm difference and define the common good in any but the most minimal terms?

It takes a community to have a common good. A lot hinges on what we mean by community. The very criticisms that have been leveled at covenant and common good can be aimed at closed and rigid communities. For the common good to be something better than an imposition of the powerful on the powerless or a mere protection of individual preferences or a guarantee of minimum conditions to everyone's advantage, a community needs to have some shared values that make room for difference and pluralism and reach out to include those who might be left out or disregarded.

These very issues of commonality and difference are addressed by the definition of community offered in *For the Common Good* by Herman E. Daly and John B. Cobb Jr. Community, they acknowledge, is a matter of degree, but its presence is contingent on four requirements: (1) Membership in the society that is a candidate for community must contribute to the self-identity of the members, but not necessarily totally define that identity. (2) Members participate extensively in the decisions that direct the community's life. (3) "The society as a whole takes responsibility for its members." (4) The diverse individuality of each member is respected.[7]

Clearly, community as Daly and Cobb define it goes beyond linkage by mutual self-interest to commonality that provides shared identity. H. Richard Niebuhr stressed that we always relate to others in the presence of and in relation to some third reality, that is, some place, some group, or some shared center of value or loyalty. We are drawn together in relation to something that affects our mutual identity.[8] This triadic structure of human relationships requires a third for connection but not for antagonism. Some common bond or center of value or common point of reference sets a community apart; otherwise, it is indistinguishable from everyone else. The others, however, do not have to be regarded as enemies, but rather can be seen as potential dialogue partners, possible allies, or friendly rivals. Our skins identify us and set us apart from others, but our skin is also our point of contact and even embrace with the other. People are often united by their hatred of a common enemy, but that form of cohesion is extremely unstable. It always requires finding new enemies to fuel the flames of patriotic zeal.[9]

The other point about identity that bears elaboration is the statement about total definition of one's identity by community membership. In this connection, it is worth recalling Walzer's caution about problems that arise when one membership totally defines one's identity. The person who is dominated by a single source of identity, "the singular self," is apt to be an ideological or religious fanatic. It is better for our identities to be constituted by plural centers of belonging and thus to internalize plural critics.[10]

Why accept Daly and Cobb's definition of community? It seems to achieve that delicate balance between individual liberty and communal solidarity that we seek. Equal participation in decisions and respect for the diverse individuality of each member mesh with the American founders' core democratic values of liberty, equality, and mutual respect or toleration. The stipulation of community membership as constitutive of personal identity and of the community's responsibility for all of the members underlines the self's social connection. Contribution to self-identity avoids the overidentification that worries deconstructionists, among others, and respect for individuality avoids the fusion they fear. Participation in decisions avoids the hazards of hierarchy, and assumption of responsibility affirms binding obligation to the other. The covenant tradition at its best envisions such community, and the common good carefully construed is embodied in such community. To the lingering question about who is left out, Daly and Cobb respond with their concept of a global "community of communities," which will be crucial for our later explorations.

Understanding the common good as something sought by a community with the characteristics that we have noted makes it more a community process than a prearranged principle or a finished product. Based on the previous chapter, we can also say that covenants should be dialogues in progress rather than simply regulations in stone. We turn now to some current appeals to the common good, either by name or by implication, to see how well they pass muster in light of the understanding of community that we have adopted.

Constitutional Protection and the Common Good

Traditional liberalism has emphasized the protection of plural definitions of the common good. Western constitutions articulate shared values, but the values are primarily protections against infringements on individual liberty. Rights are conceived more negatively than positively. The implication is that we have more to fear from the loss of liberty than from the erosion of commonality. Comparing the Canadian Constitution and the U.S. Constitution shows that there may be more to community and thus to the common good north of the border than in our own country. There, individualism is much more qualified by community membership than is the case in the United States; equality gets more emphasis in relation to liberty in the quest for justice. The health care systems of the two countries testify to this difference in fundamental assumptions about the self's relation to community and the government's role.

Corporate Bodily Harm

In her book *Only Words*, Catharine MacKinnon brings a law professor's and a feminist's perspective to bear on constitutional protections of pornography, racial and sexual harassment, and hate speech. She uses the Canadian example. Although a distinction is often made between acts of intimidation, subordination, terrorism, and discrimination on the one hand and words on the other, MacKinnon insists that words are acts when they constitute the enacting of power by one social group over another. When women are subordinated through pictures and words, something has been done to them. The verbal and physical environments cannot be separated. As she states, "Pornography has to be done to women to be made; no government has to be overthrown to make communist speech."[11]

In our own national setting, the constitutional defense for such words and pictures is sought in the First Amendment protections from infringement by government on free speech, but that amendment is often interpreted as though the Fourteenth Amendment did not exist, with its guarantee of equal protection of the law. Supposedly the marketplace of ideas benefits all, but the free speech doctrine in fact protects the speech of the dominant instead of making equality a common good that can be violated. All voices are not equal, and speech should not be considered in isolation from its power source.

Although MacKinnon does not use the term *common good*, she considers "harm to women as harm to the community." She points out that the Supreme Court of Canada has ruled against the constitutionality of hate propaganda in a case involving anti-Semitic group defamation because of its "antiegalitarian meaning and devastating consequences," and in favor of the obscenity statute in a case against a pornography store because the law promotes sexual equality and "harm to women . . . *was* harm to society as a whole."[12]

In Canada, equality is defined more substantively and positively than in the United States. The law promotes it; it is "a compelling state interest."[13] It is not a matter of indifference there whether a subordinate group is the one being hurt or helped. The harm of free expression is not reduced to offensiveness. A free speech defense is qualified by the law's commitment to equality. Thus the law assumes the political community's responsibility for all members. It sets a context of constraint on what the more powerful can do to the less powerful, even by word of mouth. Distasteful visions of speech police come quickly to mind, but it does matter who is talking and who is being hurt by the talk or by the visual objectification of other human beings that pornography constitutes. Sexual exploitation of the vulnerable will be a central concern in chapter 3.

Diversity and Dissent

Another feminist voice, that of Paula Cooey, makes an equally strong argument for constitutional protection of the vulnerable and especially of diversity in *Family, Freedom, and Faith*, but she chooses to emphasize those aspects of the U.S. Constitution that provide such protection. As it was in the beginning of the American experiment, according to Cooey, "The Constitution restricted the equality of all men to a certain class of predominantly Anglo-European males, viewed as free, autonomous individuals entering voluntarily into a compact with one another. Furthermore, the compact worked to sustain their economic, racial, and gender privilege as a compact among states not to infringe on the free trade of money."[14] This constitution was, however, subject to change. It was a compact set within a covenantal religious tradition as well as a social contract tradition, and it was, like any other covenant, as Cooey puts it, "a partial covenant," set in a particular time and place.

Despite its limitations, however, this covenantal context acknowledges the finiteness of religious people's values in the face of the infinite source of all value and affirms the equal value of "all men." In this democracy the people consented not only to representative rule but also to the rule of law, and this rule of law had two features—modifiability and the right to dissent. Modifiability meant that the coverage could be broadened, and protection of dissent meant that difference was defended.

By prohibiting the establishment of religion and protecting its free exercise, the Constitution protected minority voices. What the Christian Coalition might want to dictate, the Constitution resists granting. Looking at such issues as flag desecration and prayer in the public schools, Cooey cites the Constitution for support of free speech and minority rights in terms of religious expression and for intervention on behalf of children who are endangered by their families. Despite its inaugural narrowness, the Constitution's community has been broadened, and it does offer backing for the protection of the vulnerable as part of the family of the nation. In her treatment of the U.S. Constitution, Cooey finds a concern for the common good of a national community that protects the safety and individuality of all its members by the legal framework it erects. The Constitution and the legal system then both express and shape a community's understanding of the common good.

Both of these constitutional views address the problem of power imbalance in the development and interpretation of constitutions. Both point out how the rule of law can protect the less powerful when equal justice is given substance beyond protection against government interference with free expression. One refuses to allow harm to the community to be protected because it comes clothed as diversity of opinion, while the other underlines protection of diversity as essential to community. Both view the interpretation of equal protection of the law as a process rather than a fixed and finished conclusion. Both, in effect, make the community where the vulnerable are protected and dissent is allowed the common good in which all have a stake.

A problem implicit in both discussions is that of identification with a national community. If one feels unrepresented and even victimized by the constitutional process and the legal system because of its past biases, one's sense of identity is not constituted by that membership. Many African

Americans' perception of our legal system is a case in point. To the extent that one feels included, protected, and respected in one's difference and individuality, one will identify with the common good that is constitutionally constructed and with the national community for which it stands. The growing presence of women and, to a lesser extent, minorities in the bar and on the judicial bench will no doubt continue the evolution of that legal common good.

Community as Commons and as Common Good

Community requires something held in common, and uses of the language of "the commons" offer another way of exploring the viability of the common good as an ethical norm. Garrett Hardin has been a prominent voice that has bemoaned "the tragedy of the commons" from an ecological perspective. According to the example often used, if anyone can graze sheep on the village commons without cost, what is to prevent the rapid destruction of the grassy plot that sustains the livelihood of the village by the excessive use of selfish people's gobbling sheep? Division and privatization of the land make people become good stewards of their portions and prevent disaster. But what if the air and water we share are the commons? They cannot be privatized, and we continue to add more people to use the earth's limited resources with impunity. The common good then is tied up with the limited resources of the earth and the preservation of the commons.

Global Human Commons

Ecological economist Neva Goodwin is a contemporary writer who speaks of "the global natural commons [that] are increasingly threatened by human action that is based on self-interest." She urges us to turn to the "global human commons" for solutions. By this *global human commons* she means "behaviors and motivations tending toward 'cooperation and sharing in the interest of pan-human, or even biosphere-wide, welfare.'"[15] This commons is to be found in institutions built and shared by representatives of the human, and even the ecosystemic, family rather than one particular government or business. Universities, international treaties, and the United Nations are expressions of this global human commons. This "third sector," which is neither government nor business, can expand the way we think about self-interest. It is not dictation by an elite with parochial loyalties. It is a decentralized, bottom-up, pluralistic expression of a civic virtue that thinks globally. In chapter 5, we shall use the term *global civil society* to designate this sector. As envisioned by Goodwin, its understanding of the common good is not fixed by a powerful elite and foisted on unwilling subjects. Rather, the global community is in the process of defining the common good.

This third sector is engaged in constant reassessment of the common good, recognizing that different people conceive the common good differently and that these understandings are subject to change.[16] It may seem utopian to project such a sector that is not linked to the particularities of tribe and trade because we all have plural communities and loyalties. Nevertheless, Goodwin is seeking a way to match the ultimate inescapability of our global natural commons with a global human commons. She is suggesting that the community itself and its institutions are the commons. This commons both potentially includes all and allows for difference in renditions of the common good.

It is regrettable that religious communities and institutions are not cited explicitly as part of her global human commons. The fault is not only with her, but also with them, however. The United Nations and international treaties seem very remote to most of us, and the global commons needs local manifestations, lest the larger loyalty to global community and identification with it lose out. To the extent that they foster loyalty to global community, religious communities could be such local manifestations.

Corporate Community Commons

Another recent source that specifies the communities found in human institutions as the commons is philosopher Edwin M. Hartman's *Organizational Ethics and the Good Life*.[17] Combining an Aristotelian focus on humans as social animals with appropriation of John Rawls and Albert Hirschman, Hartman fashions his own brand of communitarianism, which is set in the business organization instead of Aristotle's political locus. Ethics is about the good community, he believes, and the culture of the business organization that employs us, rather than our political context, is often the most definitive determinant of our vision of the good life. With the later Rawls, Hartman does not believe that people's values precede their membership in communities.[18] Being a part of a community or organization affects what people want and expect from it. Such organizations are different from markets. Therefore he concentrates on the ways in which good management strives to effect a corporate culture in which self-interest is defined or redefined to harmonize with the interests of others in the commons, in which personal autonomy and good citizenship in the community are not antithetical. According to Hartman, "There may be reason to be moral if everyone's being moral will make people in the aggregate better off."[19] He may be overly optimistic about the coincidence of interests, but he prompts an effort by corporations to strive for all the coincidence that a genuine community can discover and create.

Although Rawls's liberalism is called contractarian, Hartman criticizes the limitations of contract and believes that the later Rawls goes further. The commons is more than consent driven by protection of each other's self-interest. Loyalty to the community involves interest in each other's interests. Like Rawls, Hartman is a constructivist exploring "how rational people would organize things in a certain sort of community," but the rationality is not individualistic and unaffected by community solidarity.[20] Loyalty goes beyond insurance against free riders in the commons to a definition of happiness in corporate terms.

It is not necessary or even desirable that all members agree in their visions of the good life in this commons. No comprehensive view of justice or utility need dictate the definition of the common good. Unlike Alasdair MacIntyre, Hartman does not believe that everyone in the community must agree on what is most important, but some consensus is necessary. Each person is accorded the right to have her or his own conception of the good as long as others have that same right. Writes Hartman, "We can think of a good community as one in which people negotiate and accommodate in their best interests according to rules that represent what Rawls (1993) calls an overlapping consensus and preserve the commons." The structure of the community is crucial for the support of the moral life, and that structure is the primary concern of justice.[21] The commons is a process of mutual influence on preferences, values, and interests; it is not the case that any definition of interest or of the common good is as good as any other. Hartman is a pluralist, not a relativist.

From Albert O. Hirschman, Hartman draws the minimal conditions of the ethical community—exit, voice, and loyalty.[22] The less viable choice there is to exit, the more important voice becomes; the more voice one has, the more loyalty one is apt to feel to the community. If there is absolutely no way to exit, the idea of community is meaningless. Assumptions about the freedom to find other work can make businesses in "employment at will" settings unconcerned about due process and participation in decision making, which build in fairness and voice. As Hartman summarizes, "We have good reason to want to be contributing members in an effective organization that permits the disaffected to leave by participating in a labor market, earns the commons-preserving loyalty of participants, and encourages reflection and discussion about issues of ethical importance, including the nature of the good life."[23]

Hartman's confidence about finding community in business organizations does not enjoy universal support by any means. In the era of downsizing, persistent relocating to the sites of cheaper labor, leveraged buyouts, and insistence on the quickest and largest return on investment, images of the workplace as a community sharing a vision of the good life may sound naïve. The big fish keep swallowing the little fish, and the big fish are corporations that most find more bureaucratic than communal.

It is too easy, however, to write off the possibilities of community in large corporations or large public agencies. As we shall elaborate on in chapter 4, if a nation can be a community of sorts, why can't a company? To celebrate smallness as though small business organizations and small-town public-sector offices cannot be just as antithetical to community as the giants are is a mistake. Size may complicate the possibilities for community, but it does not, in itself, eliminate them. Nor should we settle for a dualism that reserves community for the face-to-face intimacies of private spheres of endeavor and consigns the marketplace and the public square to faceless forces that destroy or distort community. Daunting tasks are not necessarily impossible dreams, and it is not true to say that if you have seen one business organization you have seen them all.

Both Goodwin and Hartman make community a commons, and thus they make fostering a community a common good. Both of them see the definition of the common good as an open-ended process rather than a fixed point of arrival. If organizations with cultures characterized by the minimum conditions that Hartman and Hirschman name are genuinely friendly to women's participation, for example, and do not relegate women to "mommy tracks" or other stereotyped roles that perpetuate glass ceilings, the common good that unites such a commons could indeed be good for women. We can say the same about racial, ethnic, and other minorities. If loyalty to the community commons of the business organization becomes all-encompassing, however, the larger loyalty cited by Goodwin and other legitimate communal and institutional loyalties get negated in disastrous ways. Walzer's "singular self" has taken over. Members bring commitments, loyalties, and priorities from their various communities or noncommunities that either impede or facilitate the process of seeking a common good in the community or communities of a workplace. Both the impeding and the facilitating can at times be beneficial, but plural community memberships are realities to recognize and address.

Religious Covenant and the Common Good

A religious covenant may be one of the commitments that a person brings to the communities of discourse and concerted action in global society and in the corporation. How does this ultimate or inclusive commitment relate to the common good? As examples, we cite, finally, two Christian theological approaches—the post–Vatican II expression of the Roman Catholic moral tradition and a recent feminist rendition of the Reformed tradition.

A Roman Catholic Combination of Covenant and the Common Good

According to the Vatican II definition, the common good is "the sum of those conditions of social life which allow social groups and their members relatively thorough and ready access to their own fulfillment."[24] This comprehensive good occurs when the various institutions of society function to promote the dignity and fulfillment of each person and when each person has the material and spiritual resources needed to be a full participant in the civic community. Three key features support this idea of the common good. The first is human dignity, which is rooted in each person's creation in God's image. The second is interdependence, which is rooted in each person's membership in various communities. The third is participation, which entails other entitlements to what is required for participation (such as food, shelter, and education) and also duties as a participant to contribute to social, political, and economic institutions.[25]

The U.S. Catholic bishops' pastoral letter on the economy, *Economic Justice for All*, posits creation in God's image, a calling to be God's covenant people, and the reign of God's justice as theological-ethical underpinnings of what David Hollenbach calls a combination of liberalism and communitarianism, which would capture Hartman as well.[26] The biblical norms that make life in community as a covenant people possible are "reciprocal responsibility," "mercy" (especially toward the vulnerable members of the community), and "truthfulness." Life in covenant is life in freedom from oppression and co-responsibility in community. Christian love should issue in civic virtue, which acknowledges both "one's dependence on the commonweal and obligations to it." Social justice should be "contributive." All who are able have the duty "to help create the goods, services and other non-material or spiritual values necessary for the welfare of the whole community." To overcome marginalization and powerlessness, a commitment to justice demands that each person be assured the minimum requirements for participation in the life of the community. This obligation grows out of our social nature and our "communitarian vocation" as human beings.[27]

For the bishops, the minimum conditions for life in community can also be called human rights. To deny those basic human rights to persons not only harms them but also harms the community, just as Catharine MacKinnon claimed. The common good as well as personal injury is at stake. The other side of the commitment to the common good is the duty of helping to build up the commonweal.[28] Educating oneself to develop one's talents, contributing through one's vocation, and training one's children for citizenship are all important dimensions of this positive duty. A special obligation is owed the poor and the marginalized since it often takes extra effort to see that they gain the education, economic security, health, and so forth, necessary to contribute fully to the common good. This familiar "preferential option" is therefore closely tied to concern for the common good. Instead of regarding this "option for the poor" as a way of pitting class against class, the bishops' readers are to understand that "the deprivation and powerlessness of the poor wounds the whole community."[29] To the extent that we are a true community, the inability of any part of the community to participate fully always wounds the whole.

From this perspective, one's work is done on behalf of one's family, one's nation, and the whole human family, not just for oneself. It should contribute to the common good. Striving for the private good of one's firm is not enough to make one's work a vocation; vocation requires commitment to the public good.[30] The right of property ownership is qualified by "the demands of the common good." Good government intervention in the life of the society and the economy "helps" other groups and institutions to contribute to the common good. Directing, urging, restraining, regulating, and consensus building are all forms that this helpful intervention may take where appropriate.[31] These are themes to which we shall return in chapter 4.

The bishops and the tradition they represent stretch the common good to the reach of the entire human community, and they lift up the particular importance of enabling the participation of the poor and marginalized. For them the common good is the needs of the community and that criterion that balances rights and duties.[32] As Karen Lebacqz observes, they keep the concern for human dignity from "dissolving into a 'rights' language that is purely individualistic."[33] They also insist on human interdependence and solidarity in ways that correct utilitarian versions of the common good. The grimness of the oft-cited feminization of poverty and the bishops' emphasis on enabling the full participation of those who have been marginalized make the "preferential option" important for women and others who have been ignored or neglected in some versions of the common good.

On the other hand, the bishops have been faulted for shortchanging the power of self-interest in their harmonization of the personal and the communal, and Warren Copeland is among those who find sin "underdeveloped" in their document. (One might say the same about Goodwin and Hartman, but they do not set out to build a theological basis for the common good.) Copeland also regards their view of community as insufficiently dynamic and pluralistic.[34] Their assumptions about solidarity and community perhaps reflect so much the tribal heritage and the monarchical heritage of the biblical tradition and the realities of an inherited community as opposed to those of a newly shaped community that they have tended to sanctify an earlier social context. The bishops heard a lot of testimony by experts in the process of developing their several drafts of the letter, but how much listening to the poor themselves occurred? The radical implications of their biblical foundational statement got dulled by the adverse reactions of some of their dialogue partners. In the end, their model is too organic and not respectful enough of difference and the need for continuing dialogue about what constitutes a good community and thus that community's good. A particular version of the common good gets the upper hand over covenant.

Anne Patrick's egalitarian-feminist voice from the same Catholic tradition is a necessary objection to hierarchical authority that binds the conscience instead of respecting responsible dissent.[35] Natural law can easily become identified with a traditional society's vision of the common good. Openness to change may be compromised, particularly with respect to women's roles. In Hirschman's categories, loyalty may thus be elevated to the neglect of exit and voice. Dialogical authority, rather than hierarchical authority, should be the covenantal model.

To the extent that the bishops' rendition of the common good endorses the traditional social order, the duties they emphasize for all to identify with some authoritative rendition of the common good and to take responsibility unselfishly for other members of that common community could be problematic. For example, they could translate into an obligation for women to fit in and to rein in their visions of different communities and plural versions of the common good. Participation may not always include enough voice, and interdependence may not be insistent enough on respecting individual uniqueness and difference. Identification with the community and its "common good" is thereby threatened.

A Reformed Feminist Combination of Covenant and the Common Good

Paula Cooey's feminist and Reformed call to "think difference differently"[36] provides a promising theological balance to the tendencies in the bishops' statement that we have criticized. It does so in the context of the very affirmations about creation and covenant that *Economic Justice for All* employs as foundations for its treatment of the economy in tandem with the common good. In *Family, Freedom, and Faith*, Cooey posits that the nation is an all-inclusive family and that each individual family, regardless of form, should be protected. While the Religious Right wants a specific people of faith setting the terms for the country (determining the common good), Cooey wants an emphasis on the people of God as an inclusive family that values difference.

Creation in the image of God means that the good of every member of the human family must be sought. Creation as male and female means that difference is essential to covenant, not that heterosexuality is the only acceptable norm for marriage and family. In her words, "That God created *all* humans in God's image establishes a kinship among humans that forms one of the two necessary conditions for all particular human relationships, namely commonality. That God created humans different from one another, as witnessed by the creation of Adam and Eve, constitutes the second necessary condition for all particular relationships."[37] Without difference, there is no conflict, no relationship, and no covenant. Difference is an asset, not a liability. Sin does not introduce difference; it turns difference into division.[38] Faith requires the transcending of division by loyalty to the entire human family of kindred creatures in the image of God and to the earth from which we come.

Both our religious tradition and our national political tradition of covenant making, noted earlier, require that we "think difference differently." We are bound to mutual protection by our social contract, and we must cease to think in terms of a mainstream and a margin. All covenants must be pressured to "exceed their partiality."[39] They must be pushed beyond their contamination by sexism, heterosexism, slavery, and ethnic prejudice. "Christian" definitions of the common good should be viewed with suspicion, but the commonality of our creation and the value of our difference make a covenantal approach to national politics promising. Building community is the challenge, and, as Cooey puts it, "Community today, as in the past, depends on a willingness to commit to the covenants we make with God and with one another."[40] All covenants need not exclude; they can include. They need not submerge difference; they can encourage it. In a participatory democracy, we can resolve disagreement by negotiations in which the so-called people of faith are not allowed to disqualify some but rather multicultural coalitions give voice to the dispossessed. Cooey equals the bishops in her attention to the poor and the vulnerable, especially children; her feminist perspective helps heighten her attentiveness to them.

The ingredients of community that we have cited all get attention in Cooey: identity, participation, responsibility, and individuality. She also faults the idolatry of our claims to religious superiority and our absolutizing of the family values agendas of either the right or the left on the political and religious spectrum. To regard the nation as one family and to embrace the earth as part of a global family does not require adherence to a particular religious vision, and some religious visions pose more impediments than pathways. Still, one has to wonder how people become convinced of the verities about commonality and difference that are rooted in creation and covenant by Cooey without any acknowledgment of their bases. Getting everyone to converge theologically is not possible or desirable; but without the infusion of religious vision, our sense of national and ecological solidarity may grow perilously thin. This position will be critical for issues raised in the next two chapters.

Covenantal Connections with Constitution and Community Commons

We have seen how representatives of both Catholic and Protestant traditions are bringing covenant and common good together. It is also possible to combine covenant with the approaches to the common good by way of constitutions and community commons that we have explored.

Covenant and Constitution

Without arguing that a common theology is the national unity we should seek, one can still notice that the constitutional and commons views of the common good have covenantal dimensions and make a public argument for a covenantal understanding of the national community. We have recalled H. Richard Niebuhr's characterization of the founding vision of the nation as covenantal and as biblically rooted, and Daniel Elazar describes our American polity as "founded on the Reformed Protestant covenantal tradition in its Puritan expression and its secularized Lockean form."[41] Cooey refers to the U.S. Constitution as "covenant" because of its emanation from this tradition of covenant making. At the same time she cautions that all covenants are partial and that every constitution should be subject to modification.[42] Covenant with God, for Christians, should give special priority to the most vulnerable citizens and their suffering. Constitutions must continually be subjected to critical scrutiny on behalf of the vulnerable. The ongoing civic dialogue must expand the common good. Otherwise, our partial covenants and our relative constitutions become idols.

Dean McBride's analysis of Israel's covenant as presented in Deuteronomy provides a useful illustration. McBride calls Deuteronomy "the archetype of western constitutionalism." The "comprehensive social charter" set forth in that book was "something quite distinctive " in the ancient world, something "perhaps uniquely appropriate to the peculiar covenantal identity that Israel claimed for itself and which was the product of mature reflection on this identity."[43] Covenant and law (Torah) are not in polar opposition but in inextricable connection. Constituted by the mutual swearing of oaths, this "constitution" was directed to a corporate entity but also to a conglomeration of individuals. It was not a decree from a political power figure, for Israel's monarchs were tolerable only if they stood under it, not above it. In McBride's words, it sought "to empower a broad constituency of the community whose integrity and political independence it seeks to protect."[44]

Rather than impose social control, it appealed to the experiences of its public, a people with a slave, sojourner, and outsider background. As stated in the previous chapter, its policies above all protected the sanctity of life and worth of individual persons—including males and females, children and adults, natives and sojourners, law-abiding citizens and criminals, landowners and laborers and refugee-slaves (Deut. 20). Although its guarantees are clearly imperfect, egalitarian justice was its crux; this justice was embodied in appropriate procedures and measured by tangible results. The officers of its city courts were chosen by and for the entire population. It assured due process for those who had violated others' rights and whose acts had threatened the larger community (the common good). McBride points out that even in the cases of public offenders and warfare, there are some indications that the worth of all living things was to be respected, but the "holy war" mentality cited earlier contradicts such an estimate.

McBride emphasizes the attention given to situations of conflict (Deut. 19–25). "Egalitarian justice," he writes, "like political life itself, can only be practiced in a social arena where basic values collide and concrete decisions must be made between divergent human interests."[45] Thus understood, law in Israel's constitution comes off less as absolute rules than as an expression of a more basic set of relationships. Identity, participation, responsibility, and respect for diversity are all present to some degree.

Still, all covenants are partial, and all constitutions are as well. Deuteronomy was a constitutional breakthrough, but any effort to absolutize it breaks down. Every legal rendering of a community's covenant obligations should be subject to change in light of the community's later experience. Freedom to dissent and respect for difference must be built in to make the ongoing dialogue possible. Covenants require institutional form in law, but the law cannot fully capture the covenant—nor should any particular version of the law be mistaken for it.

Covenant and Commons

In the case of the commons, the centrality of community is also apparent with the conditions of exit, voice, and loyalty. In light of our religious examples, we can now allege that these conditions are also covenantal. Israel's covenant, as analyzed by May, Elazar, and others, has dimensions of both gift and choice. It is a response to prevenient grace, but it is also a consensual relationship. You swear your way in, and there is a way out. Participation does not reach full democratic scope, but it is there. And then there is loyalty—surely a central covenantal virtue.

Covenant and Common Good

The common good can provide a corrective to the nearsightedness and exclusiveness of some covenants, but it can also succumb to its own forms of the same constrictions. It seems that the two need each other. Both depend for their normative value on the quality of the community that they express and inform. Both ground obligation in the presence of others whose worth and interests are not reducible to ours. What covenant does for the common good is keep it rooted in relationships—in what Edward Farley, following Buber, calls the interhuman, that reality between individual agency and social institutions.[46] Appeals to the common good can submerge the vulnerable other. Some collectivist organic models of society and the ecosystem correct the faults of individualistic models at the cost of erasing the faces of individuals. Max Stackhouse cites as examples the "gene-pool communalism" or "spiritual-organic communalism" of the Hindu caste system and the individual-effacing espousal of the Party as representative of the whole of society and of humanity in the inverted hierarchy of East German Marxism-Leninism.[47] Elazar's observation is that an organic model makes rights depend on one's standing in families, tribes, or villages from which the organic society develops.[48] The common good can be an abstraction if it is divorced from the compelling face of the other, especially the marginalized other who lacks voice and visibility.

Limiting covenant to the familiar faces of the active membership leaves it only a contract. Losing covenant behind an impersonal whole invites oppression and neglect. As stated by James Nelson at the beginning of the chapter, "Without the organic the covenantal becomes contractual, just as without the covenantal the organic becomes tyrannical." James Gustafson makes a similar point in his preference for an interactional model instead of either an individualistic-contractual model or an organic model.[49] Recently, raised ecological consciousness has led appropriately to a greater reliance on an organic model as a corrective to Western anthropocentrism, but Sallie McFague, who argued for such a corrective in *The Body of God*, cautions that we need a community metaphor that envisions a common good "where justice and environmental integrity come together."[50] In tandem, covenant and common good work well to offset the pitfalls of excessive individualism and a communitarianism that submerges difference. Covenant takes the common good personally; the common good can stretch a covenant universally. Both are only as exemplary as the quality of community constituted by the covenant and encompassed by the common good.

A Concluding Example

As an illustration of the value of using the common good as an approach to a specific problem, affirmative action works well. As Miriam Schulman has observed, discussions of affirmative action have often focused on justice as protection of rights. The issue is defined in terms of whose rights are being protected or violated and how compensatory justice or fairness can be served in redressing past discrimination. It is better, she believes, to ask whether affirmative action programs are "in everyone's best interest." If we view ourselves as members of the same community and ask what kind of society we want to become and how we propose to do it, affirmative action looks different. The poverty, crime, and alienation that disproportionately affect minority communities are surely blights on the society we have and clouds over any future society that continues to foster them. Instead of talking about where guilt resides or what compassion demands, we should ask whether affirmative action efforts can help make a society less ridden with those problems that end up burdening the entire society.[51] We could ask similar questions about nutrition, health care, and other programs for our poorest citizens.

The trick of course is to get people to view themselves as members of the same community, as kindred-sufferers who are vulnerable to illness and unemployment. If they do not have that sense of commonality, the conversation about the common good in general and affirmative action in particular cannot happen. That is the identity question. The identity question in turn hinges on the presence of the other three elements from Daly and Cobb—opportunity for participation, assumption of responsibility for all members, and respect for individuality and difference. To the extent that the last three are present, the gulf between margin and mainstream will be bridged, the common good will be understood as a community quest and not a given, and the sense of community identification or loyalty will grow. But unless the powerful think of the common good of the whole community, how are the participation, responsibility, and respect for difference and individuality to occur? The widespread current antagonism toward affirmative action as well as the war on the poor that has characterized some features of welfare reform do not give us great cause for hope on this score. Women in general and marginalized women in particular continue to be disadvantaged. Minorities continue to buck structural or institutional racism. If there is not such a thing as a commons in which we all have a stake, an inclusive community with a common good in process of development through continuing dialogue, we all are left poorer in the process.

Cooey rightly warns that all covenants are partial; idolatry and exclusiveness are always hazards of our covenants. There are ways, however, to think covenantally about a bond with the whole of a nation, with the whole of humanity, and with the earth. That bond becomes easier to incorporate into one's identity if one believes that the voices and values of one's smaller communities or identifications are given a hearing and a secure existence provided they will accord other communities that same respect and space. To envision with Daly and Cobb a global "community of communities" is to affirm a common good that includes plural common goods. This common good will need to take constitutional expression, as it does in such forms as the United Nations Declaration of Human Rights and various international treaties and conventions, both as an act of participation and as a construction of influence. It will need to regard communities as commons, where voice is made more crucial by the difficulty of exit and where interests merge in a process of seeing and seeking coincidence between self-interest and the interests of others. It will also need a sense of covenant to give context to constitution and to foster loyalty to the commons. Chapter 5 will consider these possibilities.

We do look differently at each other if we move beyond our contractual notions of temporary and instrumental arrangements to the more confining challenges of living in a global village, a national family, and even a corporate environment where exit may be a very limited option for many. This sense of community will ultimately require not only the constraint of constitution and the push of necessity, but also the pull of conviction about human solidarity and environmental solidarity, about commonality and difference. Affirmations about creation in the image of God and covenant with God are one way of enunciating such convictions, but plural religious communities may yet find common cause toward a common good from uncommon starting points.

3

Homing In on Family Values

From different perspectives, both Catholic and Protestant traditions have seen that marriage is at once a natural, religious, social, and contractual unit; that in order to survive and flourish, this institution must be governed both externally by legal authorities and internally by moral authorities. From different perspectives, these traditions have seen that the family is an inherently communal enterprise in which marital couples, magistrates, and ministers must all inevitably cooperate. After all, marital contracts are of little value without courts to interpret and enforce them. Marital properties are of little use without laws to protect and value them. Marital laws are of little consequence without canons to inspire and legitimate them. Marital customs are of little cogency without natural norms and narratives to ground them.

The Western tradition has learned, through centuries of experience, to balance the norms of marital formation, maintenance, and dissolution. . . .

The Western tradition has recognized that the family has multiple forms and that it can change over time and across cultures. . . .

The Western tradition has also recognized that marriage and the family have multiple goods and goals. This institution might well be rooted in the natural order and in the will of the parties. Participation in it might well not be vital, or even conducive, to a person's salvation. But the Western tradition has seen that marriage and the family are indispensable to the integrity of the individual and the preservation of the social order.[1]

— John Witte, *From Sacrament to Contract*

*N*ewsweek carried an item in June of 1998 about a woman who had looked in the mirror in the presence of a gathering of family and friends and said marriage vows to herself to affirm that she was "happy with herself."[2] She still wanted others involved in her celebration, but the union did not require a partner. Did it take this long for solo nuptials, or did the previous mirror marriages just not draw an audience or make the news? The event happened in Nebraska, but it could have happened lots of places given the individualistic state of marriage today.

Marriage Becomes Contracted

That contracted state to which marriage has been reduced is captured well by John Witte in his survey of marriage, religion, and law in the Western tradition, cited at the beginning of the chapter. What now reigns is the contractual model—born in the Enlightenment, nurtured in the nineteenth century, and legally come of age in the twentieth. Stripped of all visible means of support, people enter intimate associations through private negotiations. Within the laws of civil contract and the general norms of society, people largely set their own terms for getting together. In this contractual world, Witte concludes, "Couples should now be able to make their own marital beds, and lie in them or leave them as they saw fit."[3]

In the story that Witte traces from the Middle Ages through Catholic, Lutheran, Calvinist, and Anglican models to our contractual era, church authorities and civil authorities had varying degrees of jurisdiction and supervision, but the community's stake in the institution of marriage was unmistakable even if the lines of jurisdiction were arguable. God, church, state, family, and nature had a say. The Mass Mutual television ad that ended with "We help you keep your promises" could have been attributed to entire communities as well as to their official representatives. Marriage was a communal matter. The order of nature and the commandments of God were at issue. The common good of the community was at stake as well as family survival and standing. Society has traditionally sought settlers who would put down roots, not the accidental tourists or "nomads," to use Wendell Berry's label, who want to live together without commitment or reduce marriage to human relations and emotions.[4]

Despite Berry's legitimate lament, one does not have to read about all the restrictions, interventions, condemnations, oppressions, and sanctions documented by Witte to know that the contractual revolution brought a bushel of benefits along with its liabilities. People were freed from parental arrangement and consent. Just watch almost any period movie to see how much that means. Wives moved toward genuinely equal partnerships with husbands.

Family planning was a private matter. Both women and children enjoyed legal protections that enabled exit from marital entrapment and recourse for spousal and child neglect and abuse. Consensual sex increasingly became a private matter between any combination of persons who had reached legal majority, and nonconsensual sex was progressively denied any vestiges of resigned acquiescence or toleration even in the marital bed. What men and women had decided to join together neither church nor state was going to rend asunder, and when people decided to rend relationships asunder, there were fewer social supports and sanctions that would keep them together.

Contractual freedom and sexual privacy are mixed rather than unmitigated blessings, but a long, hard look at "the good old days" makes it hard to long for them. Call it "nomadism" or one of Michael Walzer's Four Mobilities, we could not have left home, in the sense of establishing our independence, without it; and *No Exit* is not an inviting sign over the doorway to marriage for most Americans. Marital security could turn into maximum security. On the other hand, when people do not intend to stay married forever from the start, they tend not to—and our divorce-inclined society is the result. We have gained some welcome freedom, equality, and protection; in fact, the struggle is not over for full contractual freedom and sexual privacy. Nevertheless, we are also up to our eyeballs in problems, and the fact that both neoconservatives and neoliberals are sprinting to hoist their banners highest on the summit of advocacy for family values suggests that we sense something must be done.

The divorce rate has flattened, but it is still 40 percent of new marriages and over 50 percent of all marriages. The proportion of single mothers who have never been married has grown from 33 to 41 percent in the 1990s, and the number of households headed by single mothers has risen from 16 to 18 percent in this decade, although the pace is slowing. The number of single fathers heading families grew 33 percent between 1990 and 1997, but single fathers head only 5 percent of households with children, and single mothers 23 percent. More teenagers are becoming sexually active earlier, although the recent decline of teen pregnancy is attributed in part to a lessening of sexual activity.[5]

Don Browning, director of the Religion, Culture, and Family Project at the University of Chicago Divinity School, speaks of ours as a "culture of non-marriage" beset by "the male problematic" and "the female problematic"—the first, "the tendency of men to drift away from families," and the second, "the tendency of females under some conditions to suppress their own needs and raise children without paternal participation, sometimes under great stress and at great cost."[6] In the 1990s a quarter of the lives conceived in our society were aborted, a third of the children born had single mothers, and half of such mothers currently fall below the poverty line. Between a fifth and a fourth of our children are born into poverty. The estimates of the number of "lost children" in our society, that is, those born into poverty and broken households and likely to drop out of school and finally out of society, have reached fifteen million.[7] Although many couples seem to want what Ted Peters terms "designer babies," ours is a culture that neglects children, not to mention abuses and exploits them.[8] And finally, abortion and homosexuality, the supposed litmus tests of family values, continue to wrack our religious communities with division and our political debates with acrimony. Our culture wars are, in large measure, family values wars, and peace is not threatening to break out.

The other main zone of contention in these family values disputes is feminism, which is accused by its detractors of everything from wrecking the family to destroying male self-confidence and defiling (by rewording) favorite hymns. From various brands of feminists, there is also growing concern about sexuality, marriage, family, and children's welfare. The statistical diagnosis of our malaise, however, often starts in a different place from the preceding list. Up front, we must understand that from a third to a half of women suffer rape or attempted rape in their lifetime, 20 percent of wives are victims of physical abuse by husbands, one in seven married women is sexually abused by her husband, 59 percent of battered women have been raped by the batterer, a third of female children are sexually abused before reaching eighteen, one of every nine children is abused or neglected by a parent or guardian, three of every hundred children are threatened by parents with a gun or knife, two thousand abused children die each year, and two and a half million elders (mostly women) are abused by caretakers each year.[9] Feminist women and men, in whose number I count myself, believe our attention to family values should focus on the violence and desire to possess and control that plague our land, on the sexism and heterosexism that pervade our thinking, and on "the second shift" and "the double day" that working women take on in the domestic sphere because there is no justice in the home.[10]

In the family values debates, the language of covenant and common good (for instance in support of the equality of women) keeps cropping up. It surfaces as the writers in the Family, Religion, and Culture series, produced by the University of Chicago project mentioned above, search for common ground. It is also in evidence as opposing positions unleash their responses to the contractualism and hot pursuit of reciprocal pleasure and to the systemic oppressions and injustices that undermine the health and welfare of our society. It is not surprising that covenant talk appears on several sides of the issues, but it could hearten us if a common language offers hope for discovery of some common ground despite deep disagreements.

Sex In and Out of Covenant

Sooner rather than later, the family values discussion gets around to sexual mores. Before embarking on an exploration of varieties of sexual ethics, we should admit from the start that none of the viewpoints that we will explore will be identifiable with the sexual mores of Sitcom City as depicted on television. If there is a moral maxim at work in that world, it would appear to be one characterized by my graduate school mentor Waldo Beach as "Let your glands be your guide." Every cell phone contact with a possible companion for an evening seems to be made with the hope that "with this ring I thee bed." French royal courts look like convents in comparison with some of the workplaces and apartments featured on the tube.

Without trying to explore the vast literature on human sexuality, we can instead explore some views that connect to our themes of covenant, community, and common good. At the outset, we acknowledge two fundamentalist positions that either elevate law instead of covenant or equate law with covenant instead of seeing it as a particular institutionalization of covenantal obligations. Both of these fundamentalisms tend to focus on inherently and unexceptionally immoral acts that natural law or biblical rules proscribe. For the physicalist school of the Catholic natural law tradition, sexuality's natural function is procreation, and any act that is "unnatural" in light of that end or purpose is absolutely wrong. The corner into which this position can paint itself is illustrated by a citation from Thomas Aquinas provided by Catholic ethicist Anne Patrick.[11] Using the unnatural/natural distinction, the giant of medieval scholasticism held that masturbation and consensual homosexual acts were more heinous sins than heterosexual rape or incest. Bodily organs are properly used only for "natural" purposes of procreation, and at least with rape and incest, there is a chance that procreation could occur. Obviously, from this perspective, contraception and sterilization are out of the question. The quality of a relationship and the effects on all concerned are not the issue; the issue is "unnatural acts."

One quickly adds that revisionist Catholics, such as Patrick, do not accept such an uncritical view of "nature" and stress reason rather than the physical purpose of organs in their use of natural law. Most Catholic moral theology now places an equal emphasis on the unitive function of sexuality along with the procreative. It sees sexual expression as good because it strengthens the covenantal union between a husband and a wife, not just because it produces more souls for salvation.

Biblical fundamentalism also mistakes law for gospel in sexual matters. Instead of seeing law as a way to spell out the demands of covenant and making the rules secondary to the relationship, biblical literalism makes the biblical prohibitions regarding sexuality absolute without attention to differences in historical circumstance and cultural ideology and developments in human knowledge. Selecting certain parts of the Bible and emphasizing the New Testament (except in the homosexuality debate, where the testaments get equal attention), these Christians allege that confining sexual intercourse to married couples is right because God says it and they believe it. The regulatory implications of covenant are as much absolute revealed truth as the covenant-making grace and the covenant-embodying relationships of justice and love that stand behind them. The marital covenant is the law when it comes to sexuality.

To illustrate the differences between the two fundamentalisms here described, one could use the example of oral sex. What a natural law physicalist would say about it seems apparent. What a certain high public official, showing some effects of a fundamentalist upbringing, is reported to have said is that his careful study of the Bible had produced no evidence that oral sex was forbidden. Being well versed, the official found the biblical witness to his satisfaction.

As we have already seen, the covenant tradition pays considerable attention to vulnerability. In the faith of Israel, a bunch of strangers, sojourners, and former slaves were given an identity as a community. The shape of God's grace conditioned the shape of their covenantal obligation to the vulnerable. The vulnerable face of the other, to use Levinas's language, summons the self to compassion and obligation.[12] The other makes covenant possible and obligatory. The other can be abused or killed, but the presence of that other subject puts us into an unavoidable zone of responsibility. A covenantal ethic of sexuality does well then to begin with the vulnerability of the other because our interhuman vulnerability is epitomized and intensified in our sexual relations. We can start either with the common good as the kind of community we want to promote and argue that harm to girls and women by the objectification of pornography hurts all members of our corporate body or with the vulnerability of the other as a potential covenant partner or rape victim, but vulnerability is at the heart of the issue in either case.

A different set of prohibitions from those of the two fundamentalisms discussed can be derived from a covenant model. Argued from a feminist or a liberationist perspective, the expressions of covenantal outrage deal more with matters of social justice and the common good than with the moral choices of people in love. If we are going to talk about what kind of community we want and what harms that community, we should start with rape. In this vein, Rebecca Chopp dissects "the ravishes of sin":

> Viewed through sin, rape is seen as a complete distortion of relationship, as the mockery and devastation of what religiously "relationship" might mean. The betrayal of creation and the refusal of any sense of covenantal relationship, rape physically, emotionally, culturally, and structurally wounds the innocent victims and alienates the humanity of the perpetrator. Rape is not just a legal and psychological act; it is a spiritual act in which the connectedness of humans with one another and with God is violated and broken, and the reality of defilement, guilt, responsibility, terror, alienation, and separations will take years and years to be made whole again.[13]

The issue is the violent use of power to take advantage of another's vulnerability and powerlessness. If gift and choice are characteristics of covenant, no measure of either is present in rape. As the antithesis of covenant, rape is totally wrong.

The Uniform Crime Reports of 1996 state that 71 of every 100,000 females in the country was a reported forcible rape victim, and that rate was 15 percent lower than in 1992.[14] That statistic of course does not tell the whole story. There was a 128 percent increase in reported rape between 1972 and 1991, and the rate of forcible rape increased by 88 percent. The 1992 report of the National Victim Center and the Crime Victims Research and Treatment Center, *Rape in America: A Report to the Nation*, provides sobering information from respondents eighteen and over at the time of the survey. Thirteen percent of the women had been a victim at least once, and 39 percent more than once. Twenty-nine percent of the forcible rapes occurred when the victim was less than eleven years old, and another 32 percent between eleven and seventeen years of age. Only 22 percent were assaulted by someone they had never seen before or did not know well.

Husbands accounted for 9 percent, fathers or stepfathers for 11 percent, boyfriends and former boyfriends for 10 percent. Only 16 percent of the rapes were ever reported to the police.[15] Even conservative estimates indicate that at least one in three women will be the object of rape or of a rape attempt in her lifetime, one in six college females will experience rape or attempted rape during her college career, one in seven males will experience sexual abuse, rape, or attempted rape, and one in seven married women will be sexually abused by her husband.[16] The use of the "date rape pill" is now a practice of which people are increasingly aware.

Rape is but the ugliest manifestation of a larger social illness—a pattern of dominance and subjection in male–female relationships that pollutes the common good and poisons individual relationships. The sex slavery and other forms of exploitation of both females and males beginning at increasingly early ages in the global sex trade at least matches its ugliness. The objectification of girls and women (and to a lesser extent of boys and men) in the hard-core pornography industry is another obvious example. Ours has been called "a rape culture."[17] In a 1981 study of teenagers, over 50 percent of the males and almost 50 percent of the females considered it acceptable for a teenage boy to force sexual contact if a couple had dated several times and the girl first said she was willing to have intercourse and then changed her mind. In still another study, 60 percent of the men said that they would force sex on a woman if they could get away with it, and 20 percent still agreed when the word *rape* was used.[18] A climate of systemic violence, control, and objectification surrounds much if not most sexual interaction in our culture. In response, a covenantal norm can just say no to any form of domination where there should be mutual, uncoerced consent.

Covenantal concerns about using power to take advantage of the vulnerable go much further than rape. Feminists have raised our culture's consciousness about the offensiveness of so-called consensual intimacy where vulnerability has been exploited by someone who occupies a position of trust and responsibility in relation to the other. Sexual exploitation by parents, stepparents, uncles, and other relatives is a flagrant example, but in numerous professional relationships there is also a clear power disparity and a high degree of vulnerability. Teachers, pastors, doctors, psychologists and other counselors, lawyers, employers or superiors in the workplace, and coaches are all in relationships where a covenant of trust and protective concern should be assumed even if it is not expressed. It is also notable that teen pregnancies often involve more experienced men in their twenties. Boys and men can be the victims as well as the perpetrators of betrayals of trust in such cases. For example, my Centre College ethics colleague Rick Axtell reports that in an urban transitional homeless shelter for thirty men in which he was case manager, there were never fewer than 10 percent of the men who had been sexually abused as children. The fact remains, however, that girls and women have been the usual victims and men and boys the usual perpetrators. A covenantal ethic insists not only that the feeling be mutual, but also that the field be level for a healthy sexual relationship to develop.

Karen Lebacqz takes the vulnerability and power consideration a step further. Sexuality is, she perceives, inextricably bound up with vulnerability. When we desire another person, we become vulnerable; to enter a sexual union, we make ourselves vulnerable. We let down our defenses and open ourselves to the other. In our openness and vulnerability we lose control and in effect allow ourselves to be carried away. Sexual intimacy exposes us. Our bodies laid bare, our awkwardness magnified, our secrets revealed, our inability to "perform" manifested, we are at each other's mercy. That vulnerability and the enfolding of it instead of taking advantage of it constitute the grace, wonder, and peace of our intimacy. Lebacqz speaks of "appropriate vulnerability" where the vulnerability is equal; neither person is using power to take advantage of the other. It is not only the opposite of rape, but also the opposite of seduction. In both these instances, vulnerability is violated and power is imposed by the perpetrator. Sexual expression in marriage may or may not be an appropriate mutual enfolding of vulnerability, and some expressions outside of marriage could be such expressions. The vulnerability of the other should be a restraint, not an opportunity. Remembering efforts on some college campuses to teach mutuality by insisting that every expression of intimacy be preceded by asking permission, we may detect a new legalism in them, but their point is important. Sexual intimacy from the first touch should be a welcomed gift and not a wanting grab.

Although Lebacqz does not lavish explicitly covenantal language on this relationship of mutual vulnerability, she does refer to "a covenant of fidelity" as providing a context of security for appropriate vulnerability. "Marriage at its best," she writes, "ensures that the vulnerability of sexuality is private and that our failures remain protected in a mutually vulnerable and committed relationship."[19] We could say then that placing sex in the context of a long-term commitment would be the ultimate erogenous zone because it is a zone of security where people can share their vulnerabilities without fear of loss because of fumbling ineptitude, inability to perform on command, failure to present a perfectly sculpted body, or showing the effects of aging.

Because single people lack such a context of security, their sexual intimacies are fraught with greater reasons for anxiety. She wonders then whether we need a different sexual ethic for young unmarried people than for older unmarried people, assuming that the very young are very vulnerable and thus more susceptible to inappropriate exploitation of vulnerability. There are probably young adults who are more secure in their sexuality than some people of more advanced age, so age may not be the key issue. Although she does not take such a step, one could argue for the general rule that sexual intimacy belongs in the context of a covenant of fidelity at any age. We turn now to disagreements about whether that covenant must be actual marriage.

One version of the traditional limitation of sexual intercourse to the covenant of marriage is offered by Lewis Smedes. He does not offer a legalistic rationale for saying that sex outside of marriage is wrong, although he believes that it is. Instead, he argues that "adultery is wrong because sexual intercourse fits with marriage." He does not discuss the claim that adultery was considered wrong in the Hebrew Scriptures because it involved taking the property of another, but he does mention the Kantian rejection as a fall from rationality, the Thomistic rejection as an effort to avoid procreation, and the consequentialist rejection because people get hurt. We need better reasons than those because, according to Smedes, we could even reach the point where people were so tolerant of adultery that no one got hurt. His reason is that sexual activity, being the way it is, belongs in the covenant of marriage, being what it is. They fit. A life-sharing union needs a life-unitive act, namely, sexual intercourse. For Smedes, "Without any sex at all you have no marriage at all." He further states, "Sexual activity, with all its joy and sorrow and tedium, fits within the wholeness of the covenanted partnership." The mystique of coitus, which is something only faith in the Creator's design can fully appreciate, is such that "it signifies and somehow seals a personal life covenant." No matter how great or ordinary the sex is, the very nature of the act is essential to the marital covenant. Sex outside of marriage is not fitting, whether it is adulterous or not.[20]

A further variation is found in those positions that sexual activity can be fittingly covenantal before it is officially marital. The traditional argument has been that even engaged couples have not made the final commitment that should accompany the final intimacy. A revisionist version argues for a pairing of covenantal commitment with total sexual intimacy, but allows that the mutual promises of two people, usually recognized in engagement, can constitute their marriage in a moral sense. Full sexual intimacy prior to marriage can be fully covenantal under these circumstances.[21]

A final covenantal standpoint makes the least use of explicit mentions of covenant as such, but it still holds on to fidelity and commitment as essential to a responsible sex ethic. To varying degrees, however, people of this general persuasion open possibilities that might, albeit to varying degrees, trouble not just some but all of the people we have cited. James Nelson's work on sexuality has given helpful expression to a new paradigm that sees sexuality as intrinsic to the divine–human relationship rather than incidental or detrimental and sees salvation as inclusive of recovered sexual wholeness. Love provides criteria for evaluating specific acts, but it is not captured by lists of forbidden acts, and sexual rules should be seen as presumptions rather than absolute prescriptions. Love, including sexual love, is self-liberating, other-enriching, honest, faithful ("expressing an ongoing commitment to this relationship, yet without crippling possessiveness"), socially responsible to the larger community, life serving, and joyous. One of its principles is "that the physical expression of one's sexuality with another person ought to be appropriate to the level of shared commitment."[22]

We are not dealing with normlessness here. The commitment of people who are not intent on marriage includes fidelity and openness, but it seems, as Philip Turner objects, to be "well-suited to a limited engagement,"[23] and fidelity does not absolutely rule out other partners. Covenantal fidelity has usually been thought more demanding than Nelson at times seems to make it. Still, he wants fidelity to be a normative virtue, and his love has principles even though they are not absolutes. It is significant that he employs specific references to covenant when he discusses the community of the church. Both organic and covenantal, with each metaphor balancing the other, the church should be a community that models mutuality rather than subordination, accepts diversity rather than imposes sameness, and affirms the goodness of our sexual bodies rather than perpetuates a body–spirit dualism. In such a covenantal community of promise keeping and responsibility, the best sex education occurs. This education should not be the promulgation of rigid pronouncements but the exploration together of responsible possibilities. A covenantal context will both challenge the sexual violence in the society and nurture sexual integrity and fidelity in the fold.[24]

When we arrive at Marvin Ellison's *Erotic Justice*, we seem to have moved about as far toward covenantal minimalism as one can get and stay under the umbrella, but his line is as hard as any other feminist's when it comes to domination and abuse of power. First of all, a sexual ethic must be justice centered, and justice is "communal right-relatedness."[25] Injustice roots in the desire for possession and control and expresses itself in racism, sexism, heterosexism, capitalism, and other structural ills that distort love and block equality and mutuality in social relationships. A sexual ethic must focus on unjust structures as well as unloving acts and avoid systematized rules and regulations in order to liberate the power of "morally principled eroticism" from dualism and domination.[26] Score one for social justice; and as "communal right-relatedness," that justice might be a community's definition of the common good.

The guiding principles or central values honored by this ethic are the goodness of the body and sex, bodily integrity and self-direction (as opposed to possession), mutuality (being with and feeling with instead of domination and control), and fidelity (which maintains trust, honors commitments, and depends on mutual openness and honesty). These principles and Ellison's assignment of priority to a climate of justice for sexual expression and to the quality of relationships rather than prohibition and control affirm important features of both covenant and common good at their best, but some of his implications are tunnels through which one could drive almost anything.

Mutual pleasure is surely the desired end of our intimate relationships, but is it an adequate norm for all intimate relationships, as Ellison suggests?[27] When he speaks of "egalitarian, justice-bearing marriages" as offering "a framework of accountability and a relatively stable, secure place in which to form durable bonds of mutual trust and devotion" and as requiring "a high degree of moral responsibility, mutual commitment, and willingness to respect the diversity of each partner's needs," we are in covenant land, but he goes on.

Ellison believes that some marriages can make room for other sexual partners, while others thrive on exclusivity. What "relational fidelity" requires will have to be worked out in each relationship. He writes, "For some people, the covenant bond will most likely be violated not by satellite friendships or 'outside' sexual friendships, but rather by refusals to keep faith and give priority, within a multiplicity of relationships, to the marriage commitment."[28] It should be possible then for a couple to make an open marriage covenant or a long-term covenantal commitment that could be faithfully kept without requiring exclusiveness in sexual intimacy.

There may have been couples who have made and kept covenants of this kind in a manner than was mutually satisfactory, but there is a strong likelihood that both partners seldom stay mutually happy with such arrangements over the long term. Given what we have said about shared vulnerability and security, it is very hard to see how such inclusiveness would work out in a mutually agreeable way, much less qualify as fidelity. There is an ecology in sexuality as well as in nature that makes it hard to do just one thing. Everything has a ripple effect in other relationships. Adultery makes waves, which is why James Luther Adams called it a violation of a larger covenant with the community.[29]

When Ellison speaks of "a moral wisdom about the erotic" and calls "bodily intimacy among friends a prime location to gain the strength . . . to resist injustice and oppression," one wonders whether there are any limits to appropriate bodily intimacy among friends. In what surely is an invitation to rationalization and uninhibited experimentation, he states, "For some people, physical touch, including genital touching, will take place primarily or exclusively within a committed relationship. When all goes well, sex enhances an intimacy already established. For others, sex will be an initial avenue for exploring bodily connection with another and for opening up the possibility of further intimacy and friendship."[30] There is so much to applaud in Ellison's social ethic of sexuality that you find yourself wanting to follow his direction, but he finally runs out of covenant. Now sexual intimacy is a nice way to make new friends.

Societal policy and regulation should focus where Ellison does with matters of power abuse and injustice and stop where he does, short of invading the privacy of consenting adults, but covenantal moral formation should keep intimacy and commitment together and make coupling of total intimacy with total commitment its aim. One does not even have to limit sexual intercourse to marriage to make that statement, and one does not have to deny any gracious possibilities in intimacy short of such commitment to make it. Our concern here is to explore the ramifications of covenant for sexuality, and some of Ellison's suggestions leave covenant behind.

Homosexuality, Covenant, and the Common Good

Thus far the issue of homosexuality has been mentioned in passing, but not addressed directly. It is the occasion of intense debate and deep division in religious circles because some people of faith believe that the Bible clearly condemns it and therefore that they are bound to repudiate it. Others either interpret the Bible differently or believe that advances in human knowledge should lead our religious communities to recognize homosexuality as a sexual variation rather than a perversion. As a consequence, they accord gay, lesbian, and bisexual people the possibility of accepted, affirmed, supported, committed sexual relationships in the same way that they accept, affirm, and support heterosexual marriages. In the public policy arena, accepting same-sex marriage and allowing fringe benefits for domestic partners is seen by one battalion of culture warriors as an attack on the traditional family, however revised the standard version of it has become, and therefore an undermining of the bedrock institution of church and society. The other unit argues for acceptance of diversity in our definitions of marriage and family and tolerance of difference in sexual orientation in housing, the workplace, military service, and parenthood. Both forces of faith think the truth is at stake as well as the meaning of morality, and both political battalions believe that the common good understood as societal well-being is also at issue.

Meanwhile, the consequences of being gay or lesbian remain dire for many. In 1997, the reported number of antigay crimes rose 7 percent at the same time that the overall crime rate dropped 4 percent. The horror of Matthew Shepard's torturous murder in October 1998 is a recent case in point. Discharges of gay servicemen and servicewomen increased 67 percent between 1994 and 1997. Over half of the states have outlawed same-sex marriage, and more bills are in the pipeline. Maine has become the first state to reverse a law prohibiting discrimination against gays in housing and employment, and it is not apt to be the last. Loss of child custody, denial of credit, denial of service in public accommodations, denial of access to housing, failure to gain approval as an ambassador or other high government official, and loss of employment are very real possibilities solely because of one's sexual orientation.[31]

To return to the spectrum of stances that was treated earlier, we can say that we know where both forms of fundamentalism stand. Natural law physicalists make homosexuality and the intimate acts performed by people with that orientation Exhibit A for sins against nature, as contrasted with natural law revisionists who argue for a more sophisticated view of "nature" that takes into account new developments in scientific knowledge. Biblical literalists believe that they can "re-verse" any efforts made by liberals to reinterpret, contextualize, or relativize those select passages that are the landing fields for the forces of righteousness. Whether one relies on biblical law or natural law, God's law is clear for either form of fundamentalism.

In most feminist and some liberationist ranks, the oppressed, the marginalized, and the discriminated against include gays, lesbians, and bisexuals. (Latin American, African, and Asian liberation theologians have tended to be silent on the issue, although concern for gays and lesbians as marginalized people would seem to be a logical extension of their positions on social justice.) For almost all proponents of equal rights, the common good should include them, social justice must respect them, true community will affirm them. The language of liberation is usually articulated less in terms of violated covenants than of denied rights and structural evils, but there is surely also a sense in which one could argue that a national covenant that should include all of the people has betrayed or excluded the homosexual minority and that the denial of social support for same-sex unions constitutes a denial of community support for same-sex covenants. If stable covenants benefit the people involved and the larger community, we should be affirming such covenants instead of rejecting them.

Opponents may argue that some covenants hurt society if they reinforce behavior that is inherently immoral and destroy societal support for the traditional family. We have admitted that all covenants are not laudable, and attackers of same-sex marriage are convinced that the line must surely be drawn here. At least one counterargument grows out of personal knowledge of committed same-sex couples. When you see loving, just, mutual covenant relationships between people of the same sex who are trying to remain a part of their religious traditions, you feel like Peter on the rooftop at Joppa, seeing a vision of animals that you have been taught are unclean and wondering how you can call profane what seems to be blessed by God's Spirit (Acts 10:15).

To pursue the matter in covenantal terms and in terms of legal guarantees of rights, we can turn with profit to the contrasting positions of Cooey and Stackhouse. Both writers place themselves in the Reformed tradition, both take the Genesis creation stories as their bases, and both make covenant their central norm; but there the similarity stops. Stackhouse discovers or sees revealed an ontotheological order in the creation stories in Genesis and other biblical sources that is, at its deepest level, institutionalized in heterosexual marriage. Sexuality's primary patterns and purposes are found in the theological-biological norms of fidelity and fecundity and in the sociotheological norm of family. Some same-sex relationships may have more integrity than many opposite-sex ones, but anything other than heterosexual, monogamous marriage open to procreation is out of order and not worthy of the home-keeping seal of approval. The predominant judgment of the church affirms what should be clear even apart from revelation, and those who say otherwise are "false prophets." As churches and as a society, we should protect human and civil rights but not approve of any homosexual behavior or same-sex partnerships.[32]

Mining the same Genesis stories, Cooey concludes that their normative claim is about difference rather than about heterosexuality. Creation as male and female in the image of God signals kinship or commonality among people, since we are all created in God's image, and difference. Difference, but not sexual difference, is crucial. Difference is necessary for covenant; division is what sin does with difference. Where Stackhouse stresses order, Cooey urges process and dialogue. Where Stackhouse cautions against heresy, Cooey fears idolatry (whether religious or secular) in our definitions of family and faith. Where Stackhouse defends a public theology that should be advocated as a political guide in the public arena, Cooey seeks governmental sponsorship for a continuing dialogue of difference lest family values be equated with a national will.[33] The scholarly work of Stackhouse has contributed consistently and very significantly to covenant ethics, but Cooey's elevation of difference and relationship over law and order in this instance holds more covenantal promise for the common good.

If sexuality and covenants are as complementary as we are arguing, and if sexual orientation is as much a given as scientific studies are increasingly indicating, both church and state need to find ways to surround sexual union with covenantal vows. To equate gayness with promiscuity forgets all the ways in which our society has withheld covenantal support and failed to recognize covenantal commitments by people of the same sex.

The Covenants of Marriage

Even when we talk about people who are married, covenant talk does not dispel controversy. The 1998 Southern Baptist Convention directive to wives to "submit graciously" to their husband's "servant leadership" is one familiar version of what the marital covenant should involve for women. One hears rumors of a new hymn to the tune of "Blessed Assurance" with the title "Perfect Submission." Here we have the marital covenant according to James Dobson and Focus on the Family. The man's place is the headship of the marriage and the subsequent family. The woman's role is to "love, honor, and obey." Love, at least for the woman, requires self-sacrifice, self-abnegation, and, in some worst cases, the suffering of abuse.

The biblical admonitions to subjection in First Timothy and First Peter are given absolute status, and Jesus' challenges to traditional women's roles get short shrift. The cruciform conclusion of the servanthood of Jesus receives normative status as a mandate for the endurance of suffering. Even accepting spouse abuse can be viewed as an imitation of Christ, and men have argued that uppity women have provoked the husband's discipline by rejecting their God-given roles. In the required self-abnegation of the wife, the self is still the center, but the focus is on the self as the suffering victim.

The opposing egalitarian model of a covenant partnership elevates mutuality, equal respect, and dialogue. As William Everett has explained it, marital communion produces two types of covenants—the egalitarian bond of the marriage itself and the hierarchical bond between parent and child, which also aims at culmination in equality.[34] In a dialogue of equal regard, all speak, all listen, all seek to identify with the feelings of the other, all open themselves to be reached and corrected by the other. No one gives up on keeping the dialogue going. This "covenant of dialogue," as presented by Don Browning, Bonnie Miller-McLemore, and the other authors of *From Culture Wars to Common Ground*, is normative for loving relationships in general and for marital relations in particular. For these authors, the idea of covenant is one of those "powerful religiocultural symbols that evoke commitment."[35] This symbol helps marriages to persist and be renewed, and the religious context that informs it is God's relationship with the world in creation and redemption. Covenants help us keep our promises—especially the covenant making and keeping of a God whose steadfast love endures forever and the covenantal reminders of communities rooted and grounded in that gracious promise keeping.

The characteristics of a community, articulated earlier, can also serve as the characteristics of a true communion in marriage and of a covenant that maintains that communion.[36] The partners' relationship is constitutive of their identities, although not totally constitutive of them. They are both full participants in the decisions that affect their life together. They assume responsibility for each other. They respect each other's individuality and diversity. The difference of the other is respected. Both partners feel accepted, affirmed, supported, heard, cherished, enfolded, and enjoyed. Secure in being loved, they can give themselves without losing themselves. Such love does justice. The work of the home is shared. Traditional gender roles are not allowed to perpetuate inequity and unfairness.

H. Richard Niebuhr distinguishes among three kinds of marriages, which correspond to three kinds of community. The first type, marriage as an association, is a contract based on a coincidence of common interests. The parties may get what they bargained for, but they remain fundamentally unchanged by the relationship. The second type is a society of interested individuals prompted by a desire for complete community of life. These marriages issue in similarities of speech, taste, opinion, and values and in common memory and hope. In fact, they see a complete merger of personalities. The third type is a commitment to faithfulness in covenant between selves, but it is not a merger of personalities. Difference is important. Mutual respect, independence of each other, trust, and assumption of responsibility for each other characterizes these covenants. The same common interests of the first type and the common tastes and opinions of the second may be present, but the fidelity of covenant maintains responsibility to and for each other, even if and when the commonalities fade and the good of the other is not necessarily the common good between them.[37] A good community and a good marriage require a good covenant of mutual respect, not merger or subordination.

A Covenant with Children

If mutual vulnerability comes into bold relief in relationships of sexual intimacy, prototypical vulnerability of the other is exemplified in the face of the child. A covenant with children is not required to justify a marriage, but it is required to justify parenthood. This assertion departs from a "no sex without babies" strand of the Christian tradition.[38] The ultimate expression of this view is the continuing prohibition of artificial means of birth control by the Vatican. Much further over on a continuum of views that keep sexuality and parenthood together are Lisa Cahill and Max Stackhouse. Without denying that loving and responsible unions can occur between people of the same sex, Cahill claims that sexual fulfillment for heterosexual women should be connected to motherhood or its possibility.[39] Fulfillment outside of that possibility may occur, but it is accidental. Stackhouse makes fecundity and family part of the ontotheological order surrounding sexuality "that everyone almost knows, although a few deny it."[40] For both, marriage without children is somewhat disordered.

A marital covenant should reach beyond itself to others. Total absorption in each other by a couple limits identity to one relationship and belies love's outreach to expand its circle of inclusion. That said, Ted Peters appropriately separates the parental covenant from the marital covenant.

Conjugal acts, as he avers, have their own independent value. Children do not have to figure in to make it responsible. What is more, the "inheritance myth" (Peters's term) that fulfillment requires that our entitlements include having offspring who share our genetic makeup is not only mistaken but idolatrous.

Parenthood should be a choice accompanied by covenantal commitment. Especially in light of the fragility of today's marriages and the pervasiveness of a self-actualization ethic, the additional responsibility of children should result from a conscious commitment to put children's welfare ahead of even that of the parents. Both parents should make such a commitment to "mothering." Both share the responsibilities of homemaking and domestic maintenance. Equality in mutuality means that neither parent is a stranger to the child, that neither is a shadowy figure who disappears before the child is awake and reappears when the child is asleep for the night.[41]

What often receives little or no recognition in people's calculations about the havoc children can wreak on parental self-actualization is the immeasurable personal fulfillment that children bring to parents' lives. They may occasion great sacrifices, but they also return great satisfactions. A recent assessment of how crucial a father's presence is for a child was inconclusive, but it was very conclusive about the value of a child's presence in a man's life.[42] On a practical note, there is also evidence that fathers who get more time with children are more willing to pay child support because of what the relationship means to them. President Clinton's directive of August 4, 1998, enabling poor couples to receive Medicaid and not automatically be disqualified if they stayed together or worked full time was so right for family values that it makes no sense to have ever allowed the automatic disqualifications.[43] Both government programs and public and private employers need to get the message about the importance of both parents to children.

The covenant with children should involve more people than two parents. Paula Cooey proposes that churches make the godparent idea mean something. Hillary Clinton has reminded us that "it takes a village to raise a child." Kurt Vonnegut has argued that we need at least eighteen people for a family and conjectured that maybe then we would not have so many divorces. Everyone needs a gang, and joining a church should be a quick way to get in one. (One can imagine a college student telling his or her fraternity or sorority members, "You are the gang I never had.") Vonnegut voices the frustration of finding no Vonneguts in the phone directories of towns he visits and insists that we all need ready-made relatives anywhere we go. In Vonnegut's novel *Slapstick or Lonesome No More!* one of the characters, Wilbur Rockefeller Swain, runs for president on just that platform and wins. Everyone is assigned a new middle name (such as Daffodil or Chipmunk) so that everyone will have relatives everywhere. When the book ends, the nation has crumbled but those families are still standing. Being stuck with each other has promising (or shall we say covenantal) possibilities.[44]

Children do need more covenant than two parents can provide all alone. Churches and synagogues have covenants with children. School systems do in effect. Nations should, and the global community ultimately must. The Children's Defense Fund provides these statistics to remind us how imperiled children are in the United States alone:

> Every 9 seconds a child drops out of school. Every 10 seconds a child is reported abused or neglected. Every 14 seconds a child is arrested. Every 25 seconds a baby is born to an unmarried mother. Every 1 minute a baby is born to a teen mother. Every 2 minutes a baby is born at low birthweight. Every 3 minutes a baby is born to a mother who received late or no prenatal care. Every 15 minutes a baby dies. Every 2 hours a child is killed by firearms. Every 4 hours a child commits suicide. Every 5 hours a child dies from abuse or neglect. Among industrialized countries, the U.S. ranks 18th in the gap between rich and poor children, 16th in the living standards among our poorest one-fifth of children, 18th in infant mortality, 19th in low-birthweight rates.[45]

Religious communities are crucial contexts for the nurture and protection of children, but their coverage is far from universal; in fact, their coverage for those in their membership is often inadequate. At their worst they can even be contributors to children's ills by protecting parents' "rights" to mistreat children or by subjecting them to abuse in a cult atmosphere, as in the case of David Koresh and the Branch Davidians.

Faith Traditions and the Family, one of the volumes in the Family, Religion, and Culture series, reveals that the churches have more reflected than guided the course of the family in the last two decades. Virtually all of the denominations covered show (the Latter-Day Saints least) the incursions of individualism, divorce, single parenthood, changing women's roles, and new forms of the family, but their attempts to respond to the new realities have not been reassuring. Eileen Lindner's article contrasts the differing approaches to family policy by the National Association of Evangelicals and the National Council of Churches, yet she concludes that "neither has developed a comprehensive policy concerning the family or sustained any ongoing program to address family concerns." Neither recognizes with Lisa Cahill that "the family is an appropriate and timely lens through which to examine the bearing of gender and sexuality on the common good."[46]

What Daphne and Terence Anderson report about the statements of the United Church of Canada has a familiar ring to people in mainline denominations in the States. Beginning in the early 1980s, the reports reflect a lack of emphasis on the church as a moral community, except in discussions of sexism; a reluctance to advocate a distinctive way of life, particularly in sexual expression; a lack of conversation with the historical Christian tradition or early reports from its own denomination or ecumenical partners; an individualization and privatization of sexuality; a failure to link sexual intercourse with moral commitment; a lack of references to the family as a domestic church; a view of children as optional extras; and a failure to appreciate the involuntary aspect or givenness of the family as a core human experience that is not a mere human invention or an option to be elected if it serves the ends of individual fulfillment.[47] Religious communities need to adjust to the changing face of the family and still reinforce the importance of that institution as a covenantal context for children, a school of faith, and a setting where people balance mutuality, self-sacrifice, and self-fulfillment. African American religious communities have often helped to model a broader network of kin, neighbors, and people of faith to care for children in ways that most predominantly white denominations have not.[48]

School systems also have a large role to play. As one public official once said to me in response to community expectations that the schools solve all of the problems of the young, "After all, the schools are where the students conjugate." (I had thought that "conjugate" was the only thing students did not do at school, in either sense of the word.) The schools' support and supplementation of the family can make a huge difference. For example, the Family Resource and Youth Services Centers that are part of educational reform in my state assist in addressing family needs ranging from clothes and dental care to jobs and education for parenthood. Looking broadly and deeply at what keeps children and youth from learning, these centers put families in touch with the agencies, employers, and other persons that can assist with a wide range of problems and dysfunctions. The schools can be a front line of assistance to implement a national covenant with every child, but they cannot do it all, and they cannot replace the family.

Disagreements over discharging society's obligation grow out of disagreements in defining that obligation and even out of disagreements about what constitutes a family. Conservatives have invested their efforts in the protection of parental rights and religious expression (school prayer) from government intervention and limitation and on the movement to limit or ban abortion, but they have largely neglected violence in the family. Liberals have devoted their energies to the protection of individual rights of both children and parents against family violation, but they have neglected the welfare of the family unit. As Cooey has explained, between these conflicting camps with their respective rights platforms stretches a vast void in the definition of mutual responsibilities between parents and children. She suggests the development of covenants that link rights and responsibilities for both.[49]

Court cases regarding medical attention for children over parents' religious objections, the responsibility of drug-addicted mothers, the parental use of corporal punishment, and sexual abuse in cults can belatedly define outer limits, but if we wait for the courts to decide, we are always reacting to irresponsibility, neglect, and cruelty instead of anticipating problems before they develop. What we need as a nation and as a globe is the secular equivalent of a designation of all people and all families as the people of God or as persons entitled to equal respect, equal protection, and equal opportunity. Our most vulnerable, including but not limited to our children, should be given priority.

As Cooey points out, the Christian Coalition has defined the people of God as the people of faith and attempted to designate that faith for the nation.[50] For the sake of the common good, religious communities should use their thicker particular covenants to support a somewhat thinner covenant of overlapping consensus that has no creedal boundaries, does not limit families to heterosexual married couples with children, does not exclude children because their parents are legal or illegal immigrants, and even encompasses the earth around us in its vulnerability as well as the people among us in theirs. This universal political covenant will get more attention in chapter 4.

Abortion, Covenant, and the Common Good

The covenants of marriage, family, and national political community provide the right context for discussing abortion, which can be effectively considered as a covenantal matter from several angles. Two noncovenantal approaches to abortion should be set aside from the outset—not because they do not have to be addressed in both religious and political debate but because they are beyond the scope of our focus on covenant, community, and the common good. The first, articulated anew in the encyclical *Donum Vitae* of Pope John Paul II, is the creationist argument that God creates a new soul for every person at the moment of conception. This claim is troubling for several reasons. One is that the cause of pregnancy by a violation of covenant (rape or incest) does not matter; a soul is a soul. Use of a morning-after pill is no different from a partial-birth abortion in the last trimester. The second is that the clear differentiation of an individual occurs only with the appearance of the primitive streak between the second and third week of gestation. The zygote, which becomes a blastocyst in the sixth or seventh day after conception, is not yet an individual. Its cells are undifferentiated, or unassigned to a part of the body that they will become. During the third week cells begin to differentiate so as to form different body parts. The nervous system develops at the same time and generates the first reflex response. A distinct individual life has now emerged with the development of the primitive streak, and twinning is no longer possible.[51] Such Catholic ethicists as Thomas Shannon and Allen Wolter have found support in their own tradition for allowing abortion before that point, and Catholic Lisa Cahill calls it "counter-intuitive" to vest a zygote or pre-embryo with equal rights when you see microscopically the appearance of this stage of life.[52] Using a relational understanding of personhood, which is appropriate for a covenantal argument, we shall base our position not on genetic determination but on relational readiness.

The other position to set aside morally if not legally is one that considers the common good only in the sense of present societal well-being. Taking a social consequences position to the limit, this view puts the burden of proof totally on the new life to justify its entry into the human family. Abortion then is simply another means of birth control or another weeding-out procedure in the quest for the ideal child, and even newborns have not gained full rights to protection if they lack relational support. The term *soul* should probably be reserved for a life in relationship to others, which arguably can precede birth, but the mere presence of a potential for personhood stakes a claim that should be acknowledged, although it need not be accorded an absolute right to life.

Between these two poles are at least three covenantal arguments. Since covenants involve both gift and choice, it is not surprising that the arguments weight those aspects differently. On the gift side stand Paul Ramsey and William Werpehowski. Personhood is God's gift, not a societal or parental choice. Just as God chose a vulnerable Israel and made a church where there was not a people, we should accept the givenness of the vulnerable life in the womb. Its extreme vulnerability and inability to make its own claim increases its moral claim to protection.[53] This position commends itself by its presumption in the fetus's favor and its making all abortion tragic, but its omission of consent or choice does not do justice to the other parties to the potential covenant.

Beverly Harrison's position locates itself decidedly on the consent or choice side. Unless a "covenant of love and affirmation" exists in a community into which a baby will be born, the child frequently does not have a life worth having. Every child is entitled to be born into such a caring community, and it is not fair to a child to bring it into an anti-life environment. For the parent, "freedom to say yes, which of course means the freedom to say no, is constitutive of the sacred covenant of life." Women's freedom is as essential as the new life's right to a pro-life environment.[54]

Harrison's position is instructive about what it means to be a pro-life society and what a society's covenant with its young ought to entail. We should promote a society friendly to the flourishing of children even when the baby's own family does not. Her position indicates why laws concerning abortion should honor the woman's freedom at the same time that they protect fetal life as it reaches viability. The freedom and community care dimensions are closely related because a community that is truly pro-life will free more potential parents to say yes by its support of child care, medical care, and flexible work schedules. What Harrison does not affirm adequately is the goodness of the life that comes as a gift and not simply as a burden and the presumption in its favor that should surround decision making.

Revisionist Catholic Marjorie Reiley Maguire offers a third covenantal option that combines gift and consent in a developmental position. It supports a growing claim to full fetal protection and status as a person as the new life develops. Maguire locates consent not in society but in the potential mother and her pregnancy process. "The personhood begins," she believes, "when the bearer of life, the mother, makes a covenant of love with the developing life in her to bring it to birth. . . . It is the mother who makes the fetus a social being by accepting its relatedness to her. After that point its life is sacred because it is sacred to her."[55] She does not fix exactly the time of the consent, but she argues that consent can be presumed from the start if the pregnancy is sought and otherwise when the brain and nervous system have developed and the fetus is at the threshold of viability. Even then mitigating circumstances (such as danger to the mother or radically altered economic conditions) could justify withholding or withdrawing consent. People should not be obliged to complete pregnancies to which they did not consent, but the longer the life develops, the more consent can and should be presumed. Personhood comes from being personally related to others, from being in community, but she emphasizes the growing claim of the fetus. Since 58 percent of fertilized eggs abort spontaneously before implantation and 12 percent after implantation, leaving only 30 percent to survive, she finds it hard to regard early abortions as the rubbing out of persons or souls. For a pairing of the gift and consent in a covenantal position, the best options seem to be Maguire's position and that of Ted Peters, who inclines toward drawing a line for policy purposes at the development of the primitive streak as a good way to combine a relational view of personhood with a recognition of a biological given.[56]

A Sacrament of Family Values

As William F. May has reminded us, covenants in the biblical tradition require ritual occasions of renewal. Where do family values get their ritual reinforcement save in gatherings with one's religious community? The family meal could be such a ritual. Our society has perfected the working breakfast and the power lunch, and when the schedule closes in, we revert to the drive-thru dinner. What about the sacred supper? If the commons or the common good of the family is the community it builds, the term *dining commons* takes on new meaning. In their plea for greater attention to the institutions we inhabit if our democracy is to flourish, Robert Bellah and the other authors of *The Good Society* bemoan the devastating effects of the market mentality and the job culture on the family. As glaring evidence of the family's peril, they cite the fact that more and more American families never have a meal together. The microwave oven symbolizes the malaise. If we are going to "pay attention" to the family meal, this vital institution must take place as "the chief family celebration, even a family sacrament." They acknowledge that the family members' celebration of each other and what they have prepared at these meals will be accompanied by numerous manifestations of conflict, but that give-and-take only highlights the role of these meals as covenant conversations and as schools of democracy. Despite these inevitable conflicts, "learning to resolve them, to listen and be listened to, is part of the indispensable educational function of the common meal."[57]

This very sacramental and covenantal vision may offer clues for the recovery of family values and for the renewal of the civil society whose decline is now loudly lamented in many quarters. This family sacrament, which begins with the trust engendered by the earliest feedings of babies by mothers and fathers and others, like the liturgical Christian eucharist, is significant both for the reality of its present communion and for the ideal to which it points—a universal inclusive communion. As a present reality it should be a community of conversation where all members are respected and all voices are heard, where we learn how to speak and how to listen, where we learn to see from the place of the other. The discourse ethics of Jürgen Habermas and Seyla Benhabib has emphasized the "necessary conditions of argumentative speech." Benhabib designates these conditions from Habermas's work as "the principle of universal moral respect" and "the principle of egalitarian reciprocity." The first welcomes all who are able to participate; the second accords to all the opportunity to engage in the full range of speech acts—to bring new things up, to ask questions, and so forth.[58] Following this lead, each person, as she or he becomes able, would become a full participant in democratic discourse marked by procedural justice.

This sacrament recognizes tradition and generational differences, and it is an occasion for offering thanks in acknowledgment of a transcendent source of the gifts being shared. It should engender justice as the foundation of a caring community not only by the rules of its discourse but also by the fairness of the distribution of responsibilities for the meal. Writes Susan Moller Okin,

> I shall argue that unless the first and most formative example of adult interaction usually experienced by children is one of justice and reciprocity, rather than one of domination and manipulation or of unequal altruism and one-sided self-sacrifice, and unless they themselves are treated with concern and respect, they are likely to be considerably hindered in becoming people who are guided by principles of justice. Moreover, I claim, the sharing of roles by men and women, rather than the division of roles between them, would have a further positive impact because the experience of *being* a physical and psychological nurturer—whether of a child or another adult—would increase the capacity to identify with and fully comprehend the viewpoints of others that is important to a sense of justice.[59]

If we begin to ask questions about who gardens, who shops, who prepares the meal, who cleans up after it, and who gets heard at it, issues of gender justice are on the table. To the extent that such sacramental events occur, they become a countercultural critique of those scenes where Mom is the only kitchen help, where children are seen but not heard, where women know their place, and where there is more interaction with the tube and the microwave than with the people.

Not only does charity begin at home, but justice must as well, and the two must be kept together. Care may exceed justice, but it should presuppose it. Civil society also begins at home; the family is the foundational mediating structure. Rule by majority may not begin at home, but democracy should in the sense that moral and political discourse are nurtured in that setting.

Lisa Cahill's writing about the family as the primary medium through which the individual relates to the common good draws on the idea of the family as the "domestic church," which is found in her own Catholic tradition (starting in patristic writing and renewed by Vatican II and John Paul II). Puritanism, as Stackhouse shows, has a similar strand. Jesus and the early Christian movement challenged the family as believers' primary identification and as an instrument of social domination that reinforced patriarchy. Nevertheless, according to Cahill, the Christian family today can "break up the power relationships that control gender." She argues further, "The domestic church image can potentially make the family itself the social educator of its members for solidarity and service outside the family." Thomas Shannon fears that applying the domestic church image from his Catholic tradition risks bringing in hierarchy and inequality instead of mutuality, but his justifiable fears can be answered with due care.[60]

Even in their incompleteness, family meals can point beyond themselves to a larger family, a larger community, a larger covenant, a larger common good. They can model listening to and remembering voices that might not be heard in the cozy confines of our conviviality. In Judaism, a glass of wine is poured for Elijah at the Passover meal, and a child goes to open the door for him. He represents the coming of the messianic age and the great banquet. Elie Wiesel tells of the setting of an extra place at the Sabbath meal in his childhood. The family looked in the streets for anyone who might have nothing to eat and believed that they might, in receiving a poor guest, be entertaining one of the twelve anonymous Just Ones who wander the earth. A traditional Christian blessing asks Jesus to "be our guest." The church at Corinth was accused of "eating and drinking judgment against themselves" by Paul because they had overeaten and overdrunk and left others to go hungry, thus not discerning their sisters and brothers as "the body of Christ" (1 Cor. 11:29).

Somehow our meals should remind us of the hungry, our sharing should remind us of the lonely, our speech should remind us of the silenced. Our meals should occur against the backdrop of a sacramental feast at which everyone has enough and none too much, and where everyone is welcomed and none is excluded. A covenant's rituals should point beyond themselves to gifts that constituted that covenant, to promises that maintain it, and to obligations that stretch it to a more inclusive community. The household might even become again the bedrock of society that Witte's statement at the beginning of the chapter described.

4

Covenants of Work, Family, and Welfare

Living in our speech, though no longer in our consciousness, is an ancient system of analogies that clarifies a series of mutually defining and sustaining unities: of farmer and field, of husband and wife, of the world and God. The language both of our literature and of our everyday speech is full of references and allusions to this expansive metaphor of farming and marriage and worship. A man planting a crop is like a man making love to his wife, and vice versa: he is husband or a husbandman. A man praying is like a lover, or is like a plant in a field waiting for rain. As husbandman, a man is both the steward and the likeness of God, the greater husbandman. God is the lover of the world and its faithful husband. Jesus is a bridegroom. And he is planter; his words are seeds. God is a shepherd and we are his sheep. And so on.

All the essential relationships are comprehended in this metaphor. A farmer's relation to his land is the basic and central connection in the relation of humanity to the creation; the agricultural relation stands for the larger relation. Similarly, marriage is the basic and central community tie; it begins and stands for the relation we have to family and to the larger circles of human association. And these relationships to the creation and to the human community are in turn basic to, and may stand for, our relationship to God—or to the sustaining mysteries and powers of the creation.[1]

—Wendell Berry, *A Continuous Harmony*

These reflections by Wendell Berry in his "The Likenesses of Atonement (At-One-Ment)" were first published in 1970. Their integrative vision of a husbandry that unites people to each other, to their work, to this good earth, and to God may sound hopelessly nostalgic, romantic, and even sexist to urban, secular, postmodern ears. *At-one-ment* is hardly the word we would use for these several relations and their connections to each other. Alienation, fragmentation, division, and even exploitation might come to mind first. We feel torn between work and family, driven in our jobs, and hard on each other and the earth. Despite the lack of atonement that surrounds him, Berry persists by his lifestyle, his fiction, and his nonfiction in expressing a vision of life as stewardship of the land in which love and work connect in a community of kindred spirits. Life's covenants connect. For him, "There is only one value: the life and health of the world,"[2] and he manages to make covenantal and organic models mutually enriching. Does his integrative vision hold any relevance for people in our condition?

The Covenant of Work

Jesus told a memorable parable about three slaves who were entrusted with differing numbers of talents or amounts of money (Matt. 25:14–30). The crunch at the end comes for the person with the one talent who had carefully hidden it in the ground but had not garnered returns on the master's resources as the more "talented" other two slaves had. This story does not support moralizing about taking risks and buying growth stocks or about missing one's special calling to be a musician or an engineer. It describes a case of lost identity or buried treasure. Israel's calling or identity as a people was to be a light to the nations, to be a beacon of justice and peace, and the parable depicts Jesus' own people hoarding their election as a privilege to be protected instead of a vision to be shared.

To become part of a community is to take on a distinct identity, and for Israel and for the Christian community, that identity had a covenantal shape. Graced by being given an unearned identity as people of God, they had a vocation that obligated them to God and to each other. It pointed them toward the outsider and the stranger who were part of no people just as the covenant people had previously been no people.

This community identity was set in the midst of a human identity and calling "to till and keep" the earth (Gen. 2:15) and to multiply and "have dominion," not domination, over it (Gen. 1:28). Creation provided a "global natural commons," to use Neva Goodwin's term, and electing grace pointed toward a "global human commons," although ancient Israel often narrowed the scope of its global reach. Vocation in covenant community is an encompassing vision that involves working in response to a working

God, but it includes more than work. It gives an integrity (Berry's "atonement") and purpose to life. It establishes priorities. Covenant constitutes the community of identity and provides a vocation to work, worship, and rest in a commitment to the reign of God and its justice that encompasses all of life.

What we make of work, worship, and rest in relation to God, the community, and the earth is another story. In our hands work becomes drudgery, alienation, exclusion, and exploitation. At our hands, the earth becomes ours to consume instead of ours to husband or to wife. Our religion too becomes consumption rather than communion. Our rest becomes distraction instead of recreation. We live in a world too polarized between those who work too much and those who work too little; in both cases, there is too little good work.

The 1995 General Assembly of the Presbyterian Church (U.S.A.) approved a study document entitled "God's Work in Our Hands: Employment, Community, and Christian Vocation." It speaks of a "covenant of work that assumes mutual responsibility between employers and employees, producers and consumers." It states further, "Ours is a global covenant-partnership of work. When we work in conscious fidelity to our far-flung work partners, we live up to our calling. No neighbor on earth is irrelevant to that calling."[3]

Clearly, the vision of vocation articulated here makes one's daily work a calling, one's vocation the totality of one's response to God and neighbor, and service to the common good the obligation of one's work. In similar fashion, the 1988 U.S. Catholic bishops' letter on the economy, which was described in chapter 2, speaks of a communitarian vocation to contributive justice. This form of justice "stresses the duty of all who are able to help create the goods, services and other non-material or spiritual values necessary for the welfare of the whole community."[4] For work to be a vocation, it must contribute to the common good. Striving for private gain and corporate success is not enough. Participation in work is a crucial means of full participation in the common life, and people are owed the preparation and opportunity for that participation.

In contrast to this vision, work is many other things to many, probably most, people. It may be the minimum wage job that you have to take to leave the welfare rolls and that does not provide an adequate living for you and your family. It may be working at subminimum wage pay on that half of women's garments sold in the United States that are made at least in part by subminimum wage workers. It may be child labor in sweatshops with sixty-hour weeks, two bathroom breaks a day, and pittance pay (such as $1.60 a day to help provide the $2 worth of labor to make $180 shoes).[5] It may be one of Dilbert's cubicles in a corporation that is always subject to "downsizing," "rightsizing," or "brightsizing." Dilbert's creator, Scott Adams, expects that people will be "happysized," "splendidsized," and ultimately "orgasmsized" if present trends in euphemisms continue.[6] It may be a place where you are contracting black-lung or carpal-tunnel syndrome or being subjected to sexual harassment or stopped by a glass ceiling. It may be part-time work with no fringe benefits because your employer believes cutting those corners is necessary for the bottom line. It may be sporadic work as part of a day labor pool—handy for employers, but often conducive to homelessness for the "employee."

You may be among the 25 percent in one survey who said that their companies ignore ethics to meet objectives or the one sixth who said that their companies overtly encouraged misconduct.[7] Or your workplace may be one of those addictive organizations, described by Anne Schaef and Diane Fassel in *The Addictive Organization*, where tunnel vision, control, dishonest communication, denial and projection of problems, trust in quick fixes, nonparticipation in decision making, a permanent crisis mentality, and preoccupation with structure to the detriment of mission are deeply embedded in the culture of the workplace, causing an institutional quicksand that only the wariest can avoid.[8]

Such situations are clearly not good work. They may be work that is producing big payoffs for stockholders and CEOs, but they are not communities of cooperation serving the larger community. Some might argue that a workplace cannot afford to be a community and that to have such expectations is to attempt to turn a corporation into a church or a workforce into a family. The counterargument of others is that they have experienced community in their organizations of work. If the rejoinder to some of us who make such claims is that we have spent too much of our lives in education and other nonprofit sectors of the economy, we can object that community does not always come easily in those realms either and that bottom-line pressures that can clash with community are not strangers there.

The fact is that people find community in workplaces of all sorts. Do those experiences demonstrate only that subversive activity in a business organization may create a bond of brotherhood and sisterhood that is at cross-purposes with the profit maximization that drives enterprise, or can a corporation be a community if it has good management, as we found Edwin Hartman saying in an earlier chapter?

Where work is good work, where it is part of a covenantal vocation for the common good, it will be done by a community, in a community, and for a community. It will be more than a way of "moving on up." It will have the characteristics of community that we have cited. Employees will find at least part of their identity in it. They will participate extensively in decisions that direct the life of the community. The corporation and the workforce will take responsibility for its members (by providing good fringe benefits, for instance). The diverse individuality of the employees and their families will be respected. In addition, the members of the community will share more than a coincidence of self-interest in the profitability of the organization. They will find a harmony between the interests of the other employees and stakeholders and their own interests that gives them a common bond, a commitment to shared values.

Both the Presbyterian statement and the Catholic bishops' statement spell out the covenant of work in more detail. Since good work is such a good thing for one's vocation for God and neighbors, employment should be full, fair, sustaining, and participatory, according to the Presbyterian statement,[9] and the Catholic statement makes similar points. For employment to be full, everyone should have the opportunity to work. The requisite preparation, education, and health care should be available to all. Some may not be able to work. Others may be carrying family or educational or volunteer responsibilities that make full-time paid work impossible or inadvisable or undesirable. They may be fulfilling their vocation and contributing to the common good effectively all the same. The point is that a society should not rest until everyone who can and will work has that possibility. If making that possibility available means shortening the workweek or upgrading distasteful and unrewarding jobs or creating more public-service jobs or paying people to care for the young and the old in their extended families, then sharing the privilege and the duty of performing good work is worth it.

To be covenantal and benefit the common good, employment should also be fair. A good job carries just compensation. It is made available without discrimination to racial and ethnic minorities, to women, and to people of different sexual orientations. Where diversity is lacking due to institutional racism, sexism, ageism, and heterosexism, affirmative action efforts should be made to restore justice in the workplace. Responsibility extends beyond those who are included in the community of work to those who have not been included or appropriately represented.

Good work should also be sustaining in its effects on human and nonhuman life in the present and on the prospects of future generations. Finally, it should be participatory. Participation, as stated in the Presbyterian document, means "sharing in the common life" both in internal decisions and in the larger commonwealth of work.

Both our Catholic and our Protestant examples make covenant and common good instructive norms for the definition of good work and useful guides for enlightened management of corporate life. In this respect, they join a contingent of ethicists who have advocated for making corporations covenantal. William F. May and Charles McCoy have urged expansion of corporate obligation beyond the requirements of contracts to the welfare of the full range of stakeholders who are affected by the business. Max Stackhouse and Douglas Sturm have stressed the importance of democratic structures in the corporation. Elsewhere I have presented attentive respect, inclusiveness, and empowerment as norms for a covenantal corporation and have joined May in arguing that covenantal virtues can be institutionalized in the workplace. Laura Nash has advanced a "covenantal business ethic" that approaches problems with a concern more for relationships than for products and makes profit and other organizational gains secondary to the service objective founded in Judeo-Christian values.[10] The list could go on, but even some covenant advocates express some qualms.

Stewart Herman, for instance, considers most applications of covenant to corporations unrealistic but still believes that covenants can be built in corporations. The covenant advocates often err, he believes, in their premature jump to higher loyalties before dealing adequately with the establishment of mutual trust in environments dominated by an exchange model of contract and the politics of power and influence. Unlike contracts, covenants change the parties involved; however, without acknowledgment of mutual vulnerability by the parties involved, covenants become paternalistic because of an imbalance of power between management and labor. In other words, without a mutual recognition of mutual vulnerability, a corporate covenant can be unhealthy.[11]

Ken Estey is even more dubious of the covenant crowd's optimism. Scrutinizing "employee–management participation programs" in particular, he finds that the establishment of covenant relationships between management and employees can be "the first step toward management's acting unjustly and with impunity." When management supports a nonadversarial partnership that operates on trust and transcends the need for exact account keeping, the interests of workers tend to get short shrift. The language of company loyalty and teamwork and development of subordinates' gifts and talents may create greater efficiency and productivity, but it covers persisting conflicts between labor interests and management interests with a veneer of cooperation. Inequalities of power and privilege that contracts should address get papered over with covenantal language about dealing with each worker as an individual or with teams of workers as small groups.[12] As Herman also cautions, power realities should be addressed and not belied. In other words, when the covenant talk starts, beware!

Another danger of covenantal language is its appropriation in connection with addictions to work. In workaholic addiction, people do not really feel alive if they are not working, and the measure of their vocational seriousness is their willingness to come earlier, stay later, and sacrifice all of the other features of their lives as they lose themselves in their work. In the age of law firms that never sleep and a stock market someplace that is always open and coaches that think you can never do too many repetitions, hold too many meetings, call or write recruits too many times, or watch too much film footage, workaholics have their work cut out for them.

When a covenant of work can be invoked to give added impetus to such addictive behavior or when blind company loyalty can be made synonymous with dedication to one's work, the door is open for both exploitation of and rationalization by employees. And the nobler and more vital the cause (the work of the church, the care of the sick, the good of the law firm, the good of the team), the more convincing the need to sacrifice all else on the altar of one's profession.

If the elevation of covenant over contract can end up being a tool of the powerful used to the detriment and disservice of the vulnerable, what does this danger say about efforts toward covenantal workplaces? It all comes back to one's conceptions of covenant, community, and common good. Healthy covenantal communities not only allow dissent, but encourage it. They raise up their own critics. Healthy, nonaddictive companies and organizations find nonthreatening ways to get bad news instead of suppressing and punishing it. They make participation genuine rather than symbolic; it is not for display purposes only. They seek to empower rather than take advantage of vulnerability. They take into account the welfare of all the members. Contractarian elements will be required to protect the vulnerable and level the power imbalances, but a covenantal workplace will be characterized by going beyond the minimum out of mutual respect and mutual loyalty. One possibility for community of the best kind is the company that offers workers a meaningful voice in the setting of company policy and a share in ownership.

In *Modern Work and Human Meaning*, John Raines and Donna Day-Lower assert that our society has been keeping two sets of books—one measuring capital gains and another assessing what is going on in community. If work is to be good work that carries human meaning, the sets of books must be brought together.[13] In today's global market where racing for the bottom of the labor pool in terms of pay scale, downsizing, leveraging, relocating, and quick maximization of profit are reigning realities, it takes constant and concerted effort to keep the well-being of community within and without the organization high on the priority list. Some companies are doing a far better job than others, and it gets harder and harder to keep score. Wal-Mart, for instance, manufactures goods in more than fifty countries, using thousands of factories. Walt Disney products are being made in more than thirty thousand factories worldwide, and Nordstrom has more than fifty thousand contractors and subcontractors. Whatever codes of conduct these companies have are self-generated and often only self-monitored or monitored by third parties that are actually a company's own "exclusive buying agents."[14] Vigilance on the inside and from outside of such corporations is a mammoth task if anything approaching covenantal communities for the common good are to characterize our workplaces.

The Home–Work Bind

The moral life involves the weighing and sorting of competing claims on time, attention, energy, and financial resources. Some of the involvements that beckon us are seductions that waste what we have to give on activities that diminish us without renewing us, that distract us without making us more attentive, that divest us of resources without investing us in anything worthwhile for others or ourselves. Many of the hours that people spend in front of the television screen would qualify for criticism on this score. Some sober reflection will usually bring a conscientious person up short on this score, although it will not necessarily lead to any radical changes in our personal waste management.

What puts conscience in a bind in even more troubling ways are the conflicts between competing loyalties in which both covenants have legitimate and convincing claims on us. Marriage, family, church, friendship, race, ethnicity, gender, class, nation, region, city, global community, school, team, club, professional organization or standards, employer, labor union, political party, social cause, and the environment or nature all may have claims on us and may have received explicit or implicit promises from us. In an almost infinite variety of combinations, these plural loyalties can and do come into conflict. Our dilemma is the weighing of priorities among competing goods. All of the claims may have a measure of legitimacy and appeal. What do we do when we cannot spend time, money, and effort on all claimants equally? How do we adjudicate among covenants?

Joseph Allen's book *Love and Conflict* covers a great range of covenantal conflicts and offers useful guidance for resolving them.[15] For example, we can opt for the more inclusive covenants that protect the rights of all instead of restrictive ones. Or we can tilt toward the entity that is closest to the problem, using the principle of subsidiarity, and leave the family alone when it can manage on its own. Our main concern now is with two covenants that Allen calls special, as opposed to inclusive—our work and family commitments. Dual-career marriages are a particularly sticky example and one that will be uppermost in this discussion, but the plight of the single parent in the home–work bind is equally important, especially with the greater likelihood of poverty entailed. In 1995, 60 percent of married couples had dual careers, and in 1996, 62 percent of mothers with children under the age of six were in the labor force (92 percent of the fathers were). We know that this bind stands at or near the top of stress producers for most working women. One study of working mothers, conducted at Duke University Medical Center, found that their stress-hormone levels rose when they woke up and remained high until bedtime. The level was the same regardless of the number of children or one's married or single status, and the central cause was the "second shift" of child-rearing and household duties that waited for them when they left work.[16]

Now the men are getting into the act, whether they are assuming more of the "second shift" burden or not. A 1992 Mass Mutual study of working fathers showed that one half of them regarded work–family conflict as their central dilemma, and half of the men in a 1996 survey by IBM found balancing personal and work life a struggle, a major increase from 20 percent ten years earlier.[17]

One could argue that every marriage is a dual-career marriage if both people are working to meet the needs of the home and also to contribute something to others beyond the marriage and family. The problem of course is that much of the time the financial rewards for carrying the major share of the domestic responsibility have not been commensurate with the work done.

The first thing to consider is what can be done to lessen the conflict between home and work if few of us are headed toward family farm partnerships in the spirit of Wendell Berry. On the work side, many adjustments can be made by employers that really want to advance family values or be family friendly. Many employers have taken positive steps, and those who have done the most have tended to be large companies and those with strong representation of women and minorities in their leadership. The measures taken, however, are usually limited to no-cost and low-cost steps, and the dents made in the overall problem are in most cases hardly visible to the naked eye.

The first comprehensive study of work–family programs was completed in July 1998 by the Family and Work Institute. The study found much room for improvement despite widespread lip service to family friendliness. Among the one thousand companies surveyed, nearly 90 percent allowed workers time off to attend a school play, half let a worker stay home with even a mildly ill child without loss of vacation and sick days, and more than two thirds allowed flexibility of work hours to enable people to cover family responsibilities. Only a third, however, offered maternity leaves of more than thirteen weeks, and a mere 9 percent offered child care close to work.[18] A 1997 survey by the U.S. Bureau of Labor Statistics, which included companies with as few as one hundred employees, found only a small slice of workers eligible for family benefits—2 percent for flexible time programs, for instance. Professionals were much more apt to get such benefits than blue-collar workers.[19]

The Family and Work Institute study reported that many companies lack work–family policies, fail to communicate well with employees about services that are offered, and do not include sensitivity to family concerns in evaluation of managers. It is noteworthy that the employees' loyalty to the company grows appreciably when the employer corrects or avoids such failings and the employee likes the job itself.

Even when better policies are in place, however, the culture of the corporation may discourage the use of them. As Karen Geiger, president of Karen Geiger and Associates, put it, "This is war; . . . you gotta be here all the time."[20] A woman does not want to be subtly relegated to the mommy track, meaning that she is considered content not to move on up as long as she has flexibility for family responsibilities. The women that crack the glass ceiling seem to have learned to play the game the way the men play it, and that means going all out all of the time. In 1996, 19 percent of the labor force worked part-time; only 18.5 percent of that number were managers and professionals.[21]

The woman who became chief executive of Autodesk in 1992 found out she had breast cancer two days after taking over and feared that having a "female illness" might provide ammunition for those who did not think a woman should have the top job. Her response was to have a stopgap lumpectomy so that she could keep working for another month before having a radical mastectomy and then returning to work in four weeks instead of the recommended six to eight.[22] Whether she was unnecessarily wary or not in her situation, the attitudes she feared are still with us.

In her book *Time Bind*, Berkeley sociologist Arlie Hochschild, who also wrote *Second Shift*, found that both men and women suffered in the "family-friendly" Fortune 500 company that she studied if they leaned the family way. "Family man," she found, was a term in the company for a worker who was not a serious player.[23] One's own family may send similar messages. More than one young father who has elected to use flextime options to help with children due to his wife's educational and professional commitments has been warned by concerned parents that he will not be considered professionally serious by present and potential future employers. In such an ethos, it is no wonder that we get what Ellen Goodman dubs "the two workaholic family," and the laptop computer and the cellular phone make it possible to make life into wall-to-wall work.[24]

Another of Hochschild's findings was that the burdens of home often seem so daunting that work becomes one's haven, thus reinforcing workaholism. The workplace culture as well as its policies are keys to the resolution of our conflicting covenants, but the home front has to change too. Domestic tranquillity is not threatening to break out in the midst of the strains and conflicts of a growing multitude of homes.

Justice has to begin at home. If the greater presence of women in the workplace (50 percent of all workers) has not produced an adequate response by employers, the greater demands of the "second shift" at home have not produced an adequate response by men. As Okin has spelled out in *Justice, Gender, and the Family*, the idea that care is the reigning norm in the family and therefore justice is not necessary must be challenged.[25] Justice is the precondition of an ethic of care, not a desired outgrowth or an unnecessary additional mandate. Without justice, there is no true care. When ethicists separate an affectional ethic of the private, domestic sphere from a systemic justice ethic in the public sphere, they not only relegate the public sphere to a carefree existence, but also ignore the necessary inseparability of justice and love.

In the wake of such a split, women are left vulnerable to abuse, exploitation, and oppression, if not in the name of love, often in tandem with protestations of love. Any children in the picture not only may suffer their own abuse and oppression, but also most definitely lose the opportunity to see justice modeled in the privacy of their own homes. If the marital covenant is the mutual and equal partnership that any good friendship should be, it will change the context in which the partners struggle with the home–work bind. A marriage should be more than fair, but it should not be less. Participation in decisions, shared responsibility, and respect for difference should be learned at parents' knees.

On a certain professional football team, some coaches criticized another coach on the staff who allowed a player in training camp to return home to be with his wife when their child was born and then to remain two additional days because there were complications. They argued that they did not miss practice when their children were born. The culture of the workplace was wrong if the birth of one's child is not more important than a couple of days in preseason camp, and the culture of the marriages was wrong if suffering in silence was the expectation among coaches' wives. But who does the "homework" is a much more lasting and pervasive issue than time off for the kid's birth. The feminist revolution has taught us that the personal is political, and the politics of the home require an establishment of justice even when it is "just us."

If the home and the workplace should both be communities, all of the characteristics of a strong community become relevant. If both being a part of a particular profession or organization is an essential part of one's identity and being a part of a family is an essential part of one's identity, it is important that one's entire identity not be totally consumed by either of those bonds. One should not become totally institutionalized by either set of relationships, and a measure of the health of either institution is its recognition and even insistence that there is more to life than any single institutional or community connection. Just as children need other adults in addition to their parents with whom to connect and from whom to learn, a person who is totally absorbed by one relationship or set of responsibilities suffers deprivation and probably acquires tunnel vision. The perspective that varied relationships and community affiliations bring to a person's life is a powerful insurance policy against not only tunnel vision but blind loyalty and idolatry. How can we get our bearings if we are always enclosed in the same situation and encircled by the same influences?

If a commitment to justice and a concern lest one set of responsibilities or one covenant completely subsume and consume one's life can be established in both the home and the workplace, what might constitute some concrete evidences of these commitments? In *The Dilbert Principle*, Scott Adams proposes OA5 (out at five o'clock).[26] That rule gets to the heart of the matter. Of course flexibility is desirable, and in this electronic age, some people can do significant portions of their work at home and not on site. The point is that we need to institutionalize ways of saying, "Enough already!" If the assumption is that everyone leaves at five, no one feels pressure to stay as long as the boss, and the boss feels no pressure to demonstrate staying power and dedication in terms of hours logged. People can have a life after work! Adams is convinced that nothing necessary or worthwhile really gets done after five anyway. Granted, some of us are night people, but all of us need some way of setting limits on the suction toward work addiction, whether it is largely self-generated or generated by addictive organizations and institutions.

Another way to make the point is to limit paid employment that takes both parents out of the home to a total of sixty hours a week. Jean Bethke Elshtain and David Popenoe make this proposal in *Marriage in America: A Report to the Nation*, a 1995 study published by the Council on Families in America.[27] This guideline is one part of their general campaign to turn back "the divorce revolution" and the unwed parenthood boom by reclaiming the marriage ideal. They urge that every child needs a father and that parents must spend more time with their children. The sixty-hour rule certainly sounds ideal, but how are parents to negotiate who works less and thus may signal less professional seriousness? How many pay levels necessitate two full-time jobs? How many employers will support such a move when downsizing has often meant fewer employees doing more work? And what about all that work that many of us take home, either from necessity or from choice?

Still another way to talk about limits is to reexamine the meaning of the Sabbath in the biblical tradition. It guaranteed that, for at least one day out of seven, no one worked. The free adults did not, the children did not, the servants did not, the animals did not, and the strangers at your gates did not. There needed to be a limit. The sabbatical year was another part of Israel's covenant. The land was allowed to lie fallow, and indentured slaves were freed. Even nature deserved a break. These institutions affirmed that the land ultimately was not ours, that we did not own each other, and that work did not own us. Without imposing the same rest period on everybody at once, we need to institutionalize ways to let people off, to allow life to have rhythm and renewal.

Change will not come easily. In part it will not come easily because we all want everything we want to be available whenever we want it. It also will not come easily because you have to be holding some high cards to be able to buck the pressure to be a grind. Some people have quit jobs or bargained for part-time employment so that they could have time for children. To do that, a person needs options and therefore leverage.

You need some financial cushion, perhaps in the spouse's salary, and some impressive credentials, either for this employer or for the next one. People with power in organizations need to lead the way in spelling out relief, but sometimes they are the most addicted of all. Here and there, people are cutting back, scaling down, and reordering priorities, but they have to swim against the stream to do it.

One name for that stream is the global market. This market is making us a global village in spite of ourselves, and it is generating a cornucopia of wealth for those on the receiving end of its bounty. The blessings are distributed with drastic unevenness, however, and they are produced with an often-dubious efficiency. As companies restructure, reengineer, refinance, downsize, split up, and merge their way to prosperity, they are often squeezing more out of fewer people in a pell-mell rush toward a competitive edge. The cornucopia can also be a maw, devouring the participants.

Markets are not inherently evil, competition is not inherently bad, and bigness is not an inevitable bane, but it takes more than friendly persuasion to check the momentum of either a producing juggernaut or a consuming public when the market makes war zones out of many workplaces.

One power center that has already made some difference in American life is women. Twenty-five percent of all workers work for a woman-owned business, and women employ more people than the entire list of the Fortune 500. Women-owned businesses account for $2.28 trillion in our economy. Women purchase 85 percent of all consumer goods, and women comprise 50 percent of the workforce. There is power there if women do not simply imitate all of the shortcomings of the rat race they have increasingly joined. And their supposed bargaining power still has big barriers to cross. Eighty percent of women workers, for example, still earn less than $25,000 a year, and they comprise 70 percent of the world's poor.[28] Women and children need multitudes of male allies in the effort to recover or discover an at-one-ment between work and family based on a shared commitment to individual well-being and the common good of both this generation and the next one. The forging of strong marital covenants committed to justice in the home and the support of family values in the workplace will be of critical importance in this effort.

The Covenant of Welfare

If work can be a major problem, lack of it is perhaps even more troubling. Work is usually one's entrée into full participation in our society, and we have argued that everyone should have both the opportunity and the obligation to do work that contributes to the common good as well as to personal fulfillment. Good work is not a punishment; it is a milieu of meaning and a partial former of identity. How does a society assure such an opportunity for everyone? How do we enable people to be ready for such opportunities? And what do we do when sufficient opportunities do not exist or when people are not inclined to avail themselves of the opportunities that do exist? What do we do about people who are unable to work at all or cannot handle the jobs available, or who carry family responsibilities that consume all of their work time? What about the dependents of the unemployed and underemployed, when nearly 25 percent of American preschoolers live in poverty? Since we know that not all work is good, how can it be made better, and what obligation does a society have to get bad work done until it gets better?

The American answer to some, but not nearly all, of these questions has been the welfare system. It has been our way of assuming minimum responsibility for those who cannot, should not, or will not work and their dependents. Since the welfare reform of 1996, we have been reducing funding for this safety net and upping the incentives to enter the workforce. People have two years to get off the welfare rolls or be put off, and they cannot accumulate more than five years on welfare in a lifetime. People in school have been given only one year of continuation before they have to do at least twenty hours of work a week. Block grants to states have replaced federal programs, and services are being reduced as the funding belts are tightened. Some funds were made available for job training and work readiness programs, but no funding was allocated for job creation, and there was no guarantee of a job to those whose assistance eligibility ended. Each state could do its own program of assistance or nonassistance.

An important post-reform breakthrough came with the passage of the Workforce Investment Act in August 1998 after five years of arduous bipartisan effort. The act reworked the nation's job-training system to equip workers with the skills needed for existing unfilled jobs. It consolidated sixty existing federal programs into three block grants with considerable flexibility for the states. It cut through a maze of regulations by giving workers training vouchers and sufficient information on the placement record of schools in their area to enable wise choices.

The good news of the 1996 reform was that people who married no longer lost their benefits and that the people most ready, willing, and able to leave the welfare rolls did move into employment in significant numbers. Twenty-eight percent of adults on the welfare rolls began working in 1997–98. The economic boom helped; those leaving the rolls have often been the people who live in communities where employers and social agencies, such as family resource and youth services centers in the school system, are most active in assisting with this transition.

The bad news is that people least ready, willing, and able, who are often located in communities or noncommunities with greater levels of unemployment and much lower levels of cooperation and support from employers and community organizations and agencies, have not followed the script prepared by welfare reform. Disproportionately nonwhite and urban, this harder core of the unemployed will only enlarge when the economic boom subsides. People with physical and mental impairments or with less education and work experience will require more services to leave the rolls, not fewer, and more expenditure of public funds, not the assignment of welfare dollars to other programs. Child care assistance lasts only two years after a person gets off welfare, and 8.75 million eligible children failed to receive assistance in 1998 due to insufficient block grant funding.

The other bad news is that women leaving the welfare rolls (and they and their children comprise most of the welfare recipients) usually qualify for and receive low-paying service, administrative, and clerical positions, mainly at minimum wage. Such jobs do not enable them to climb out of poverty. Sixty percent of all U.S. jobs created since 1979 pay less than seven thousand dollars a year (typically less than eight dollars an hour, and often less than six dollars an hour). Sometimes the work requirement has forced people with children to drop out of school rather than continue to equip themselves for better jobs in the future. Sometimes the work requirement has led people to leave the welfare rolls without finding work because they cannot afford the day care and transportation required if they take jobs, and the stipends for these purposes are too meager.[29] Sometimes their job training has been received from employers who would not or could not hire them but used their cheap labor during training and then moved on to another shift of such workers. Because some people cannot believe that a living-wage job is or will be available for them in their area and because some strongly resist leaving the area where all of their family and friendship connections are, they sometimes simply try to wait out the crisis, assuming or hoping against hope that public assistance will be continued or restored when the crunch comes. Another complication is that parents who do not comply with work registration, and their children as well, can lose Medicaid coverage as a means of receiving health care.

One supervisor in the welfare system for forty Kentucky counties indicated that there were more changes in the two years after the reform in 1996 than there had been in the previous twenty years, and that the timetable pressure was simply too much too fast for many of the most difficult cases. Some people need the kind of impetus that the reform provided; others need much more than minimal help to break out of dependency. Welfare system cooperation with other community agencies and organizations is an important outgrowth of the changes and a promising return to practices in the 1970s, but what if communities lack such resources, and what if it takes more than two years to reverse longstanding and entrenched patterns?

One successful form of assistance, the Earned Income Tax Credit, has been targeted by some as a "handout" that should be discontinued. According to the Center for Budget and Policy Priorities, 4.6 million people (2.4 million of the children) were lifted out of poverty in 1996 alone by this credit, which offsets some or all of federal income tax and payroll tax for the poor. Such assistance is a dire need for the working poor if they are to escape poverty.

One of the reasons that critics of welfare reform fear that the war on poverty has been superseded by a war on the poor is that our nation's outlays on welfare for the poor are dwarfed by other forms of welfare that often seem sacrosanct. We spend 85 percent of our government benefits on the middle and upper classes of all ages. An *Economist* editor observed in February 1997 that the welfare state is not giving too much to the old, but to the rich. Tax breaks on home mortgages and other governmental concessions to the nonpoor assist and encourage individual families, but there is also what is often called corporate welfare. The libertarian Cato Institute identified $86 billion of such "welfare" in 1995 alone—about two-thirds found in special subsidies to businesses and one-third in tax breaks to industries. For the average CEO to make 173 times the average worker's income in 1995 and the CEOs at major companies to get 419 times the pay of the average blue-collar worker in 1998 amounts to still another form of welfare for the rich.[30] The welfare system certainly needed revamping, and all subsidies to business should not be summarily scrubbed, but the point is that welfare reform left the major portion of welfare benefits untouched.

How should covenant, community, and the common good figure into our political conversation on the welfare system? The covenantal tradition offers combinations of gift and obligation, of limitation and choice, of rights and responsibilities. One's being part of the community is not earned but given. Everyone has worth as a creature in the image of God. People are assumed to be deserving even if they do not always prove to be so. The gift or grace of inclusion involves obligation, a grateful sense of duty to contribute, to do one's part. The limitation part recognizes that people do not start from scratch, that they are shaped by historical, economic, sociological, and genetic realities that they did not choose. On the other hand, people do make choices. A covenant is an offer that can be refused, although it is not self-generated, and opportunities to overcome the limitations of one's history can be accepted with some help from friends. These changes are often slow in coming and require long-term help to occur. Human dignity entitles people to life's necessities, but life in covenant with others entails responsibilities even more than it guarantees rights.

An emphasis on community posits that we are people in relationships, not isolated atoms. We begin in connection; we are members of bodies. Healthy communities and the empowerment of all members to participate in them should be our aim. Freedom is not an abstract value; it should be the means of our full participation in the human community in its several manifestations. One community should not submerge all of the others. National political communities should encourage and protect the communities of smaller localities, religious communities, civic organizations, families, neighborhoods, and interest groups. Government and other communities should work together rather than in mutual exclusion. Any healthy community will seek to include all members in full participation, take responsibility for all members, and respect the diversity and uniqueness of all members.

The pursuit of the common good would affirm a shared good, a community in common, that is more than the sum of its individual parts and private interests. It would endeavor to make everyone a contributor to the common good by guaranteeing education and work and health care to all so that they can contribute to the common good and a minimum income for all so that they can participate meaningfully. Other ways of contributing to the common good besides paid employment should be recognized and rewarded. The poverty of any impoverishes all.

In their respective analyses, Warren Copeland and Frederick Glennon have assessed the main positions on welfare using some of these very convictions and affirmations.[31] Copeland combines the values of freedom and community in his analysis; Glennon uses a covenant model, which he finds closest to a communitarian position but not identical with it. Both posit that we are social selves whose personhood is realized in community; both aim to recognize and enhance personal freedom; both want to affirm the good of work for everyone without limiting people's worth to their work. Both find the main positions on welfare suggestive in part but lacking in some respects.

We can use former secretary of labor Robert Reich's morality tales, which have informed American culture and politics, to distinguish these positions. In *Tales of a New America*, Reich suggested that both conservatives and liberals live by their versions of four shared morality tales—"The Mob at the Gates," "The Triumphant Individual," "The Benevolent Community," and "The Rot at the Top." They might define "the mob" differently, for instance, but they have placed themselves in these tales. Despite their value, Reich believes that they no longer mesh with interdependent global reality.[32]

The libertarian or individualistic position of Charles Murray, Edward Banfield, and others pairs "The Triumphant Individual" with "The Rot at the Top." People are completely responsible for what they make of themselves, and their problem is that the welfare system has reduced the poor to a state of dependency. People will do what is in their interest, and the government has made it in their interest to take handouts. All we owe people is an equal opportunity to achieve happiness. We should get the government off people's backs and give them the freedom to sink or swim.

This position recognizes the severity of the dependency problems found in what has been labeled the culture of poverty, and it holds out admirably for personal uniqueness and responsibility. Nevertheless, these folks greatly exaggerate how self-made we are. Assuming that people are poor only if they want to be and that the government has given them incentives to be poor is a gross oversimplification. Carrots and sticks are sometimes necessary, but the libertarian stance sells short people's desire to contribute and to make something of themselves if there is true opportunity. From this perspective, the common good need not be anyone's concern, especially not the government's. Providing and finding good work is up to the individual employer and potential employee. Life is a series of contracts; covenant, community, and common good are out of sight and out of mind here.

A liberal, egalitarian position lifts up Reich's "The Benevolent Community" and "The Triumphant Individual." Lisabeth Schorr, William Ryan, and Herbert Gans could fit here. Again we start with individuals and not with community membership. The problem is that people have been deprived of what they need to succeed and to enjoy equal rights with others. This type of liberalism provides a sober assessment of what people lack and an optimistic estimate of what they will be able to do if government services and entitlements are provided at an adequate level. The emphasis is less on true equality of opportunity than on equality of benefits, rights, and resources. Adequate national governmental solutions can fix the problem.

The recognition of deprivation and the aim for greater equality are assets here, but there are also glaring liabilities. Community and mutuality are neglected out of deference to equality. The emphasis on individual rights, including economic and social rights, neglects the entrenched systemic character of the dilemma of the poor and the solutions that are needed. The duties and responsibilities of each to contribute to the common good and the uniqueness of each get short shrift in the push to gain the same for everyone. National collective governmental solutions get most of the credit. The common good comes into play in terms of the loss to the nation occasioned by the inability of the deprived to contribute, but the depth of the analysis of how the poor can be empowered is disappointing. The mood remains more contractual than covenantal, and more individualistic than communal.

The communitarians come in even more varieties than the other two positions. The neoconservative type represented by Lawrence Mead seems to have adopted the morality tale "The Mob at the Gates" along with a particular version of "The Benevolent Community." In this instance the mob is the legions of welfare recipients. The common good of the society is of primary concern, and chaos is the threat. The culture of poverty has ruined the poor, and it is their fault. They need to be inculcated with society's central values by a parent government. Self-interest alone will not bring the desired result; people must be required to meet their obligations to society even at the cost of some personal liberty. They will change only if forced, and they must be brought back into the community's order for their own good as well as to avert chaos. Daniel Patrick Moynihan in a less coercive way also aims for integration into the social mainstream as the best cure for poverty. William Julius Wilson, who has been appropriated by neoconservatives but is more of a liberal democrat, has still a different take on the separation of the poor from the mainstream. He believes that the isolation of the poor is the problem and that the values they have make sense in their environment. To get them back to involvement with the mainstream through a full-employment guarantee by government would accomplish a value stretch that Mead wants to be effected coercively.

As Warren Copeland writes, "There is no grace in Mead,"[33] although he does recognize the need for communities to hang together and support each member's contributions. This is not a community that values diversity, but rather one that enforces order. Copeland calls this position graceless because it first blames the victims (the poor) for their plight and then, in effect, punishes them into changing if they are to change at all.

Communitarians of a liberationist or democratic socialist bent have a different version of "The Rot at the Top" than does the libertarian group but a no less decided one, and they link it with a version of "The Benevolent Community." Frances Fox Piven and Michael Harrington are examples. This time the rot is the economic system, which needs a certain level of unemployment to function efficiently. Solidarity with the poor will bring one into conflict with the privileged class. Alienation from community is the problem, and systemic or structural economic realities are its cause. Governmental transfer payments are a way of quieting unrest and also assuring a minimal ability to participate in society. Full employment will guarantee both participation and personal fulfillment. Piven is more pessimistic about change, and Harrington more optimistic about the possibilities and effects of full employment.

Among the shortcomings here, as cited by Copeland and Glennon, are a tendency to neglect the intermediate institutions between the individual and the bureaucracies of big government and big business, the depths of behavioral dependency among significant portions of the poor, and the obligation each person should feel to work for the common good. From one perspective, inclusion and participation through a job or a social wage (guaranteed income) will restore one to community, and the common good will inevitably be enhanced. From the perspective of a conflict model, one takes what one can get from a system that is not apt to change except under duress.

Placing people solidly in community makes some version of this latter position most attractive to both Copeland and Glennon, yet not fully satisfactory. Max Stackhouse wants to put some distance between a covenantal model and communitarian-liberationist models because he believes that a covenantal model is less susceptible to the in-group/out-group inclinations of tribal forms of communitarianism and more antagonistic to Marxist collectivism, which undercuts the family and other mediating institutions just as surely as libertarian individualism does. He tends to lodge all communitarian and liberationist thought with collectivisms spawned by Marx and Hegel and tar it all with the same brush.[34]

One way to get at the shortcomings of all of the positions is to recall Reich's insistence that all of the traditional American morality tales are out of touch with the interdependence of our global social and ecological existence. All four morality tales, like all of the positions on welfare that we surveyed, have something going for them. "The Triumphant Individual" underlines the uniqueness and creativity of each person. "The Benevolent Community" mobilizes the cooperative spirit and the philanthropic generosity of a people. "The Rot at the Top" reminds us that power corrupts just as powerlessness does, and that it does more damage when unbalanced and unshared. The word *sin* is the theological label. "The Mob at the Gates" reminds us that people who have been down may not be content to stay there and that they may not always follow the establishment's rules when they come after their piece of the action. Sin can wear all of the hats.

The tales are behind the times, but not just because of unavoidable interdependence. Reich asserts that there is no mob and there are no gates in our shrinking world. They are also failed guides because they in some way pit "us" against "them," even when some of "us" are doing benevolent things for some of "them." Historical developments have created a certain kind of solidarity whether we like it or not. We need to learn to tell better stories about ourselves as a nation that affirm our common membership one with the other as well as our commonality with the world's peoples. We need solidarity beyond class, creed, color, or nation. As Ronald Thiemann observes, "A free democratic society can only endure if its citizens share some sense of public good and common destiny."[35] Without something in common, we cannot even argue.

Although Reich makes no references to covenant as such, that tradition can affirm a universal solidarity if it is inclusive enough. The model of a national community or family can affirm universal solidarity if it makes room for diversity within a community of communities. The common-good tradition can confirm such solidarity if it is separated from hierarchical determination of that good and wedded to an understanding of the common good as a search carried on in dialogue. We need stories that couple freedom with responsibility, equality with solidarity, order with diversity, and participation with obligation. Models of covenant, community, and common good not only grow out of such stories, but are communicated beyond particular faith traditions to larger societies and other associations in a society.

We have observed that at least one approach to the welfare system lacked grace, and we have also claimed that grace, or a sense of indebtedness for unearned gifts, is pivotal in the covenantal tradition. How exportable is grace? After all, we cannot tell every American that God brought you out of the land of Egypt, the house of bondage, as the prologue to a new covenant, and we should not attempt to build a national covenant on the announcement that Jesus offers a new covenant in his blood. We noted earlier May's description of the debt owed by physicians because of what they have received from scientists, teachers, patients, and government grants. They are not just possessors of skills; they are recipients of a tradition and of considerable help from others.[36]

A more general reminder of indebtedness was provided by a certain father who went to his daughter's college campus for family weekend. He was a magazine editor, and he had been working on an article on welfare cheaters. He drove to his daughter's campus in time to enjoy a concert on Friday night, a football game and reception on Saturday, and other weekend activities. He concluded the visit by attending church with her before heading back home. When the church service ended, he tarried in his pew, still lost in meditation. Growing rather embarrassed, his daughter asked what was wrong. His answer was as follows: "I have been sitting here thinking about my visit. I drove here through snowy weather over cleared roads and arrived safely and on time. I came to this college where I would be paying only two-thirds of the cost of your education if I were paying the whole tab for room, board, and tuition, and where you are receiving the fruits of the perennial quest for knowledge. I listened with you to some of the greatest music that human artistry has created and performed. And here I have worshiped beside you because our forebears made untold sacrifices so that we could have the freedom to follow the dictates of our consciences and worship according to our convictions. I think I am going to have to rewrite the piece that I am doing on the welfare system because we are all on welfare."

Somehow our education for citizenship should and can convey a sense of our community as a graced people for whom the welfare of all us is bound up with the welfare of each of us. That would make us partners in a covenant of welfare. Our religious communities and our families must be prime movers in such consciousness raising, but our educational institutions and our civic and professional organizations must play key roles. We are talking about civil society, to which we now turn.

Civil Society and the Welfare System

The current discussion about civil society often defines it as everything between the individual and the state, and the state via the welfare system is charged with having undermined rather than supported the civil society. E. J. Dionne, a *Washington Post* columnist, calls civil society "the organizations and places where everyone knows your name, and probably a good many other things about you, and your commitments, and your family."[37] For him these associations are outside of government and the economic markets, and they need protection from market forces as well as against the state. Government policies can actually strengthen and protect these associations from both the state and the market forces. Everyone includes voluntary associations, schools, clubs, unions, churches, softball leagues, and charities in the civil society, but some include the media, while others include businesses. Sometimes it seems that size is the issue, with the big media out and your local radio station in, the multinational conglomerates out and the mom-and-pop business in.

Perhaps the origins of the civil society discussion in Eastern and Central Europe and his own exposure to those societies accounts for the fact that Stackhouse seems less worried about the market forces than he is about government in his discussion of civil society. He acknowledges that the state can encourage as well as undermine civil society, but it certainly cannot construct civil society, and it cannot really sustain it either. He does not want to trash the whole entitlement system, but he tellingly traces an evolution from a casework system to an entitlement system that has either treated people as a class or as individual claimants and failed to look at them as parts of a matrix of relationships. With the breakdown of nongovernment institutions, which government has chiefly caused, "It is increasingly clear that the state makes a poor parent and a poor source of both income and values."[38] For Stackhouse, it seems, a corporation can be covenantal, but the government cannot. "In the long haul, the state is not capable of discovering wisdom or sustaining reason, or procreating or forming the next generation, producing wealth or meeting needs. It certainly cannot inspire trust and meaning at an ultimate level. For these it must depend on other dynamics, such as religion, culture, the family, the household and the market."

Without wanting the state to become the chief value generator in the society, one can still hold out more positive possibilities for government than Stackhouse seems to allow. John Wall articulates needed reservations about the clear distinction of roles between government and civil society on the part of traditionalists on both the left and the right: "Government itself, after all, has roots in tradition; ours in enlightenment values but also in the religious and ancient understandings of justice and the dignity of human life."[39] This depiction suggests a different possibility than either a secular state willfully devouring the functions of families and other associations or a religious state promulgating a public theology that squelches cultural diversity and religious pluralism.

When the free exercise of religion in families can include sexual abuse of children, genital mutilation of girls, denial of blood transfusions and other standard life-saving medical intervention, and marital rape, I fear less the intervention of the state where a clear and compelling interest exists than I fear the consequences of legislation sought by the Christian Coalition to protect, without restriction, the right of parents to bring up their children according to their beliefs and values.[40] The burden of proof should be on advocates of intervention, but government can legitimately assume a parental role. The state relies on the value creating and value maintaining of religious communities, families, and voluntary associations to inspire and expand the civil religion or the core values of the society, but people need protection from religion, family, and workplace as well as protection of them.

The government and voluntary associations should be partners, not adversaries, with respect to poverty programs, family problems, and environmental protection. One of the encouraging outcomes of welfare reform has been the necessity for community employers, community organizations, and voluntary associations to work together with the government offices to help people meet deadlines and to keep them from being plunged deeper into poverty. Rejection of government is not the answer. Cannot government policies reward the family-friendly business, make tax laws more family friendly, offer incentives to greater flexibility in the workplace, and assist companies who want to remain loyal to employees and communities rather than simply chase cheap labor wherever it can be found or to provide health care when the bottom line does not benefit by it? Has not government been one factor in balancing capitalist values with noncapitalist values in our democracy?

Government bureaucracies can drive a person up the wall, but so can the bureaucracy of an airline. I speak from personal experience in both cases. Hospitals, universities and colleges, and churches have generated their own horror stories as well. Bureaucracies can obscure the human faces that are supposed to be served by them, but they can also assure evenhandedness and efficiency in place of capriciousness and disarray. The big is not always the enemy of the good, but organizations can quickly become ends in themselves unless their people exercise eternal vigilance. By the same token, our individualism can wreak destruction on democracy if it keeps us from paying attention to the institutions in which our days are lived and in which our values are formed and perpetuated.

When I think of the state, I think of the government at various levels. When one of our daughters was doing research and writing for a state supreme court judge and then working for the state attorney general drafting legislation, she was part of the government. When another daughter was working in a U.S. senator's office and then working for the Office of Technology Assessment doing research on health issues for the U.S. Congress, she was part of the government. When another daughter worked in another U.S. senator's office and then taught in the public schools, she too was part of the state. Then I started thinking about our sons-in-law—the one who worked for the state attorney general and then became an assistant district attorney concentrating on domestic violence cases, the one who worked in legislative research for one state and now works in the Medicaid office of another, and the one who has worked for the Environmental Protection Agency in Washington on biotechnology agreements. They were all involved in statecraft at some level.

I think too about people in a monthly ethics discussion that I have coordinated who serve on the local planning and zoning commission and the city commission. And then there are those friends of mine who hold county offices or significant positions in the state's workforce development cabinet or the position of local police chief, whom I see at NAACP meetings and events. There is my former student who now supervises forty counties in the state welfare system and who comes back to speak to my classes. There is our recently retired state representative, who also speaks in my classes regularly and who served in the legislature for twenty-five years to the considerable advantage of our state and the considerable disadvantage of his law practice. There is the recently retired federal court of appeals judge who is a friend and trustee of our college.

The list could continue. The point is that the line of demarcation between the government and the civil society is far from clear, and the people I mentioned have been part of democratic institutions that carry on traditions, espouse values, promote the common good. What they were doing was not eroding civil society. Granted, the people I listed are members of faith communities, families, and voluntary associations that have nurtured and inculcated values, and their education and service in government institutions have involved immersion in a tradition, call it civil religion or civil liberties or constitutional tenets, that furthers and enhances democratic values.

If all people are to have the opportunity and feel the responsibility to do "good work," not just have a job, and if all members of our society are to be assured the requisite resources to enable their full participation in our democratic community, we clearly need partnership between government efforts and the contributions of voluntary associations and private institutions, not polarization. The government can work with families and not at cross-purposes. Relying on mediating or intermediate institutions alone to address the problems of the disadvantaged and marginalized will leave millions to fall through the cracks. Relying on public programs and universal entitlements alone will leave many of the roots of people's difficulties unaddressed. There are systemic and structural dimensions to poverty that neither pressures to work nor entitlement checks address. Only a conviction of common membership in a common covenant for the common good will keep us from expanding institutions at the expense of others and neglecting some institutions to the detriment of us all. As Bellah and the other authors of *The Good Society* have warned us, only by "paying attention" to all of our vital institutions—familial, religious, economic, educational, and governmental—can we have a democracy worth preserving.[41] Pamela Couture speaks of "a homelike society" where flexible workplaces are the norm, where biological parents can count on support from social parenting, and where it is possible to make time for love and work.[42] It takes a sense of community covenanted for the common good to make such a society more than a pipe dream.

5

Global Community, Covenant, and the Common Good

No era will ever succeed in destroying the unity of the human family, for it consists of men who are all equal by virtue of their natural dignity. Hence there will always be an imperative need—born of man's very nature—to promote in sufficient measure the universal common good, the good that is of the whole human family.[1]

—Pope John XXIII, *Pacem in Terris*

Although we would now ask for more inclusive language with respect to both women and the ecosystem, Pope John XXIII and Vatican II did the world a great service in giving the common-good tradition an explicitly global reach. Herman Daly and John Cobb in *For the Common Good* speak of a global "community of communities."[2] Exponents of the covenant tradition argue for the precedence of a universal covenant that includes all of humanity and even all of life on the planet. How, we now ask, do such noble visions mesh with the realities of both integration and fragmentation in today's global village?

Observing Integration and Fragmentation

A global market is rapidly making us one world. Regional and global trade agreements are bonding the lives of national neighbors who have not always been good neighbors. The electronic media and information technology are the messengers of a shrinking planet. But is this new togetherness creating or undermining community? The priority of national sovereignty still blocks international agreements on such issues as human rights, climate control, and United Nations peacekeeping. Subnational regional loyalties challenge even national identifications, and ethnic tribalism or nationalism foments bloody cleansing. National groupings suffer genocidal atrocities and hotly pursue liberation by whatever means their access to weapons will allow. Global community is clearly not about to break out.

Inside Europe

A notable example of integration found in trade agreements fostered by market forces is what began as the European Coal and Steel Community in 1951 and evolved into the European Economic Community, the European Community, and now the European Union (EU).

The opportunity that my wife and I had to live in Strasbourg, France, "the capital of Europe," greatly heightened our awareness of the integration in the EU, whose Parliament of Europe meets in Strasbourg, and in the older Council of Europe, which is based there and has its own Parliamentary Assembly. That sojourn also impressed us with the fragmentation that rivals the integration. Traveling across borders and escaping the provincial limits of much of the American press sets a person in a different world. One learns that European integration is not only persisting but growing, and one also confronts the suspicion that European integration could be a hazard to global community rather than a harbinger of it. Because of the mammoth market presence of the United States in Europe, its defense alliance with it, its role in trade agreements with it (such as the General Agreement on Tariffs and Trade), and its linkage with Western European culture, the European example has great relevance in our own country.

Life in Strasbourg can give a person more than just a better feel for Europe's growing integration and fragmentation. In the process, one also gains a new vantage point on the role of the United States in the world, on the postmodern rejection of metanarratives, on the relationship between the thick moralities of particular national and ethnic communities as opposed to the thin morality of international justice, and on the tensions between respect for difference and inclusive visions of universal community in international discourse. Is real European integration possible without some metanarrative? Is a metanarrative possible that respects difference and does not pit insiders against outsiders? Can the values of particular political and ethnic communities be protected and minorities still be protected as well?

Can a European community develop that will be a boon to the rest of the world, and not a bane?

The Council of Europe, founded in 1949 and expanded at last count to thirty-nine members, does not have the market base of the EU. It seeks to protect and strengthen pluralist democracy and human rights and to promote "the emergence of a genuine European cultural identity." Despite that announced purpose, one high official in the council's secretariat remarked to me that "the notion of European cultural identity is disappearing." The impact of immigration and the persistence or resurgence of regionalism and ethnic nationalism are important reasons for this observation. To cite one glaring example, the former Yugoslavia has made many wonder about the possibility of a truly integrated Europe both because of the EU's ineptitude in addressing its chaos and because it highlights the extremes of ethnic and religious enmity on the Continent. Disillusionment with past religious, political, and economic foci for integration could well be another reason for questioning European cultural identity.

The regional home of Strasbourg, Alsace, is generally supportive of integration moves, and its history should definitely prompt it to want close and amicable cooperation between France and Germany in particular. Nevertheless, Alsace also exemplifies continuing fragmentation or diversity. Alsatian identity is important. The Alsatian language is still heard often in the streets of the region, although it is not taught in schools. When a friend of ours said, "Vive la France!" to a waitress in a Strasbourg restaurant as a way of complimenting the food, she quickly replied, "Vive l'Alsace!" If one goes to Barcelona, Catalan language and pride are even more apparent. In Scotland, Gaelic is taught in some schools. In all these cases, a regional loyalty or former national loyalty is being expressed.

One also sees in Strasbourg why Muslims now outnumber Protestants in France. The Turkish and North African Muslim inhabitants are a substantial presence. Hate crimes against Turks in Germany and recurring French campaigns to suppress Islamic militants are evidences of a fear of loss of European identity as some define it. The upheavals in the former Yugoslavia and certain nations of the former Soviet Union have underlined the repercussions of tribalism for both victim and victimizer.

As Michael Walzer observes, the way to get people to transcend tribalism does not seem to be to suppress it, since it cannot be overcome, but to assure people "conditions of security" in which they will take on "a more complex identity" than one narrow tribal one, while demanding that the tribe accord to others what it demands for itself.[3] A healthy European community should be what Herman Daly and John Cobb call a "community of communities," and by their measures that ideal is not being realized with nearly the speed of either the merger of markets or even the collaboration of governments. As they caution, a common market does not make a community.[4] In order for European integration to be salutary both within Europe, however defined, and in the larger global community, it will have to respect difference within and without, and with immigration patterns those distinctions have become blurred. It will also need to convince the rest of the world that a more unified Europe is not an exclusive Fortress Europe of an economic kind that will prosper at the expense of others who are not in the club. The East European countries' eagerness for membership in the EU is one manifestation of that fear.

Two Camps

To comprehend the Fortress Europe problem, which cannot be separated from a Fortress America problem, the mixed picture of European integration and fragmentation must be set in the context of global North–South polarization. When our family first had the opportunity to live in France, in 1974–75, an apocalyptic novel by Jean Raspail entitled *The Camp of the Saints* was a hot topic of discussion. It predicts a world in two camps, which eventuates in the landing of a million desperate Indians on the coast of France. According to the story, the Belgian government had responded to the burgeoning famine, squalor, and overpopulation in India by agreeing to receive a number of children into Belgium and adopt them. The crush of Indian mothers offering their children at the gates of the Belgian consulate in Calcutta causes a reversal of the policy and sets off a seizure of every available ship and a forced voyage to the Riviera by masses reaching thirty thousand on a single ship. The message that came across was that the rich might have to fight the poor to avoid being overwhelmed. The wretched of the earth would not just lie there and take it forever.[5]

After our 1992–93 year in Strasbourg, the French government's 1994 response to its immigration problems gave dramatic expression to the "two camps" polarization depicted by Raspail. Cabinet minister Charles Pasqua announced a zero immigration policy that contradicted a centuries-old policy of granting asylum to refugees. At the same time that he announced the closing of the frontiers, he acknowledged that by the year 2000 there would be sixty million people in Algeria, Morocco, and Tunisia under twenty years of age and "without a future." Unemployment rates in many North African cities range between 40 and 70 percent among the young.[6] He could see "them" coming, and he proposed drastic measures to fend them off.

Pasqua's words, reported by Matthew Connelly and Paul Kennedy in their article "Must It Be the Rest against the West?" reveal only one example of a Third World (or is it now a Fourth or Fifth World?) of poor nations where populations double every twenty-five years, where people migrate to already-glutted cities, where population pyramids spread wide among the young, where labor cannot move freely where the capital goes, and where misery combines AIDS, TB, and malnutrition on the inside with desertification and civil war on the outside. (Americans may be untroubled by our population statistics, unless it is by the decline of our birthrate, but we are keenly aware that the Third World has come to our cities and that Hispanics will soon be our largest minority population group.) If only the poor could not observe Western affluence on TV! Speaking of a siege mentality in the West, Kishore Mahbubani, deputy secretary of Singapore's Foreign Ministry, observed that "no Western society would accept a situation where 15 percent of its population legislated for the remaining 85 percent."[7] Europe and North America are projected to have only 10 percent of the population by 2025 because 95 percent of population growth is in the poor nations.

The Human Development Report of the United Nations in 1998 indicates that the wealth of the world's 225 billionaires (controlling over one trillion dollars) equals the income of the poorest 47 percent of the world's people (2.5 million persons). One billion people have no safe drinking water; 842 million are illiterate; 158 million children under five are malnourished; 1.3 billion (20 percent) live below the income poverty line. One billion were unemployed in 1996. And poverty is not confined to poor nations; the report describes spreading poverty in affluent nations. The camp of those who do not have a place at the table is not geographically contained.

As Connelly and Kennedy point out, optimists about free trade in the global market see cornucopia where others fear apocalypse. They expect a rising tide of economic development to lift all of the boats and cite East Asia's economic boom (recently faltering) as their exhibit. The inundation will come from prosperity, not population. If one calls the roll of political upheaval and instability, famine, and population growth in Africa, however, and learns that it will take forty years in Nigeria and perhaps a century everywhere else for most Africans to return to their income equivalents of twenty years ago, it sounds like time for the affluent West to lower its own lifeboats and hope that it doesn't get swamped in the waves from Raspail's threatening fleet as it heads for some imagined island of protection. That's assuming that survival and not human solidarity is uppermost in the minds of this new breed of boat people. To those knowledgeable about these countries, calling the roll of Algeria, Angola, Democratic Republic of Congo, Egypt, Ethiopia, Liberia, Nigeria, Rwanda, Sudan, and Somalia does not reassure.

In light of these conditions, what would make possible a European or U.S. identity that affirms convergence rather than conflict between European community or Western community and global community? Amid the fragmentation and pluralism, can a master narrative be recovered or discovered or developed that respects difference and yet creates a larger sense of identity around commitments to common values? Can any such narrative represent the marginalized members of the global community, both human and nonhuman, and lessen the polarization between the camps of North and South?

Assessing the Health of the European Community

In chapters 2 and following, we have referred to the four measures that Daly and Cobb provide for assessing the degree to which a society is also a community. For Daly and Cobb, to be a community, the social grouping does not have to exhibit the intimacy designated as requisite by Ferdinand Toennies to set it apart from the impersonality of society. Everybody does not have to know your name. It is required, however, that members of a community have a conscious sense of identification with that particular society and extensive participation in decision making. The society should also assume responsibility for its members and respect each member's diverse individuality.[8] We have asked how we rate as a national community by these measures, and we can assess European community using these same standards.

Community Criteria

In the European Union the participatory point is being addressed at least somewhat by the according of greater co-decision powers to the directly elected Parliament of Europe alongside the European Commission, which is the supranational executive body made of two commissioners named by the larger member governments and one commissioner named by the smaller ones. Greater transparency or publicity has also been implemented in the proceedings of the union's institutions to correct what was termed the "deficit of democracy." There is, as well, direct election of representatives to the Parliament of Europe from parliamentary districts of each member country. Nevertheless, much remains to be done to make the general populace feel like European participants.

The assumption of responsibility involves, on the one hand, a debate between the richer and poorer members within the EU. The more prosperous countries of the northern tier, joined most recently by Austria, Finland, and Sweden, believe at times that they are having to do too much sharing with the less-advantaged countries, and the poorer countries question the adequacy of the assistance. As William Drozdiak wrote in 1995 in the *Washington Post*, Germany and France have sometimes faced in different directions in their anxieties over threats to their security—Germany to the power vacuum in Eastern Europe and the unrest in Russia, and France (along with Spain and Italy) to "the spillover of Islamic radicalism in North Africa."[9] Germany has convinced the EU of the need for trade and aid to raise the living standards of the East, but some concessions have also been made to the concerns of France, Spain, and Italy about opening markets and giving aid to neighbors in the South.

Some assumption of responsibility by the richer countries is understood going into the EU; the question is how robust a nation's economy has to be even to get in. The Council of Europe need not be so exclusive about membership because it undertakes no such economic obligation. When we turn, however, to the protection of individual persons in all member states, the uneven success of some of the European Commission's executive branch social programs demonstrates lack of community in many instances. Occupational health and safety, free movement of workers, standardization of education and training, and sexual equality are the bright spots. Harmonization of wages and benefits for workers, their involvement in corporate decision making, and "social dialogue" among management, unions, and public authorities at the EU level have had a more checkered record. The thorny question of who gets to become a full citizen in member nations is particularly telling about the openness of membership.

A related and even more damning issue in Europe is respect for differences. Some of the lack of respect, as seen in the treatment of immigrants, is rationalized in some quarters by denying responsibility for noncitizens and making citizenship hard to get (as with the case of Turks in Germany). Evidences of xenophobia and racism often increase with rising unemployment rates, as seen in the French example cited earlier. A 1993 UN report estimated that twenty-five million people would migrate into the European Union in the coming decade.[10] These will be people of "other" colors, creeds, and customs. The prospects of growing respect for differences are not pretty. The history of hostility toward Muslims in the former Yugoslavia and the persistence of neo-Nazi elements in Germany are two reasons for discouragement. In fact, the measure of respect for difference points more to Europe's lack of community than its progress toward community.

As for self-identification, the end of the Cold War has in a way deprived Europe of its best stimulus to a sense of European membership. If defense is all that makes you a community, what do you use as a new focus to generate a sense of being part of one another, of being defined in part by one's larger membership beyond the nation-state, when the Iron Curtain is not there anymore?

The next refuge for mutual self-interest has of course been economic; despite the abandonment of European Economic Community language for EC and now EU language, being able to compete with the United States and Japan economically has created more incentive to integration than ideals of political cooperation have. Neorealist theory points to the fear on the part of wavering nations of being left behind in the drive toward integration. The hope of neofunctionalists is that every new aspect of economic cooperation and interdependence will produce spillover that will ultimately bring thoroughgoing political union. Despite evidences that spillover does occur, although often not at the anticipated rate, the lukewarm reception of each new stage of integration, including the move to a common currency, has revealed that the average European's sense of transnational self-identification has run well behind the projections of the folks in Brussels.

What will it take to evoke such loyalty? Surely more than European anthems, holidays, and T-shirts. Loyalty to something more than the market will be required now that whole regional economies (fishing, cheese, etc.) have seen their vulnerability in the face of the push toward free trade not only in Europe but also in the world (e.g., the General Agreement on Tariffs and Trade, the European Economic Area, the North American Free Trade Agreement). Insistence on environmental standards and protection of human welfare can be conditions of trade agreements and economic alliances, but maintaining their normative importance is more than the market alone can bear.

In his article "Disintegrating Theories of Integration," Eric Gorham underlines the centrality and confusion of the loyalty question. People are asked simultaneously to be loyal citizens of their region (Basque), their nation (Spain), and Europe. Strengthening ties to Europe seems to mean weakening other strong traditional ties. "At the same time," Gorham asserts, "it [the EC] asks those citizens to reinforce their differences with Americans, Canadians, Koreans, etc. Being a European, then, means not-being something else, it means recognizing an other, and choosing to exclude it."[11] He doubts that Europeans are ready either psychologically or culturally to make this loyalty leap.

The Need for an Other

The internal identity conflict is not the only aspect of European integration that seems to require an other to exclude. The pressures of both immigration and the global market illustrate the global context in which European integration will either progress or regress, and they push the discussion of the health of the European community beyond an intramural focus to the question of impact on global community. A sobering alarm on this subject was sounded in the summer of 1993 by Giles Merritt. He observed a "European fundamentalism," which he described as "our fear and rejection of other cultures," at work.[12] Economic recession had brought defensive reactions against non-European goods and people. The actions of skinheads and neofascists had triggered tighter immigration controls instead of a push toward greater openness. Writing in 1994, Arthur Schlesinger worried similarly about a resurgent tribalism, seen in ethnic and religious fanaticism, that threatened even national identity and grew out of a search for a secure shelter from the buffets of global economic and technological forces that people have felt unable to control. Global economic integration can trigger a disintegrating politics of identity.[13]

In an effort to suggest what is lacking, Merritt wrote,

> We Europeans apparently see ourselves as a beleaguered white Christian community that is fighting a rearguard action against what we perceive as growing threats to our way of life. Long gone seem the days when Europeans wisely believed that they had a *mission civilisatrice* to help less fortunate people around the world.
>
> Europe needs a rallying call that will banish these defensive attitudes.[14]

He argued that this protectiveness against the outside world needs to give way to a more global vision. He wanted the European Commission to stop defending the status quo and take the lead in relation to the newly industrialized countries of Asia and the whole of the developing world. In its own long-term interest, Europe should allow (not a winning way to put it in Third World eyes) the economies of Eastern Europe, Asia, Latin America, and Africa to assume leadership in steel, textiles, automobiles, and other items in order to gain the capital needed to buy Europe's high-tech goods. Europe must emerge as "a force for global economic development."

What has actually occurred under the rubric of economic development has been the creation of a global interdependence that has rendered poor countries dependent, according to Gustavo Gutiérrez and such dependency theorists as Theontonio Dos Santos. The dynamics of the global market have created a center and a periphery, with the underdevelopment of poor countries becoming a byproduct of the development of rich countries. In their perceived backwardness, the poor nations become feeders of raw materials and export products that enhance the growth of the developed countries. The interdependence thus forged is disadvantageous to the dependent countries. As my colleague Rick Axtell has elaborated in some of his writing, the "structural adjustment programs" that have been required as conditions for loans by the International Monetary Fund and the World Bank have presumed that success is measured solely in terms of certain economic indicators—a 4 to 5 percent increase in the gross domestic product, increased exports, lower inflation, increased foreign investment, and lower national budget deficits through increased privatization. The growth of a country's debt burden, the swerving of its economy away from sustainability and toward the export market, the increase of unemployment, and the worsening of such important health indicators as infant mortality rates and immunization levels are not leading indicators for the measurement of success. Thus global economic development and interdependence come at a cost to community and the common good conceived in terms other than selected economic criteria dictate.[15]

Egyptian Samir Amin, in his book *Eurocentrism*, also offers a Third World perspective on Europe's heavy hand in past development that does not see its earlier civilizing mission as being as benign as Merritt does. As Amin perceives it, Eurocentrism emerged with the Renaissance but did not flourish on a global scale until the nineteenth century, when capitalism made its universal claim. Uprooting Hellenism from its ties to Egyptian and Phoenician cultures, Eurocentrism constructed a history of "the eternal West" that progressed from ancient Greece to Rome to feudal Christian Europe and finally to capitalist Europe. It asserted that "the entire history of Europe necessarily led to the blossoming of capitalism to the extent that Christianity, regarded as a European religion, was more favorable than other religions to the flourishing of the individual and the exercise of his or her capacity to dominate nature." Islam, Hinduism, and Confucianism were correspondingly treated as obstacles. Further, the arbitrary and mythic construct of the West required a counterpoint—"an equally artificial conception of the Other (the 'Orients' or 'the Orient'), likewise constructed on mythic foundations."

Amin believes that the universal claims of the West to be the beacon of material wealth and power, of the scientific spirit and practical efficiency, of tolerance, of respect for human rights and democracy, and of concern for equality and social justice are fundamentally racist and that Nazism was only an extreme formulation of the Western myth. So much for the Eurocentric metanarrative! The West tells the world to imitate us if you want to progress; faith in the global market has become the content of the dominant ideology, with religion having been reduced to the legitimizer of the social order.[16]

From this Eastern perspective, as long as the Eurocentric view of the other persists, the capitalist project will continue to envision a global game of catching up with the West, when actually the North–South gap has not changed except to widen in four centuries. It should be clear that European levels of consumption can never be a realistic possibility for the five-going-on-eight billion humans on our planet. Homogenization at the center is being accompanied by destruction at the periphery. Europe must develop a new, universalistic project that is not Eurocentric and that dismantles the debt imperialism and the dominance by mercantile competition with Japan and the United States that keep the developing world in thrall. Amin wonders whether Europe can contribute to a truly polycentric world where different social and economic paths to development are respected, and he proposes a socialist universalism "based on contributions of everyone" that "gives all human beings on the planet a better mastery of their social development."[17]

Amin's voice is important not only because he is right about Third World debt and Western consumption levels but because he pushes the question of a universal culture that is more than a Western melting pot. Economic imperialism is no more acceptable than religious triumphalism or political colonialism, and the urging of a global vision to keep the unification of Europe from being an end in itself must beware of the continuing threat of paternalism.

The problem of paternalism is illustrated by Christopher Layton in his essay "Europe and the Global Crisis." He rightly recognizes that Europe cannot address its problems of unemployment and poverty except in the larger world context, but listen for the residual superiority in his words:

> If the European idea is to recover its vitality and capture the imagination of idealists, of all ages, it must be by living Europe's larger mission in the world outside. It would provide the valid reason for new efforts towards unity, and offer spiritual as well as material satisfaction. Europe's worldwide empires and exploitation catalyzed many of today's world problems; they also made the world a global village. It is time Europe's gifts of statesmanship, generosity, and knowledge of the world were mobilized to help set the village straight.[18]

"Setting the village straight" is not an expression to gladden the hearts of many of the village's other citizenry, but the good news is a recognition that European integration takes place in a global context and that a form of integration that fails to face the responsibilities of a global context is short-sighted at best and destructive at worst. Parallels in U.S. attitudes toward our role in the global village are easy to draw. What then are the promising possibilities for some sort of universalism that includes instead of excludes and that respects difference instead of blotting it out?

Exploring Prospects for a Global Community

If European community is not to be a mere end in itself, and in the process take on some of the very liabilities of narrow nationalism writ larger, it needs to orient itself in a global context and engender a loyalty that transcends the confines of limited European identification. It also needs to respect the differences of various communities within whatever community it develops, and it seems that global free trade agreements tend to dissolve difference instead of respect it. The United States as well is faced with learning to be a national community of diverse communities within a potential or actual world community.

Pointers toward Universal Community

These needs can be approached in several ways. In *The Responsible Self,* H. Richard Niebuhr observes a self-transcending impetus in human communities. The third reality in relation to which people relate to each other may be a nation, a religious body, a political cause, or a fraternal organization, but some tie binds a community. These third realities or centers of value tend to inspire people's loyalty by pointing beyond themselves to causes, ideals, and values that transcend the narrow interests of the community. This third must at least seem to point beyond the particularity and partiality of a given group to principles and values of more universal relevance and authority in order to hold people's allegiance. Experience, he suggests, tends to unmask the idolatry of centers of value that limit our responses to our narrowed enclaves based on blood or soil or race or creed. He writes, "The societies that judge or in which we judge ourselves are self-transcending societies. And the process of self-transcendence or reference to the third beyond each third does not come to rest until the total community of being has been involved."[19] If he is right, European and American community then will ultimately merit loyalty only by an affirmation of universal community.

As was indicated earlier, Michael Walzer argues that people who feel a reasonable level of security for their tribal community feel freer to explore other types of identification and belonging that stretch them beyond mere tribal membership. Thus Niebuhr and Walzer both suggest that tribal identification and a larger community identification need not be inherently antithetical.

The discourse ethics of Jürgen Habermas and Seyla Benhabib seeks to arrive at "the universal and necessary communicative presuppositions of argumentative speech." Habermas posits an ideal community of discourse where everyone would be heard and justice in the process could produce some consensus on universally shared values. Benhabib anticipates no such universal agreement but focuses on a just process where all can participate (the principle of universal moral respect) and participate equally (the principle of egalitarian reciprocity). These principles of process will assure that strong and weak, rich and poor alike are heard and will therefore have universal reach without producing universal norms.[20]

Another avenue of approach to the need for an expanded vision of community can be found in theological affirmations about shared human dignity and solidarity, such as the statement of Pope John XXIII at the beginning of the chapter, and the writing of Douglas Sturm, to be quoted later, and in Robert Reich's affirmations of human solidarity based on the political and economic realities of global interdependence. Theological claims make all human beings members one of another because of our common creation in the image of God with all of the dignity and relationality that go with it. The nontheological or anthropological-sociological claim posits an inescapable relatedness and solidarity because we are social beings whose lives are linked around the globe whether we like it or not.

As noted earlier about Reich, he finds in the American story at least four morality tales: "The Mob at the Gates," "The Triumphant Individual," "The Benevolent Community," and "The Rot at the Top." Better tales are called for because these stories have not adapted to global reality, and all of them pit us against them. The mob, for instance, may be variously defined as illegal immigrants, refugees, terrorists, drug traffickers, Japanese imports, cheap products from developing countries, Communist governments, welfare recipients within the nation, or poor nations seeking assistance from rich nations. Reich questions the very existence of mobs and gates; the drug problem, for instance, is a shared problem rather than something some nations are inflicting on others. Instead of putting us all in the soup together, the old tales enable us to locate the problem in others. We must learn to tell better stories about ourselves as Americans, according to Reich, if we are to affirm our membership in a single national community and see our problems as shared with people beyond our borders.[21]

European-American parallels on "The Mob at the Gates" are obvious. With a little pushing and shoving, we can also relate Reich's other tales to the European setting. "The Triumphant Individual" might translate internationally as a narrow nationalism whose sovereignty must not be qualified or as small regions that covet a more fragmented independence and fear the loss of the particularity of smaller communities. "The Benevolent Community" echoes in Layton's words about setting straight the global village that Europe has created and twisted. The rhetoric of "The Rot at the Top" appears in suspicion of the perceived dominance of the Brussels bureaucracy, on the one hand, and of the irresistible muscle of international financial powers as represented in the Bundesbank, the World Bank, and the International Monetary Fund, on the other. The crucial question that emerges from the parallels is whether the cohesion of a community requires being united against or distinguished from some other.

If Europeans and North Americans are to move beyond us-against-them thinking and begin to tell stories about European (and American) and global community that recognize interdependence and affirm universal solidarity along with diversity, what are to be the better sources for the new morality tales or myths or metanarratives? Will such tales, if we tell them, carry all the negative freight of the metanarratives that postmoderns view with such suspicion? Is it possible to discover or recognize a center of value or shared principles or procedural norms that could provide the focus for the community we seek? Master narratives are under deep suspicion in our time because they become ways of dominating and discrediting diverse and divergent narratives of different cultures, ethnic groups, races, religions, genders, and sexual orientations. Single loyalties are suspect because they undermine pluralism and reinforce the power of those in hegemonic positions. What options do we have?

The Earth as a Common Home

John Cobb has a proposal that addresses both loyalty and story because it traces the different "religions" that have made bids to unify the Western world. A thousand years ago people's chief religion or loyalty really was religion. In medieval Europe, for example, Christianity was supposedly the umbrella under which everyone was gathered. Cobb is recalling an era when being Christian or Jewish or Muslim was a person's most important identification. It put all other loyalties in the shade. In the first half of the seventeenth century, this hope for human community had to be scuttled because the wars of religion reached such an advanced state of horror and ugliness. Northern Ireland and Kosovo are fresh and gruesome reminders. The successor "religion" was nationalism, which undergirded the growth of the modern industrial state; but World War II dealt a devastating blow to this religion. Hitler showed where that religion could lead. A common good confined to blood and soil was a sinister tribalism indeed. Bosnia and Kosovo again come to mind.

The next theological victor, according to Cobb, was economism. Embodied institutionally in the World Bank, the International Monetary Fund, the European Community (now Union), and the General Agreement on Tariffs and Trade, this postwar Western religion organizes the planet in pursuit of economic growth through free trade. In a manner as foreboding in its own way as Amin's warning concerning economism, Cobb states, "In my opinion the aim of increasing growth at all costs—that's basically what economism is about—will lead to global horrors worse than the ones that brought an end to religionism in the earlier period and subsequently to nationalism. Economism speeds up the exploitation of the Earth's resources and hastens the day of the collapse of the ecosystem."[22] It causes great suffering to many (the poor and even the middle class), while it inflates the wealth and power of a few. The earth simply cannot sustain this brand of growth over the long haul. The market cornucopia is great for the world's winners, but too many people and too much of the earth lose. Economism mistakenly leaves the common good to take care of itself.

Economism is on anything but its last legs; yet Cobb does see glimmers of hope that a successor could emerge—namely, earthism. This "religion" places individuals in communities instead of isolating them and puts economic theory in the service of community instead of heedless growth. In compatible fashion, Al Gore's *Earth in the Balance* proposes a new common purpose, a new organizing principle for civilization—the rescue of the environment. He believes that his "Global Marshall Plan," which replaces the defeat of Nazism and the defeat of communism with the healing of the environment, is "the essence of realism" and that public recognition of the global environment is curving up even though the needed level of response is not yet politically feasible.[23]

Both writers see a possibility emerging that could put European community, North American community, and global community in concert instead of at odds, one that could realize the vision of the 1992 Earth Summit in Rio instead of mirroring its frustrations. As Cobb and Gore both indicate, we are our own worst enemies when it comes to the environment. It is high time that we tell stories about ourselves and the rest of nature that make us members one of another instead of exploiters one of the other. These stories must provide a utopian vision to counteract the nagging narrative of our environmental past.

There are discordant notes in our perceived chorus of support for an ecological vision as a bridge between European community and global community. It is interesting that among Norway's and Sweden's concerns as they considered EU membership was the fact that the environmental standards of the EU were lower than their national ones. Their environmental concerns made them question EU membership. On another front, Third World countries have often objected that Western urgings about environmental protection would serve to stifle their efforts at economic development of the sort that the rich nations pursued in the past to their great advantage and to the further disadvantage of the poor nations. They ask when the West's level of assistance is going to make a dent on the past inequalities of power and wealth that have made global economic and political interaction a tilted billiard table that keeps the balls going into the same pockets. They also ask whether the conversation is going to be dominated by elites who can afford to gain the expertise and make the trips to have the talks. If we are to tell a better environmental story about ourselves as a global community, it better grow out of a conversation in which the voices of the disadvantaged are not muted and the North's agenda for the discourse does not make for dominance rather than true dialogue.

Human Rights as Common Cause

A second commitment that could make European community and global community not just compatible but mutually reinforcing is universal human rights. Darrell Fasching envisions such a possibility in *The Ethical Challenge of Auschwitz and Hiroshima*. For him, "The UN declaration on human rights represents nothing less than a response of the human community to human dignity as an experience of transcendence that evokes a new international covenant community-of-communities."[24] He realizes that there is no full consensus about universal human rights, but he believes that the UN declaration, now past its fiftieth birthday, expresses a "utopian narrative" that is emerging with respect for human rights at its core. The First World has emphasized "first generation" negative rights that protect against interference with individual liberties; the Second World has elevated "second generation" social, economic, and cultural rights; and the Third World has stressed "third generation" solidarity rights to development, a healthy environment, and ownership of the common human heritage. The UN Conference on Human Rights showed that these differences are still matters of conflict, but full consensus is not required for a global commitment to respect for human dignity, which is "the only one universal human right."[25] Respect for difference is of course a crucial dimension of this respect for dignity, and the West does not have to be the hegemonic arbiter of human rights issues. Listening to diverse stories about human rights is crucial.

This global commitment to human dignity is gaining increasing global support because of the convergence of two influences, according to Fasching. The first is a recognition of "the transcendent dignity of the human self" generated by modern sociohistorical consciousness. Although the self always appears clothed in societal roles, the urbanized modern self is a role-transcending self that is understood to be prior to all roles and able to choose among roles. Nature-based organic societies tended to assign and fix roles and identities within those roles to legitimate "natural" differences and inferiorities. Modern consciousness questions those reductions and challenges the equations of selves with roles. The role-transcending self enjoys then an attribution or claim of dignity that no societal restriction or denial effaces.

Fasching's second source is the convergence of the utopian narratives of a global ecology of holy or religious communities—Buddhist, Christian, Jewish, and so on—in their affirmations of human dignity, particularly that of the stranger. Communities rooted in assertions of sacredness (as opposed to holy communities) tend to shrink selves to fixed statuses in hierarchical structures; holy communities, by contrast, see the self as holy or set apart but within a community. In his opposing of the holy to the sacred, Fasching reflects Jacques Ellul's distinction. The sacred can provide a sense of order, but that order easily becomes closed and demonic and thus prevents rather than encourages the transformation of selves and societies. The holy communities espouse a utopian vision of human dignity and liberation that exerts a salutary desacralizing pull on the secular liberation of the self occasioned by urbanized, modern society. Each of these communities at its best understands transcendence as Wholly Other, which makes for a break with "the cosmological imagination of the surrounding society" and forms a utopian alternative. This alternative stands in ethical tension with the surrounding society because it welcomes "those who are the social analogs of the Wholly Other, namely the alien, stranger, or outcast."[26]

It is not clear why the idea of the *Wholly* Other is crucial since what we find in common with the stranger may surprise us, and some assertions about sacredness may be worthy of affirmation and transformation instead of utter repudiation; nevertheless, his claim about the convergence of the narratives of religious communities is an important one. *Towards a Global Ethic,* which was issued by the Parliament of the World's Religions in 1993, is another pointer toward convergence that does not make all religious ethics the same. Against those who argue that Confucian-shaped Asian societies sacrifice the person to the community, Islamic societies subordinate individual rights to religious authority, and African religions also embody a communitarianism that submerges the person, searchers for a usable past and a liberating present in these cases are claiming success. There are resources in the Confucian tradition, they claim, for supporting tolerance and challenging oppression. The golden era of Islam (the period between the eighth century and the fourteenth century, after the death of Muhammad in 632) provides possibilities for building tolerance for diversity. And African traditions show a coupling of respect for the individual and the community in the pre-colonial era. Maybe dialogue among various perspectives on human rights can discover a "reiterative universalism" or a multilingual basis for human rights in line with Stassen's suggestions.[27] Without reducing thick moralities or religions to a thin common essence, we just may be able to find common cause through a conversation that brings everyone to the table and does not let anyone dominate the discourse. In a global village, that reiteration could be the base for a thicker common story that surpasses the thin beginnings.

One thinks in this connection of a statement by Jean Bethke Elshtain as part of her remarks on "Power and Identity in Contemporary Discourse" at the 1994 Annual Meeting of the American Academy of Religion. She spoke of "political mothers" whom she had encountered in Israel's West Bank, in Latin America, in Prague, and in Kiev (near Chernobyl). As they spoke of the disappeared and the tortured and of environmental degradation, they spoke a universal language of human rights. They communicated across cultural, political, religious, and linguistic divisions.

Fasching argues effectively against the assertions of Alasdair MacIntyre and Stanley Hauerwas that efforts to support the idea of universal human rights are based on an erroneously conceived, naked, individual, bureaucratic self with no roots in any community. (It was MacIntyre who lumped belief in such rights with belief in witches and unicorns.)[28] If hospitality to the stranger is affirmed by several religious communities, the stories of others are partners in dialogue. Our community stories can by definition include other stories or function in concert with them. What urbanized society strips away in terms of constitutive communal identity can be supplied in new and better form by religious communities.

While Fasching is on shaky ground when he seems to posit a transcendent self that can define itself apart from all roles and roots, and while there are surely examples of holy communities that are more limiting of the self and less open to the stranger than some secular associations, he takes us helpfully beyond despair about consensus on human rights. MacIntyre is wrong; claims for human rights are not illusions of a technical civilization. It is unfortunate that Fasching's rendering of the naked modern self bears such a close resemblance to the one that MacIntyre blames for the futility of the human rights quest. Perhaps Walzer's divided self (divided among roles, among identities by gender, race, nationality, and so forth, and among contending values) offers a better critical distance from particular roles without being denuded. All of his inner critics are fully dressed.[29]

In a different fashion, Douglas Sturm also takes issue with MacIntyre and offers universal human rights as a possible center for global community. Modernity has produced the turn toward subjectivity, but that experience of subjectivity can lead either to subjectivism or to relationality—that is, to recognition of and participation in the subjectivity of the other. Human rights derive from the human condition as part of a network of interdependence, of giving and receiving. His context for the development of a doctrine of human rights is summed up in this claim:

> We cannot avoid our engagement in an extensive network of interdependence, human and extrahuman. . . . We are, whether we embrace the fact or resist it, citizens of the world. But we are citizens in the precise double sense that as our citizenship is dependent on what the world has provided for us, so, in turn, the shape of the world in the future is dependent, in no small measure, on the form and direction we give to our own lives.[30]

Human rights point to our connectedness as well as our individuality, and the connectedness is ecological as well as social. Beneath all of the various social roles is still a related self, not a transcendent naked self. Walzer would add that this self had best be pluralistic and not dominated, and that the same is true of its harboring society.

A Common Story Out of Common Dialogue

What the ecological and human rights proposals have in common is not just the potential convergence suggested by Sturm. Both of them move beyond the parochialism of the national community, which Fasching insists will produce either individualism or collectivism if it is the chief definer of personal identity, to global community by some other means than the economism of the market or the oppressiveness of a super state. They both do so without requirement of an other against which one's nation, race, ethnic group, or region is pitted. Both affirm a universal community by pointing toward Niebuhr's "total community of being." Both place the self in a "utopian narrative," to use Fasching's term, that envisions the changing of the world in a way that transcends all current tribalisms without rejecting difference and self-determination by communities within communities. Both propose a master narrative that includes rather than colonizes or condemns other narratives, although it does not do so uncritically. Instead of the other being a threat or an object of conquest, it becomes neighbor or even partner. Both earthism and the human rights covenant community of communities find the enemy more in ourselves than in nature or in alien cultures.

The current suspicion of master narratives is rooted in an antipathy toward definitions of reality based on a single slant and in a suspicion of conversations conducted on the terms of the powerful. The master narrative tends to be the story told by the masters—those in power or the master "wannabes." Any candidates for a narrative in which to locate a European community and U.S. community that affirms rather than compromises universal community or the particularities of smaller communities should bear a burden of proof to dispel suspicions of economic imperialism. Samir Amin's search for a universalism on other than Eurocentric terms does more to subvert the reigning ideology of the global market than it does to trace the contours of a preferable socialist universalism. What he does make evident is that Eurocentrism's need for an other is at the heart of its offensiveness. For European community or American community and global community to converge rather than conflict, some common understandings are required—an understanding of the gravity of our ecological and political (due to rich–poor disparities) peril and a commitment to respect for both human dignity and extrahuman life. These common understandings are not apt to thrive in the absence of some sense of a common story (even a metanarrative) and a shared interdependence. Like the continuing conversation about the common good, the evolution of a common story is a work in progress.

The convergent utopian narratives of religious communities will be crucial contributors to this story, but the global community needs its own inclusive mythic vision that affirms ecological kinship and hospitality to the stranger. True integration of Europe needs a narrative, but experience with its master narratives of the past reveals a need to tell better stories about itself and to hear better the stories of others. We Americans should understand that problem.

The history of the quest for European community reveals that the greatest strides toward unity occurred where community was a means to some end of mutual interest—the defeat of Nazism, the containment of the Soviet Union, or the acquisition of competitive economic clout in market competition with the United States and Japan. Reich cites the Great Depression and the World Wars as times in the United States when Americans felt a solidarity in suffering and in efforts to overcoming a shared problem rather than a gulf between us and them. Of course that common enemy in the wars was the integrating catalyst. It remains to be seen how quickly a shared fear of dire environmental consequences, a shared abhorrence of human rights violations (in such forms as ethnic cleansing in the former Yugoslavia or neo-Nazism's resurgence), or both will create a deeper identification of Europe and the United States with the family of being. One fears that waiting for necessity to mother invention will mean that a sense of global community comes too late.

Advocates for European unification and advocates for American support of the United Nations and economic assistance to developing nations as a moral duty because of its essential rightness have wanted to make community a normative obligation rather than a means to some shared end. Their efforts have, however, often gotten snagged on the horns of stubborn preoccupations with national sovereignty and nagged by persistent suspicions of unification for its own sake and of a burgeoning bureaucracy. The specter of an international superstate ("The Rot at the Top") can usually be conjured up by opponents to great advantage.

Perhaps the strongest foundations for European integration, and for other forms of international integration, are those that rely less on acts of mutual national interest and admonitions about the rightness of international cooperation than on the reality of international and ecological interdependence on a global scale. Community then will be seen as a context of connectedness and as the expression of a shared story in the future if not in the past, and not simply as a means to an end or as a norm to obey. As John Cobb reminds us, we are dealing basically and finally with a religious question when we ask whether earthism and a utopian narrative with respect for human rights at its core can replace economism as a center of loyalty in an international covenant community of communities with a universal vision of the common good. A sober realism about impending ecological and political disasters may get our attention, and a hopeful idealism may beckon us toward global expressions of community, but a sense of human solidarity and of global citizenship depends on our learning to tell better stories about ourselves, stories that do not pit us against them or attempt to make them like us. Religious communities have shown that they can tell such stories, but no one religious story is going to be adopted by all.

To the extent that European integration becomes a window toward global community, it signals hope for our troubled planet. To the extent that it constitutes a wall of protection against the other, it only reinforces a world in which every Latin American baby is born owing a thousand dollars to a foreign bank.[31] To the extent that we question how well Europe has achieved integration of the best kind, we Americans would do well not to reach for the first stone, but instead to check the materials of our own house.

Global Civil Society

National community, we saw in chapter 4, relies on intermediate communities. The health of public discourse in the United States depends on the vitality of the voluntary associations of what is termed civil society. A parallel claim has emerged in international relations theory concerning global community.[32] Above and beneath national governments, a global civil society is discernible that expresses and advances people's identification with the inclusive community of humankind of which Pope John XXIII wrote. Discourse due to formal and informal contacts among human rights activists, environmental activists, biotechnologists, and other issues networks and knowledge-based movements and organizations profoundly influences the development of international regimes. These rules, norms, and decision-making procedures are seen in international conferences on environment and development, women, and human rights where the role of nongovernmental organizations has gained growing status. Greenpeace and Friends of the Earth, for example, transcend national boundaries, and the World Wide Web has facilitated ever-increasing levels of interaction among grassroots groups with common concerns. Networking on the Internet by such groups has even been credited with the passage of the land mine treaty.

International relations theory about community has often confined itself to state sovereignty as the defining reality for a particular citizenry and to societies of states. Andrew Linklater and others are now giving more attention to a sense of membership in an inclusive community of humankind that they see manifest.[33] States may link themselves in communities because of shared interests in trade or defense, because of commonly accepted conventions on immigration or human rights, or through common institutions such as the United Nations or the European Union. Neofunctionalist theories about increased integration take both top-down and bottom-up forms. Ernst Haas believed that floating international institutions by agreement among states would bring a greater sense of community between states in their wake. Elites initiate; peoples congregate. Other theorists, such as Karl Deutsch, believe that a sense of community across national boundaries must precede the formation of institutions if they are to have hope of success. Riding the wake has happened, but not to the extent its exponents anticipated. Bubbling up from global civil society as a way to integration of the second kind is now getting growing attention.

My Centre College colleague Nayef Samhat, who is an advocate for global civil society, believes that the regimes (rules, norms, and decision-making procedures) that emanate from and reflect this civil society signify the presence of a boundary-transcending international community. The regimes so signify if they are interpretive and emancipatory, which means that they do not simply accept the traditional constraints of the conventional wisdom and that they enhance human security and well-being globally. They will have at least three characteristics—commitment to ethical principles, activation of nonstate actors on the international scene, and inclusiveness of universal membership (as opposed to the exclusiveness of sovereign states). The principles are the stickiest point because of the danger that they will suppress difference in the public discourse of the global civil society. If they are arrived at by genuinely open dialogue and remain contestable and malleable, they can effect reconciliation of differences while continuing to recognize them. It makes a huge difference if the statements of human rights or environmental norms or other international regimes are produced by inclusive dialogue and are continually subjected to it. The participants remain national community members, but they are also identifying themselves as members of a larger human community.[34]

The discourse ethics of Habermas is prominent in this discussion of global civil society. What must inform it further is Benhabib's stress on the concrete conversations in process even more than the ideal speech situation.[35] If universal moral respect and egalitarian reciprocity are to characterize discourse in the global civil society, we must recognize the dominance of elites in the networks of issue advocates outside of government as well as in the circles of issue specialists within governments and within intergovernmental institutions.

As we said about the national civil society, the voluntary associations outside the state and the communities of concern within governmental institutions are not totally separate camps. There is overlap and interpenetration. The NGOs and the operatives of the UN, EU, and EPA do talk to each other. What requires eternal vigilance is the facilitation of listening that keeps stretching the reach and reciprocity of the conversation. Religious communities are in a critical position. Because of their global reach and their inclusion of both elites and ordinary citizenry, and because they avowedly have allegiances that transcend national loyalty or any other circumscribed political loyalty, they can both model a participatory and reciprocal conversation and contribute actors to various networks in the global civil society as well as the several sovereign states and the institutions of societies of states. The global conversation can be a covenant to acknowledge inclusive membership in a continuing search for the meaning of the common good. Getting the diverse voices to the table in a true community of discourse is common good in itself. At such tables, people can learn to tell better stories about themselves.

Out of his belief that moral communities are always particular, Michael Walzer has stated, "Humanity . . . has members but no memory, and so it has no history and no culture, no customary practices, no familiar life-ways, no festivals, no shared understandings of social goods."[36] He does, however, allow that we may at times be able to march in each other's parades. Could it not be the case that humanity is developing or could develop a memory, a history, a culture, and some shared understandings of social goods?

6

Covenantal Virtue for the Common Good

By contrast, the fruit of the Spirit is love, joy, peace, patience, kindness, generosity, faithfulness, gentleness, and self-control. There is no law against such things. And those who belong to Christ Jesus have crucified the flesh with its passions and desires. If we live by the Spirit, let us also be guided by the Spirit. Let us not become conceited, competing against one another, envying one another.

—Galatians 5:22–26

Virtue as Table Manners

When we set an ethic in the context of covenant, community, and the common good, what kind of an ethic are we exploring? Concern to discern and enhance the common good suggests an ethic of purpose or end. An ethic of the good is teleological; its focus is on contributing to a desired personal or social or ecological outcome. Our discussion has surely counted consequences as a dimension of morality that must be factored in, but assessing costs and benefits has not been our primary concern.

A focus on covenant can hardly ignore the obligation inherent in the Mosaic covenant tradition and its institutional embodiment in law. Duty and law suggest an ethic of the right, a deontological ethic that focuses on the relevant principles, rules, and rights to which obedience is owed. Covenant ethicists have indeed spelled out the guidance of in-principled love, and the language of obligations, rules, and rights has played a part in the preceding discussion. Covenant, however, cannot be captured in law and cannot be reduced to law. It expresses a relationship or a set of relationships that defy reduction to rules, as Paul stated to the Galatians in reviewing the fruit of the Spirit in the quotation that opens the chapter. Covenanted people incur obligations, but they also take on new identities.

As William F. May offers in this connection, they do not simply ask, "What shall we do?" Even more fundamentally, they inquire, "Who shall we be?"[1]

What relationships in community call for above all is virtue or character. This ethic then focuses on those qualities of life, those habits of the heart, those dispositions, outlooks, inclinations, passions, and patterns of interaction, that make persons the kind of selves they are and communities the kind of groups they are. The work of such ethicists as May and Patrick and such social theorists as Bellah and his colleagues deals, implicitly or explicitly, with both covenant and common good, and they all converge on virtue. Although virtue has often had an individualistic and even a moralistic reputation, these writers and the participants in the civil society discussion are placing virtue squarely in community, in public discourse, in voluntary associations, and in all kinds of institutions. Given what we have said about the importance of marriage and the family as the locus of civic formation and the import of discourse in home and school and workplace for public discourse, we could say that all virtue is civic virtue. From the family supper table to the international conference table, the rules of discourse we follow as we include, listen, address, differ, argue, and agree will exemplify who we are and what we are making of each other. Given our immersion in institutions as our natural habitat and the embeddedness of values and virtues in Bellah's "patterned ways of living together,"[2] we could say that all institutions are virtuous. They, of course, do not all exhibit the same virtues and they also embody vices, but certain virtues and vices are fostered, encouraged, and reflected in institutions.

Amitai Etzioni's responsive (to individual rights) communitarianism proposes two basic social virtues for a democratic society. These are order and autonomy. The order is a moral order that is not imposed but is "largely voluntary," and the autonomy of individuals and subgroups is not limitless but is bounded by placement in community. These two values or virtues provide the context or framework within which more dialogue can occur about equality, justice, and other principles. A society is always faced with keeping an equilibrium between order and autonomy in response to oppressive efforts at order and anarchic advocacy of limitless autonomy. These virtues are not just matters of consensus or majority preference or the practices of particular religious communities or other voluntary associations. They are the self-evident requisites for life together and for continued moral dialogue. They are the necessary components of his "new golden rule," which is "respect and uphold society's moral order as you would have society respect and uphold your autonomy." Others offer longer lists of requisite virtues; he is content to let the moral dialogue in which all of the voices are heard flesh out the profile of civic virtue. A society's constitution is critical, but the constitution is subject to reinterpretation and amendment in light of a compelling or self-evident moral order that evokes or compels agreement among the members of the society.[3]

Etzioni is trying to advance a communitarian ethic that is neither sectarian nor disrespectful of autonomy and diversity, and the context-setting virtues or values that he espouses deserve broad allegiance. His optimism about the self-evidence of compelling moral causes is, however, less convincing. His illustration of compelling moral causes or concepts with the virtually universal assumption that people have a greater moral obligation to their own children than to other children and that telling the truth is superior to lying is apt, but the rampant neglect of people's own children and the prevalence of lying suggest the need for virtue-fostering communities with their own distinctive stories to tell.

This chapter proposes to flesh out a profile of social virtue beyond the skeletal framework offered by Etzioni's "new golden rule" without attempting a roll call of all the virtues that life in covenant and in quest of the common good might entail. Rather we turn to virtues that are particularly important for life in covenant community for the common good as espoused in the Judaic and Christian traditions. Although they are part of particular stories of religious communities, we are entertaining the possibility that they have broader resonance and relevance for the fostering of civic virtue, both because they may find some coincidence in other religious traditions and because they may find adherents outside of religious communities. In addition, the point of view that has been developed here might affect our understanding of those central theological virtues of faith, hope, love, and gratitude.

Faith as Faithful, Audacious Openness

Covenantal faith as a moral virtue is a far cry from renditions of faith as intellectual assent to doctrinal truth. It is, instead, being true to a set of relationships and open to the call of the other. In the first instance, it is faithfulness or fidelity. Since the fall semester in 1960 when I took H. Richard Niebuhr's seminar "Faith as Virtue," I have been impressed with the way in which he made faithfulness the essential virtue in answer to the love monism that has often shaped Christian ethics. He believed that he was following the biblical lead in making interpersonal faith the focus of theology and ethics. *Fidelity, trust, confidence*, and *loyalty* are the fitting terms for understanding faith rather than *acceptance, belief*, and *intellectual knowledge*. People will trust in something, and they will either trust or distrust the ultimate power or powers in the presence of which they live. Faith in God as friend or companion is a trusting and loyal response to the fidelity of a power that is believed to be for us and not against us. Faith communities whose center of value or uniting Spirit is such a power understand sin as breach of trust, as failure to keep faith, and as not living up to our covenants; they understand the good life as imitation of the faithfulness of God, whose love is steadfast. This faithfulness is a way of relating to one's family, one's communities of labor and worship, and one's place on earth politically and ecologically.

Wendell Berry delineates community disciplines of two kinds—the discipline of principle and the discipline of fidelity. Faith is "the ultimate discipline" because it "holds to the propriety of one's disciplines."[4] Principle should carry the lessons of the community's past experience, and fidelity should bond a person of faith to the present living community of family, neighbors, and friends. This faith is proved by consistency between profession and practice. This fidelity or faith or loyalty is not some ethereal virtue; it is the mundane enabler of the possibility of love and joy.[5] Life in covenant then lives out of a past and tries to live up to that past among sharers of present love and work. Without the discipline of faithfulness or fidelity, the hard work never gets done; and thus we do not experience the joy of doing it. Without faithfulness, love cannot continue to flourish and bless us with abiding joy.

For Niebuhr distrust was the opposite of faith;[6] for Berry, similarly, it is suspicion. In suspicion we trust no one and rely on no one. The other is threat and not promise. The stranger is not to be welcomed, but to be resisted or rejected. We are always protecting ourselves against our current enemies and those who will soon be our enemies. Of an institution built around suspicion such as the Pentagon, Berry writes, "Trusting nobody, it must stand ready to kill everybody."[7] Some level of trust then is essential to a life not lived at each other's throats. Without faithfulness, covenant is not possible and the common good is not thinkable because suspicion can find nothing in common with others. Everyone else is part of some "mob at the gates" or some "rot at the top" that is bent on doing us in, and the ultimate expression of this distrust, as Niebuhr made clear, is a "faith" in God, or whatever one's ultimate power is, as enemy. By contrast, faith in an Ultimate Other that is for us and not against us, and in fact is for the other lives around us and not against them either, makes one open to others and even makes one hospitable to strangers.

Faith practiced in covenant for the common good is not only faithfulness, but openness. In *Winds of the Spirit*, Peter Hodgson makes openness his definition of religious faith.[8] Getting an education requires the faith to believe that new possibilities are worth the risk of having your life tampered with by the experience of exploring different worldviews, investigating different material, allowing oneself to be influenced by different people, sharing one's life with new companions in learning. So too openness to the transforming power of God's Spirit and to the transforming possibilities of genuine dialogue and interaction with people different from us (in race, ethnicity, class, religion, political ideology, nationality, sexual orientation, etc.) is an act of faith. Without difference, after all, there can be no covenant. A person has to believe that the changes that will occur because of this new exposure or encounter or openness are full of gracious possibilities. And being surrounded by a community that shares that faith does not just make the most of the difference; it makes all of the difference. That community tells itself stories about past experiences of transformation through openness to the new and different, and it will also produce new stories.

This openness is not simply tolerant of the other, or receptive to encounter by difference; it is audacious. Its hospitality is daring. It is not docile obedience; it is courageous engagement. It is not just willing; it is willful. Faith is Abraham arguing with God over the destruction of Sodom. It is Jacob wrestling all night at Peniel with the night visitor, refusing to let the other go until he receives a blessing, and receiving a blessing because he has striven with God and humans and prevailed. It is Moses contending with God on behalf of his stiff-necked people on Sinai and getting God to change. It is Job wanting an explanation. It is Jesus in the Garden of Gethsemane asking for the cup to pass. To quote Habermas on discourse ethics, covenant in these instances provides "the communicative presuppositions of argumentative speech."

Referring to Jacob in particular, Darrell Fasching calls faith *chutzpah* in *Narrative Theology after Auschwitz*.[9] The classic description of the gall of the *chutzpanik* is the man who kills his parents and then throws himself on the mercy of the court because he is an orphan, or the one who cries "Help! Help!" while beating you up. Even better is another of Leo Rosten's depictions in *The Joys of Yiddish*. The village beggar comes to the rich man's house at 6:30 A.M. when the man is still in bed. Aroused from sleep, he says, "You mean that you have come here at this hour to beg for my money?" The beggar counters, "Listen, I don't tell you how to run your business, so don't tell me how to run mine."[10] You begin to get the picture of audacity to the point of *chutzpah*. It took *chutzpah* for Jacob to demand a blessing in the midst of his culpability for fleecing his brother Esau out of his birthright and his father-in-law Laban (no small-time fleecer himself) out of flocks and household gods. He was a man of audacious and single-minded faith, though not a man of exemplary character in other ways.

A modern example of faithful audacity is Elie Wiesel, "the Job of Auschwitz." At the age of sixteen, he was liberated from Hitler's death camps after losing his parents and his sister in them. His childhood faith shattered, his image in the mirror someone he does not even recognize, he is faced with the question of faith. He cannot forsake his Jewishness because he must be the messenger of the atrocities visited upon the Jews and others in the Holocaust. If he cannot forsake his Jewishness, he realizes that he is stuck with God. As his fiction and nonfiction flow from his experience, he has characters in his writing accusing God, putting God on trial, praying for God, asking for forgiveness for God, but the argument goes on. As long as the argument continues, there is faith.

Covenant provides the context in which argument and dissent are allowed. It keeps us at the table talking and even contending with each other. Covenant assures the faithful of the faithfulness of God, but it does not equate the power of God with control. God's power is interactive and transformative, but it is not domination. Human covenants should mirror the mutuality of such a covenantal relationship. In Anne Patrick's and Charles Curran's rendition, obedience is not properly understood as submission to church authority, but as willingness to hear or attentiveness to what God may be saying through the other. Authority should be dialogical and consensual. No human authority should be confused with God, and even God's own authority is relational and dialogical.[11]

Hope as Active, Patient Anticipation

Hope too warrants reexamination and distinction from otherworldly escapisms as well as this-worldly optimisms. Covenants are long-term suppositions, and the common good is a work in progress. As a covenantal virtue seeking the common good as a future realization rather than a past definition, hope has the patience to go the distance and the expectation to anticipate more than humans can contrive in the future. It knows how to wait, but does not simply wait. It bides its time without ceasing to labor to redeem the time and without thinking that all the factors that shape the future are at our disposal.

Picture two cartoons. The first is a Trevor political cartoon from the *Albuquerque Journal.* It depicts a long serpentine voting line in the South African elections. One of the white people in the line is saying, "This is intolerable! We've been waiting five and half hours to vote!!" One of the black people is saying, "That's not so bad. We've been waiting three hundred years."[12] The other cartoon shows two vultures sitting high on the limb of a tree. One says to the other, "I'm tired of waiting. I'm going to kill something." This contrast gives dramatic expression to the political and the military, which Walter Lowe calls two different views of "the way things are."[13] Max Weber referred to politics as the patient boring of hard boards.[14] Without patience, politics is hopeless. The political process is painstaking and slow. In politics, yesterday's adversary could be tomorrow's ally, and the participants are committed to a long-term endeavor. In the military mindset, it is only a matter of time until the potential enemy becomes an actual and active enemy, so it might be a good idea to get the jump with a surgical strike. Covenants are long-haul commitments that call for and allow for patient negotiations and argument in pursuit of a common good; wars are desperate, rather than hopeful, efforts at fixes in situations where no common good is envisioned and no covenant any longer exists, if one ever did.

The patience of hope is a covenantal virtue and a civic virtue, but it is not a popular one. The media, the advertisers, and the politicians have combined to give us politics by sound bite, photo opportunity, and single issue. Impatient with the painstaking conversation in search of the common good, we want quick results and marketable news. Always desirous of news in time for the 7:00 P.M. feeding frenzy, we will create some if the daily political fare is dull and uninteresting.

Incentives to impatience abound. Advertisers cultivate our susceptibility to the lures of instant gratification. Investors want quick returns. CEOs need to show quick results. Ambitious leaders of public and private institutions need tangible evidence that they are making things happen for today's board and tomorrow's potential employer. To hear some headhunters and search committees talk, impatience is a virtue. Movers and shakers and mover and shaker wannabes don't like to wait because people with power shouldn't have to wait—wait to educate a constituency, wait to prepare the ground, wait to build consensus, wait to make the case.

People without power don't like to wait either. People who have had to contend with injustice, oppression, discrimination, and subordination object to the counsel of the powerful and privileged to wait. They say, "Look who's talking!" Remember Martin Luther King's *Letter from Birmingham Jail.* White moderates had been telling him that he should wait and let time take care of things. He responded that they had a mistaken faith in time as the solver of problems. "Time itself is neutral," he said: "it can be used either destructively or constructively." He told his opponents and his avowed, go-slow sympathizers "why we can't wait."[15] If waiting means resignation to injustice, then patience cannot wait. It is cheap talk to tell the victims to be patient and their time will come. Patience is active waiting that resists oppression of any kind without letting the oppressor set the terms of the struggle or letting the odds against change determine the depth of the resolve to overcome.

If we are looking for examples of such patience, Nelson Mandela fills the bill. In 1964, thirty years before he became his country's first black president, he was convicted of sabotage, sentenced to imprisonment for life plus five years, and sent to Robben Island in the frigid South Atlantic. There he labored breaking rocks and was allowed only brief visits (with no touching) from his young wife Winnie. He wrote that he felt like someone who had "missed life itself." And what did he do during his twenty-seven years of imprisonment? He taught himself law, history, economics, and even Afrikaans, the language of the powers that were. As young revolutionaries were sent to the island, he became their teacher. In fact, the island became known as "Mandela University." Eventually an exchange of letters and secret meetings occurred between him and the government leadership. Finally he became the president. By what journalists called "his patience, forbearance, and largeness of spirit," he became an example to his people.[16] When he told them that creating a new society would take time, he had earned the right to be heard. He was not advocating resignation, but resolute patience in effecting a peaceful revolution. Speaking in New York's Riverside Church in June 1990, he quoted Isaiah: "'We have risen up as on wings of eagles, we have run and not grown weary, we have walked and not fainted,' and finally, our destination is in sight."[17]

The word *patience* comes from the same root as *passion*, which means "suffering," but suffering is not something to be accepted while it is being endured if it is being inflicted by the powerful on the powerless. Patience suffers because it pays the price of continuing to identify with those who have been disadvantaged by others' blindness and prejudice and injured by others' cruelty and enmity.

When the Bible offers examples of patience, we quickly learn that passive resignation is not the model. Moses is called patient although he killed the Egyptian overseer who was beating the Hebrew slave and smashed the first set of tablets when he beheld his people's idolatry. He learned his patience by toughing it out for forty years in the wilderness with that bunch of complainers. To our surprise, the writer of the Epistle of James names the prophets (5:10). Amos did not sound very patient in his diatribe at Bethel, Elijah had no patience with Ahab and Jezebel, and Nathan ran out of patience with David. These people had a lion's share of righteous indignation, but they and their fellow prophets also took the long view. Hosea bought back an adulterous wife, Jeremiah bought a field in Judah when his people were being driven into exile, and Isaiah and Ezekiel took considerable time acting out their messages because they figured that neither judgment nor redemption depended on them. In *The Soul of Politics,* Jim Wallis, in a powerful passage on hope, recalls the defiant hope expressed by Desmond Tutu to the white rulers of South Africa in a sermon on March 13, 1988, when the conflict between church and state was at its height. The bishop said, "You may be powerful, indeed very powerful, but you are not God. You are ordinary mortals. God, the God whom we worship, cannot be mocked. You have already lost. We are inviting you to come and join the winning side."[18]

To top it off, James cites the "patience of Job." Job, we have recalled, complained, argued, and protested in his encounters with God over his suffering. He did not just lie there and take it; he hung in there and kept the relationship going, and God hung in there with him, although he tells him that he owes him no answers. And then there is the patient Jesus—driving the moneychangers out of the Temple and praying that the cup pass from him, yet enduring a torturous death when he could not be true to his vocation and dodge the horror.

For James and for the biblical vision in general, which is a covenantal vision, the ultimate exemplar of patience is God, who is long-suffering in compassion and mercy. Patiently creating, patiently forgiving, patiently nurturing without ceasing to oppose injustice, the covenanting God is steadfast in love. Paul Taylor suggests that we liken the 600 million years since the first algae appeared (forget the protozoa that have been around for several billion years) to a football field. At the 75-yard line, put in sharks and spiders. At the 50-yard line, put in reptiles. At the 33-yard line, put in mammals. At the 2-foot line, put in hominids, the type of mammals to which we are the closest kin. At the 6-inch line, put in the human beings.[19] The creating God has taken God's own good time. And then there is the forgiveness until seventy times seven, or seventy-seven times, depending on your translation (Matt. 8:22).

Patience is not just a requirement for public discourse and political reform in a democracy, or of prophetic endurance and redemptive suffering; it is a prerequisite for all life in covenant. It does not take patience to fall in love, but it does take patience to wait for sexual intimacy until it is the fitting expression of a lasting commitment. It does not take patience to get married, but it does take patience to build and maintain a good marriage. It does not take patience to have dreams about one's future, but it does take patience to go through the painstaking process of discovering one's vocation. It does not take patience to want children, but it does take patience to go through pregnancy and childbirth and to nurture children through their development to maturity, letting each one grow on her or his own schedule. I heard of one parent who grew impatient about the toilet-training progress of a three-year-old. The result was a plan that involved the spouse taking a day off from work to keep the baby so that the task could be accomplished with a one-day blitz. We grow impatient with what we cannot control, and parents soon realize that we lose control the day we have a child even though we keep hoping that the little folks don't find out too soon.

It often takes some patience to get a job, but it always takes great patience to make a difference in one's work situation. It may require some patience to get elected, but it requires a lot more patience to get something done in a legislature, a city council, a government agency, a court system, or a presidency. It does not take patience to give orders, but it takes patience to listen to unheard voices, to evoke others' speech, to negotiate differences, to work out compromises, and to develop some level of consensus. It does not take patience to start a war, but it does take patience to negotiate a peace and to attend to conditions that further the likelihood of war.

It does not take great patience to lecture to a class, but it does take considerable patience to assist in the education of students. It does not take patience to write a check, but it does take patience to address the causes of people's poverty and alienation and nonproductivity. Two years may often not be enough time to reverse patterns and ameliorate disadvantages that have been decades in the making for a welfare recipient. It does not take patience to make a profit, but it does take patience to make a profit in a manner that is ecologically responsible and attentive to long-term effects on all of the stakeholders in a business. It does not require patience to order tests and write a prescription, but it does require patience to listen to patients. It does not take patience to have surgery, but it does take patience to undergo painstaking rehabilitation after surgery and to live with chronic illness (both as a sufferer and a caregiver) that has no medical fix. It does not take patience to live off nature, to plunder the planet, but it does take patience to live with nature, to till and keep the earth we inhabit.

Patience may have to be learned the hard way after we have tried everything else, and it takes the long-suffering patience of those who love us to teach it. From Wendell Berry's novel *Remembering* come the examples of Flora and Andy Catlett. It is a story of how Andy, who gets dismembered when he loses his right hand in a corn picker, becomes re-membered. Andy had been in a hurry and had gotten impatient. When the corn picker became fouled, he had tried to clear it without turning it off. When it took his hand, he could not get over his anger at himself and his grief at his loss. Although Flora, his wife, and his children try to help him, "giving him patience and kindness that he knew he had not earned and did not repay," he becomes alienated from everyone in his family and farming community. Flora tells him, "You're mad at me because I can't stop you from being mad at yourself. You must forgive yourself." Fleeing everything he has known, Andy goes West. When he finally returns home unannounced, he finds Flora's note waiting for him even though she had not known when or whether he would return. The note tells him that she has gone to pick beans and visit, and she signs it, "Love, F." It comes home to Andy how blessed he is. "He feels the strong quietness with which she has cared for him and waited for him all through his grief and his anger. He feels her justice, her quiet dignity in her suffering for him. He feels around him a blessedness that he has lived in, in his anger, and did not know."[20] The impatient Andy has come to understand the patience of his home. He is re-membered.

Hope waits actively not only because it is patient, but also because it believes that the future is open and there are more possibilities in it than are visible to the naked eye. Even when all of the evidence is apparently in, hope believes that there can still be a breakthrough in the case. It knows that its labors are not in vain because it does not believe that everything depends on its labors. It expects more of the future than realism allows, but it rejects the guarantees of optimism as ill-advised, foregone conclusions based on misplaced trust in human ingenuity. As Edward Farley has explained, individual hope is encouraged by the resources of the traditioned past, the aid and effort of others along the way, and one's own inner resources, but there is also a transcendent dimension. Aided and abetted by the other resources, things could go either way. They have potential for evil equal to their potential for good. Faith affirms a power that is at work to stave off chaos and ruin, to nurture and sustain what is good, and to assure that what is worth keeping is not lost. James Gustafson speaks of "a sense of possibilities" that is a response both to the resources in us that are empowered by God and to the new possibilities that are continually opened up by God.[21] In Farley's words, "For when we hope, we call to something or someone able to direct tradition, human others, and even our own selves in the direction of peace and redemption rather than new idolatries and oppressions. Hope, thus, is directed past these finite resources to something unambiguous, something whose very being is justice, peace, and love."[22]

Some religious communities foster such a vision in the face of life's unshakable tragic dimension, of continuing reasons for despair, and of simplistic tendencies to pin hopes on a particular eschatological future or reduce them to personal wishes. Such covenant communities keep hope alive among those who have the good fortune or the good judgment to land in them.

At the grave of Robert Kennedy are inscribed these words from an address given in South Africa in 1966: "Each time a man stands up for an ideal, or acts to improve the lot of others, or strikes out against injustice, he sends forth a tiny ripple of hope, and crossing each other from a million different centers of energy and daring, those ripples build a current that can sweep down the mightiest wall of oppression and ignorance." Hope like that does not make us resigned, but it makes us patient and it keeps us going. It keeps us going because we believe that we are not alone socially but are part of a community of kindred strivers. It also keeps us going if we believe that we are not ultimately alone, that there are transcendent grounds to be of good courage. As Martin Luther King expressed it, "When days grow dark and nights grow dreary, we can be thankful that our God combines in his nature a creative synthesis of love and justice which will lead us through life's dark valleys and into sunlit paths of hope and fulfillment."[23]

Recalling the cartoon that contrasted two reactions to the long wait to vote for a new government in South Africa, we add the words of one person who waited for six hours in one of those lines. Afrikaner novelist André Brink has called those six hours "the most moving and exhilarating experience of my life."[24] People whom the reign of apartheid had tried to keep separate shared umbrellas, passed mugs of coffee, touched hands, and laughed together as they waited to vote. Wrote Brink, "In achieving, for a few hours, what had been considered impossible, we caught a glimpse of the possible." As Paul put it: "If we hope for what we do not see, we wait for it with patience" (Rom. 8:25).

Love as Compassionate and Just Affirmation

In the context of covenant mutuality and concerted quest for the common good, love takes on a distinctive coloration. It is not obligation, although it assumes obligations because of a relationship to the other. Love that is only duty is not love, but love that carries no duty is cheap. Love is also not charity, because charity offers aid to the other without really entering into the life of the other and being affected by the other. Love is also not self-abnegation on behalf of the other, because self-abnegation does not value the worth of the giver despite its preoccupation with its own sacrifice. As Edward Farley explains, we take ourselves with us as we enter into the life of the other.[25]

A teaching colleague of mine in a summer program once recounted to me her experience in going to a minister about her husband's abuse of her. The minister's response was that she should hang in there and endure suffering as Jesus did. When I asked what she did, she replied, "I changed churches." Love has important connections to suffering, but submission to indignity and violation as a requirement of love constitutes attempting to keep a covenant that has been destroyed and failing to respect both the selves that made it.

Love is first of all a way of regarding another and of regarding oneself. H. Richard Niebuhr offered this start toward a definition: "By love we mean at least these attitudes and actions: rejoicing in the presence of the beloved, gratitude, reverence and loyalty toward him."[26] This affirmation, appreciation, respect, and even joy in the existence of something or someone properly extends to everything that participates in being, including enemies, animals, and oceans. The existence of the object of this love is something to be wondered at, rejoiced in, regarded as a gift, and respected as something that is not there to be dominated or possessed, but to be appreciated and affirmed. Wendy Farley entitles one of her books *Eros for the Other*. Appropriating Emmanuel Levinas, she speaks of a consciousness of the infinity of others that is only available through desire and discourse and is never subject to our possession.[27] The presence of the other appeals to us in spite of ourselves, drawing us into the inescapable relatedness of existence, obliging us to the other before we choose it. All realities present a beauty and a vulnerability to which we must respond.

The other is not simply a gift or a presence to be engaged by and to be affirmed; it is also a fellow sufferer. Existence is not only to be wondered at, but also to be grieved. Tragedy is unavoidable amid the conditions of finitude, and in the face of finitude and suffering, people compound suffering by their sinfulness. Suffering can either isolate people from each other or bind them together. In Wiesel's *The Town beyond the Wall*, Michael returns to his hometown in Hungary, from which he had been deported along with all of his fellow Jews, because he wants to understand the spectator, the person who stood looking out the window in detached silence as the Jewish "cleansing" transpired. In the course of his pilgrimage, he learns an important lesson from his friend Pedro, who becomes his alter ego. Instead of letting the Holocaust drive him into himself and over the brink into madness, he had to resist suffering by reaching out to others. Says Pedro, "You frighten me. You want to eliminate suffering by pushing it to its extreme: to madness. To say 'I suffer, therefore I am' is to become the enemy of man. What you must say is 'I suffer, therefore you are.' Camus wrote somewhere that to protest against a universe of unhappiness you had to create happiness. That's an arrow pointing the way; it leads to another human being. And not via absurdity."[28]

Love links us to the other through compassion, which moves us to suffer with the other. Since the Hebrew word for compassion, *rahamin*, refers to the movements of the womb, the idea is not to foist ourselves upon the other, but to make ourselves receptive to the other, to accept the other's suffering. Nel Noddings writes of empathy, "I do not project, I receive the other into myself, and I see and feel with the other."[29] Although we cannot fully experience what another is experiencing, we can, nevertheless, identify with others in their suffering. I once heard Karen Lebacqz tell of an experience that she had in her doctor's office. He was performing a painful gynecological procedure, and she agreed not to scream if he would warn her each time the pain was coming. She recalled vividly the sweat and anguish on the face of the male physician as she endured something he could never experience firsthand. She felt that he was suffering with her in her ordeal out of compassion.

Without claiming to know fully what people are feeling, we can still put ourselves in their place without taking over their place. Richard Zaner calls this empathy "affiliative feeling." This act of putting ourselves in others' shoes is, he believes, "a, if not *the* fundamental moral act."[30] This "sympathetic knowledge" of others' suffering (Wendy Farley's term) issues in solidarity.[31] True solidarity is neither the escape of apathy or the condescension of pity; it is the identification of engagement. As Farley explains, even when others have brought suffering on themselves and visited it on others, compassion reaches out to them in their brokenness. Sister Helen Prejean's compassion for the man on death row, which was depicted in the movie *Dead Man Walking*, is a powerful example. Compassion does not forsake the respect and mutuality that characterize life in covenant. It stands with the other, but it does not try to take control.

Feeling others' pain does not exhaust the meaning of compassion, however. Compassion has to oppose the causes of suffering, to the extent that they are more than the unavoidable conflicts of life together in a precarious universe. In Wendy Farley's words, "Compassion is an enduring disposition of love that resists suffering." Rather than take power from the other, compassion seeks to empower the other to resist suffering.[32] Compassion does not offer condolences, it triggers transformation. Compassion toward the poor family on welfare then means solidarity for the purpose of empowering, not control or domination. Compassion enters into a covenant or recognizes an already existing covenant with a kindred sufferer instead of taking over the life of the other.

Justice must always accompany compassion.[33] Love cannot eschew politics, and therefore love and justice are partners. Justice establishes the conditions for a healthy relationship, but it cannot produce that relationship. Love has the power both to create and to transform relationships. Compassion is more than justice, and it is not constrained by the abstract principles of just distribution, compensation, and retribution. Institutional guarantees and guidelines to ensure equity and fairness are necessary because institutions can be very oppressive. Justice is an expression of compassion, but unlike justice, compassion is not blind.

The love that makes us "members one of another" (Rom. 12:5) and justice understood as right relationships transform other virtues. Anne Patrick argues for a reinterpretation of chastity as purity of heart. Instead of making it a way of protecting one's sexual purity and keeping one's lower nature under control, it becomes the singleness of purpose that focuses on justice and the common good.[34]

When we understand ourselves as "members one of another," temperance looks different as well. Wendell Berry insists that we conceive our common membership and our common good ecologically. Speaking at Centre College in 1978, he enunciated a vision that is central to his literature and life:

> Order was there long before we humans were, it will be long after we are gone, and within that order all creatures "are members one of another." Within that order the ecological axiom always holds: you can't do one thing; each event invariably compounds itself in others. Order ramifies in order; disorder ramifies in disorder. . . . If, for instance, the order that I have described is a fact, which it is, and if it surpasses human comprehension, which it does, then temperance is not just a spiritual discipline, but a practical necessity, no less so than food or water or air; and we have an infallible standard by which to measure the sinfulness of gluttony. . . . Gluttony is not sinful merely because it consumes too much and leaves too little for others; it is also sinful because it belittles what it consumes, and belittles the source. . . . Gluttony gives only the soon-jaded pleasure of the little we can consume; temperance gives the joy of inconsumable abundance.[35]

Just as chastity has to be revisited in the context of social justice, temperance must be revisited in the light of ecological justice.

Grateful, Generous Public-Spiritedness

Berry's lament about belittling the source brings us to the virtue of gratitude. Consumers use without giving thanks. Contractors bargain without acknowledging debts. Their deals are fresh every morning and new every evening. Covenanters are responding to unearned gifts. Paul lists generosity as one of the fruits of the Spirit, and generosity grows out of gratitude. This generosity is more than philanthropic elective beneficence; it is indebted, obligated, glad response to life's unearned increments and its unfathomable riches. It is largeness of spirit brought on by an overwhelming sense of life's goodness, an amazed sense of God's grace, a deep awareness of social benefit, an appreciative assessment of the past, a sustained wonderment at the earth's grandeur.

We treated earlier William May's rendition of the physician's indebtedness to everyone from the scientists who made discoveries to the patients whose trust and openness are crucial contributors to any effectiveness of the medical art. "No one," he writes, "can graduate from a modern university and professional school and think of himself or herself as a self-made man or woman." May believes that the virtue of gratitude in a physician should foster and feed the virtue of public-spiritedness. This virtue is "the art of acting in concert with others for the common good in the production, distribution, and quality control of health care."[36] The physician's covenant is not simply with individual patients; it takes responsibility for the common good.

By extension, all citizens who believe that we are "members one of another" and that we are the heirs and daily beneficiaries of more grace than we can fathom will practice the virtue of public-spiritedness or public responsibility. We have obligations to our political communities and our voluntary associations just as surely as to our religious communities. Former senator Bill Bradley, in addressing the challenge of revitalizing our national community, links public-spiritedness to the sense that we are recipients of "undeserved gifts."

> One way to encourage such responsibility is to give the distinctive moral language of civil society a more permanent place in our public conversation. The language of the marketplace says, "get as much as you can for yourself." The language of government says, "legislate for others what is good for them." But the language of community, family and citizenship at its core is about receiving undeserved gifts. What this nation needs to promote is the spirit of giving something freely, without measuring it out precisely or demanding something in return.[37]

I cannot agree with Bradley that "never in American history has a new vision begun in Washington."[38] Nor do I believe that people at all levels of government think they can solve every social problem, as Bradley alleges. However, he is right about the language we need to speak in America if we are going to be a national community. It is also true that governmental vision is dependent on a dialogue about the common good that extends beyond the confines of the Oval Office or the halls of Congress or the statehouse or the city hall, but visionary civil discourse is even possible among government bureaucrats.

If gluttony is the vicious counterpart to temperance, and desperate impatience is the antithesis of hope, and distrust and infidelity are sins against faith, and callous control is the opposite of love, what is the vice of choice among the ungrateful and the mean-spirited? Since Paul ends with it after including it on his list of "works of the flesh" earlier, envy is a strong possibility. Taking the three vices in his conclusion to the "fruit of the Spirit" together, we might arrive at "conceited, competitive envy."

Envy is sorry that others have received or accomplished something because we thought we should have gotten it. If compassion is putting ourselves in others' shoes, envy is wishing we were in others' shoes and resenting those others because we are not. For envy, life is a zero-sum game. At least it is if we are dealing with our competitors among our siblings, our fellow students, our professional colleagues, our coworkers, our teammates or opponents, and our fellow aspirants for attention, approval, recognition, grades, fellowships, jobs, promotions, or a significant other. It's the affirmative action reaction: "You got my job! Surely I deserved what you got. No one else could fill that position as well as I could. I resent what you received."

In Dante's *Inferno*, the eyes of the envious are sewed shut. Justice is blind in order to be fair. Ambition is blind because its gaze is riveted on the desired goal, and tunnel vision ignores all else. Envy is blind because it cannot appreciate either what it has or what the other has. As William May suggests, "Perhaps the specific blindness of envy is in gratitude."[39] It inflates its own deserts, belittles those of others, and cannot take an honest look at either. The other gets by luck or plot what should have been mine by right or accomplishment. It cannot see how much it is indebted to others for what it has; yet it assumes that others alone account for what the other has. It cannot stomach the idea that we are all on welfare, and yet we also get what we deserve more often than we like to admit.

In the clutches of envy, we do not just lose our ability to see what we have; we shrink. We become small in the process of cutting others down to build ourselves up. Envy eats us up and leaves very little. Instead of exhibiting largeness or generosity of spirit, it begrudges others what they have, perhaps damning them with faint praise or seeding the clouds for rain on their parades. Instead of being at a loss to count all of our blessings, we lose the ability to recognize a blessing when we see it. Ungrateful, envy stops giving.

How does this envy diagnosis relate to the world's have-nots? Should they be more conscious of their blessings and not resent the riches of others? Should they be content with their lot or else hold themselves responsible for failing to succeed or even to muster the minimal requirements for a decent life? The ideological poles on our political scene have been labeled by some as the politics of greed and the politics of envy. If one wing plays to the haves and devotes its moving and shaking to feathering the nests that are already blanketed in down, the other plays to the have-nots' feelings of having gotten a raw deal. The first feeds on greed; the second feeds on envy. In the first instance, the reward for doing well is having more. In the second, the response to having less is getting even, perhaps by pulling everyone down to my level.

If we think of envy as a spiritual problem, then we may point to the meaninglessness of the differences between the haves and have-nots. The preacher tells me that the ground is level at the foot of the cross and that Jesus became poor so that all might be rich—spiritually speaking, that is. What, though, if we match Matthew's rendition of the beatitude of the poor in spirit because the kingdom of heaven is theirs with the Lucan beatitude of the poor for whom the establishment of a new kingdom will make their lives better and the lives of the rich worse? Poor people can fall prey to envy just as surely as anyone else, but is it envy to resent the fact that your child lacks the diet, the shelter, the health care, and the education that are required for survival and equal opportunity, while the welfare system for the rich grows rather than diminishes? Surely not.

If for religious or other reasons we believe that everyone has worth and that we are all in some way part of the same human family, then we would have to regard destitution in the presence of the ability to do something to remedy it as deprivation and consider assertions of rights to food, shelter, and medical attention as legitimate complaints. A lot of what we envy others was not necessarily taken from us. Perhaps we lost out simply because our parents had only so many hours in the day to read to all the siblings, or there were only so many job openings available at that workplace, or there were only so many parts in the play. However, unless we inhabit conditions of scarcity in which there is not enough of life's essentials to go around, it is not envy to demand a place at the table; it's a birthright to have a place. People who are grateful for what they have received and convinced that "their" good cannot be separated from "ours" will not regard the voices of those asking for equal opportunity as special pleading. It is not envy to want a place at the table.

Schools of Virtue

All virtue, it seems, is public if the definition of public is broad enough. Virtue requires public expression and entails public obligation; the traditions that surround public life spawn virtues. Yet if we reduce it to a public creation, we not only will be left with a skeletal image at best, but also may be saddled with a version of good citizenship that serves the ends of the hoarders of power more than the needs of the least advantaged. Virtue is situated in stories that identify and guide communities. It is defined by communities and determines the quality of life in communities. The quality of community will foster the ranking of virtues, and the scope of community will determine the reach of virtues. If a community of communities is the aim of public life, then the virtuous contributions of plural communities are needed to enrich civic virtue.

Although virtue is nurtured first in the family, the neighborhood, the church or other religious community, the natural environment, and the school, if a person is fortunate enough to enjoy all of those associations, it should also locate people in larger communities of nation and globe. The mediating communities of civil society are the breeding ground of virtue, but they are not the only communities, and they do not exhaust civil society, which we have claimed can even extend into the government and the corporation and can have global reach. For better or for worse, virtue is being taught all over the place, but not all virtues are equally contributory to the common good and equally reflective of life in covenants of fidelity, trust, compassion, justice, and responsibility. Can covenantal virtue for the common good emanate only from the small, particular communities that have an explicitly religious center? Can compassion be taught anywhere but at the parent's knee and on the playground and perhaps at church or synagogue?

Surely, religious communities are essential nurseries for civic virtue, and there is no place like home for learning what it means to live in a democracy. Still, we have to hope that they are not our only schools of virtue. In part we say that because many children lack a nurturing home or a nurturing religious community. That impoverishment can occur because stable and loving home life is nonexistent for them, and they are not part of a religious community; it can also occur because their homes and religious communities are up to no good as schools of virtue. Estimates of how long the average child spends with a parent run as low as one hour a week; the amount of time spent with any adult outside of school as low as three hours. The average teenager reportedly spends six minutes a day with the mother and less with the father. We cited earlier the rarity of a common meal in most families.

Judith Rich Harris's recent book carries a message in its title that would seem to dismiss the importance of these laments: *The Nurture Assumption: Why Children Turn Out the Way They Do: Parents Matter Less Than You Think and Peers Matter More.*[40] Her claim has hardly won universal affirmation and for good reason, but assuming that she is at least partly right, we can venture some rejoinders. If peers, including gangs, are raising our children, they may be doing it by default, and it is not apparent that they are fostering civic virtue. For parents to put down the book and breathe a sigh of relief would be a huge mistake. At the same time, parents, churches, and schools need to pay more attention to the power of peer inculcation of virtue and vice in the various contexts in which young people interact, including the Internet.

Too often, children are not listened to. They are not attended to. They are not read to. They are not corrected or redirected. They are not commiserated with or reasoned with. They are not required or inspired. They feel no love and they encounter no limits. What their parents and other significant adults model is not faithfulness, patience, compassion, tenderness, and justice but unreliability, betrayal, impatience, apathy, callousness, and unfairness.

Way back in the late sixties, early in my teaching career, a student plopped down in my office one night. Since I was then the college chaplain as well as a teacher, he first voiced some recurrent curiosity about the possibility of being a minister because they helped people, although he thought he would have to believe more than he did for that path to be open to him. Before long we got to his puzzlement about how he ended up in a good college with promising prospects when, as we spoke, the young men that he hung out with in his neighborhood were probably all sitting out on a corner someplace drinking cheap wine and looking for some action. As he searched his past, a few simple but profoundly important factors came out. Most of his friends saw a series of different men in their houses or apartments spending time with their mothers, but his parents were married. He knew that their relationship was important to them, although their work schedules meant that they were seldom in the apartment at the same time. Both of his parents held steady jobs. And when his mother was at home, the thing she most often did was lie in her bed and read books. Two parents who loved each other and stayed together, two workers, and a love of books were enough to get one young African American male away from the dead-end streets of his friends and on track for a life of service. There was probably more to it. There must have been a reason why he would even entertain the idea of being a minister, and he probably had had teachers and coaches (he was a football player) who had broadened his horizons. All in all, a few things that might have seemed small to some and perhaps even to him loomed large in his life.

A religious community can make a big difference as a school of virtue, but it depends on the quality of its community—on the sense of identity connected to a center of loyalty, the sense of responsibility, the respect for diversity, and the openness to participation in decisions. What if the church is more of a drive-thru entertainment center than a covenant community? What if it is more of an individual spiritual fitness center than a place of public discourse where important theological and ethical issues are discussed? What if its members are more consumers of therapeutic assistance or contractors for services than covenanters in communities that see themselves in connection to other communities? Church, after all, could just be another part of the problem.

Schools can be teachers of virtue. Timothy Jackson and James Gilman are among those who believe that compassion, personal care, or *agape* can be taught in the schools through the study of exemplary lives from a variety of traditions and without religious triumphalism.[41] Building service into learning and fostering conversation about matters of civic, ethical, and religious import in which Habermas's principle of universal moral respect and principle of egalitarian reciprocity are practiced can make primary, secondary, and higher education a manifestation and a feeder system of civil society. Openness to the other can certainly be promoted by the way teaching and learning are conceived and implemented. The mind-boggling possibilities of our electronic era for information gathering and exchange may enhance this training in civic virtue, but not if sitting at our computer screens makes us less engaged in genuine dialogue and argument with each other. If the Internet links us to larger circles of public concern, advocacy, and discussion, it will have enriched our global community of communities. If it only increases the quantity of available data and the distance between those with access and those without, the malaise of civil society will worsen.

Some medical schools are demonstrating that virtue can be taught in professional school. It seems self-evident that compassion should be standard equipment for a doctor, yet some survivors of the rigorous training and practice have reported that they had less compassion rather than more when they finished their preparation before any compassion training was required. At Duke University Medical School, physicians-in-training on a geriatric rotation have gone through the experience of finding out what many elderly people experience—blurred or blocked vision, diminished hearing, abandonment, force-feeding, loss of valued possessions, threatened sense of identity, and being addressed by their first names or with pet names by people they do not know. Another doctor at Duke required his students to go home with patients for the weekend in rural North Carolina. The late Dr. Gabriel Smilkstein of the University of Louisville staged "humble rounds" in which the patients taught the medical students instead of being talked about in front of medical students.[42]

If medical training can teach compassion, legal training can build in the prisoner's point of view, the victim's point of view, the point of view of the person who got the death penalty with a court-appointed lawyer asleep in the courtroom, the divorcing couple's point of view, the grieving spouse's point of view, and the point of view of the person who is too poor and too lacking in savvy about the system to get legal assistance. Every lawyer could be inculcated with the vocation of a public defender in the sense of a protector and promoter of the common good, not just of personal fame and fortune. Likewise, corporate employers can take the places of employees, the unemployed, community members, competitors, suppliers, and environmental advocates to bring community relationships and civic discourse into the workings of the marketplace.

Our political leaders can be teachers of virtue by the way in which they provide occasions for civil civic discourse with their constituents, their fellow legislators, and their staffs. Listening and initiating, "hearing others into speech"[43] and being responsive to their needs, searching out the participants in dialogue who cannot pay their way in and who are intimidated in organizational settings where the better educated often feel at home, people in government can build civic virtue. By facilitating communication and modeling respect for difference, sensitivity to need, and commitment to the values of liberty and justice for all, they will do that very thing. In this way, civil society's vitality will be stimulated by government instead of smothered by government, and the perceived chasm between civil society and the state will be crossed. As Ronald Thiemann asks, "If democratic government cannot serve as a 'school of virtue' for a pluralistic society, where will those virtues essential to a responsible public life be nurtured?"[44]

The media can be schools of virtue. They can facilitate public discourse, dramatize public responsibility, celebrate compassion and public service, and expose public wrong. Examples of all of these public services continue to appear. Yet something else is going on that is not so laudable. The media have helped make campaigns dependent on sound bites and media events instead of genuine debate and serious moral discourse. And the role historically played by political parties has largely been taken over by the media, where the ranking of issues is apt to take place. What is more, the cost and importance of media advertising by candidates further heighten the cost of political participation and widen the gap between those who can pay to broadcast their views and those who cannot. In this media world, what Bill Bradley calls "the dual credos" rules: "If it bleeds, it leads; if it thinks, it stinks."[45] The sensational gets the attention, and the substantive often gathers dust.

The covenantal communitarianism of Clifford E. Christians, John P. Ferre, and P. Mark Fackler, the authors of *Good News: Social Ethics and the Press*, stands in marked contrast. They claim that "the press should enable citizens to act transformatively out of truthful narratives." News is the making of a covenant, and it should involve the kind of affirmative action that aims to "promote and explore the hidden people." The point is to "multiply voices, not silence them." Dialogue, universal solidarity, partnership, trust, empathy, mutuality in organizational culture, and transformative social change are the language of their commitment to justice, covenant, and empowerment.[46] To the extent that they can realize this vision, the media indeed can be schools of virtue.

Timothy Jackson considers it "possible, but not likely" that we can have "the equivalent of civic *agapism* without God and a religious description of the good."[47] Max Stackhouse is convinced that a public theology can inform a recovery of covenant in our common life. A particular religious tradition will advocate it, and others can accept it, while still respecting pluralism. Both the ecumenical Protestant and the Catholic tradition believe that what they have come to know through scripture, tradition, reason, and experience "is pertinent to the whole of society and to all people." "They feel a compelling responsibility both to interpret and to shape the common life—not just the life of those who adhere to their confession—on theological grounds."[48] One has to wonder how the project can be carried out in a way that respects difference in a pluralistic society.

My own contention is that those of us in religious communities should endeavor to interpret and shape the common life on the basis of our theological convictions, but that we should do so confessionally, not apologetically as Stackhouse does.[49] There is an important difference between trying to sell a particular theology as the public theology and giving public expression to convictions grounded in one's theology in discussion of public issues. Society is leavened in marked and crucial ways by the presence of religious communities, but a public theology should not try to impose a theological position that, for instance, rules that same-sex marriage cannot be condoned in society.

People can live covenantal lives and practice covenantal virtue for the common good without reliance on religious faith, although I suspect that they live on borrowed capital when they do. What is more, some unifying commitment to core values is essential to a political community, even if these values are merely the requirements that discourse ethics stipulates for argumentative speech (the right of all to participate and to participate equally and reciprocally). Call it civil religion or core values, we need some common commitments and common language to carry on the dialogue about the common good.

However, there is too much damage done when a particular theology is implemented as the reigning ideology of societies. There is enough religious pluralism in our own land and in the global community to make one hope that we can discover some commonly affirmed civic virtues from a variety of storied sources, including our American political tradition, and even some reiterative universal norms through dialogue, without promulgating one theology's norms as universal directives.

Learning to tell better stories about ourselves as Americans and as members of the global community will not occur if we cease to remember the stories that we tell around the tables of our familial and religious communities and of our various voluntary associations and fail to advocate the virtues embedded in those stories. Nor will the better stories emerge if we lack the willingness and ability to hear the stories of others. What is more, a nation or a global village that keeps dialogue alive will find that richer traditions result from that public discourse.

The virtues of faith as openness to the other, love as affirmation of the other and compassion toward the other, hope as the expectant patience to keep public discourse alive, and generous public-spiritedness as the manifestation of gratitude are essential to the process of table talk that sustains civil society. If our covenantal religious traditions are worth their salt, they will season civil discourse to make it more inclusive, more respectful of difference, more attentive to the well-being of the entire community, and more constitutive of shared identity that does not subsume all other identities.

Conclusion

The quest for community is the obligation of covenant, and the fostering of community of the right kind is at least one understanding of the common good. The three terms belong together; and taken together, they can approach and perhaps even accomplish that delicate balance between individual liberty and communal solidarity that revisionist liberals and societal communitarians seek. Conceived as complementary, they combine respect for difference with affirmation of commonality. Together they counter the brand of individualism that denudes the self of its social locations, historical connections, and constitutive affiliations and that reduces the self's associations to calculated protections of personal interests. Together they enrich our discussion of family values and incline it in a better direction than mere arguments about rights. Together they relocate the discussion about work and welfare in the context of what it means to have full membership in a national family, as well as membership in various voluntary associations. Together they point toward a global community of communities in which we can not only occasionally "walk in each other's parades," as Walzer puts it, but also learn together to tell better stories about ourselves as global citizens. Together they connect our ideas of virtue to the crisis of civil society. They found virtue on table manners—at the table of the family meal, the table of religious communion, the table of workplace decision making, the table of political debate, and the table of global civil society. The rules of discourse at those tables set the tone for the communities we are, the covenants we keep, and the common good we nurture.

At these tables, what language shall we use? Is the value-laden discourse of the family table and the religious table only so much table talk and so many inside stories that are not translatable in the public square and the corporate boardroom? Is it out of place, as liberalism has sometimes claimed, to employ arguments based on religious conviction in the debates of a democracy? Must the language there be limited to the minimal linguistic currency of that phantom figure, the rational person? Must the common good be left alone because there can be no substantial agreement in a pluralistic society, and because there should be no imposition of a particular religious or philosophical agenda on a diverse and separately storied populace? Must covenant be the argot only of the Passover meal and the communion table, or does it have a crucial contribution to make to public discourse?

The response in these pages to these questions has been to make the conversations of civil society and of government at all levels (and these are not separate, airtight compartments) a process of exploration of the common good, and even to regard the continuation of that process as a common good. We have argued that community is not confined to those intimate interactions where everyone knows everyone's name. Rather, it can extend to national and even global dimensions. We have also claimed that covenant is more than a household word and a biblical concept. It is a metaphor that points to the interhuman and interdependent character of our existence as a given and not merely a choice, as the ground both of moral possibility and of claims about any reality that transcends our individual needs and wants. Granted, the world has changed since the covenant tradition developed, but the concept of covenant can still be the carrier of insights without which we would be consigned to a familial, ecclesiastical, and civic wilderness with no Sinai in sight.

This claim returns us to Edward Farley's question about the continuing viability of deep symbols, those community-constituting and community-directing god-terms. It would be a mistake to value covenantal currency as the only medium of symbolic exchange. Deep symbols are contextual and may become outdated. They are also partial insights that should not be idolized. It is significant, however, that the symbols Farley chose—tradition, obligation, law, the real, and hope—have strong covenantal connections and configure themselves in relation to each other appropriately in a covenantal context. Together they can structure a community's story about itself. Tradition and hope place a community in time, giving it identity and purpose. Obligation and law, carried by tradition, convey the claim of the other on us and institutionalize the conventional wisdom about just human interaction. Obligation cannot be captured in law, but it cannot be generally practiced without law. The real and obligation both point to the other, to an existence beyond our own that impinges on us. Covenant involves an acknowledgment of what we did not create that has made us what we are. It obligates us. It is spelled out provisionally in law. Its future hope is linked to a trustworthy past and a long-suffering present.

Edward Farley's exploration of deep symbols locates what is ultimately at stake in the discussion of covenant, community, and common good, quite apart from the use, neglect, or repudiation of particular terms or concepts. The deep symbols or the god-terms originate in the sphere of the interhuman, as Buber designated it, not in the individual or the institutional spheres. Yet they connect the three spheres. The interhuman is captured in our seeing "the face" of the vulnerable other, as Levinas expressed it. This presence, which we cannot fully fathom or control, calls to us, requires our recognition, and obliges our response, even before we place ourselves under obligation or decide to assume responsibility for this other.

Being "faced" with the other does not constitute a covenant, but it creates that possibility. Assuming responsibility does instigate a covenant. Because something universal is represented in the face of the other, obligation is generalized through law. The common good of a larger community is a part of the obligation to the other. Law is not the same as the covenant, but it is a necessary, provisional expression of it as social policy. When the face of the vulnerable other is eclipsed by the law, the law has overshadowed the covenant.

Not all theologians ground deep symbols in the concrete relation to the other being whose existence and experience are beyond the questing self. Some attempt a rational leap to the very structure of things, to the order of Being itself. If we start with the interhuman, our focus on covenant, community, and the common good becomes more important than the terms themselves. If hospitality to the stranger is the prerequisite for covenant, it is also essential to any community that respects difference. It is the beginning of moral obligation. We start from difference to discover kinship. If hospitality to the stranger is the prerequisite for genuine dialogue about the common good and about anything that people believe to be good or real, it is not only a moral obligation, but also a theological or religious necessity. Wherever people are going to talk about substantive matters of shared concern, they will need to have recourse to deep symbols, and communities of discourse cannot talk without some common language. We cannot leave home without it.

As a society, we already have some shared symbols, just as we do as families or as religious communities or as other voluntary associations. We could not be getting along without them. People with nothing in common cannot even argue. Our ability to converse in public depends on shared symbolic expression; moreover, these shared symbols will determine how our communities live out their covenants for the common good in the future.

The critics of the traditions of covenant and common good and of the idea of community have done Christian ethics a great favor. One testimony to the vitality of these traditions is that they have raised up their own critics. A further test of their vitality will be the extent to which they practice hospitality to the stranger from other traditions. If God does meet us in the other, then we can anticipate that the stories of varied communities will find points of convergence and places of concord without presenting themselves as duplicates of one another or seeking to become fused into a single story or diversity-absorbing identity.

If what we hope to become is a global, national, and local community of communities, the stories that we tell about ourselves will not be rival candidates for hegemony as master narratives, but shared accounts of what covenants brought us to the table and reciprocal testimony about what common good the table talk is and seeks. Without covenantal commitments, we would not share the setting of the table or stay at the table together or care about the table fare. Without community that affirms and respects difference, the table would be reserved for the in crowd and offer only limited seating. Without the valuation of the table fellowship itself as a common good, there would be no continuing conversation about what it means to take responsibility for everyone who is at the table or belongs at the table. We would get no practice at minding our manners.

NOTES

Introduction

1. Richard Gula, *Reason Informed by Faith: Foundations of Catholic Morality* (New York: Paulist Press, 1989); Antonio Moser and Bernardino Leers, *Moral Theology: Dead Ends and Alternatives*, trans. Paul Burns (Maryknoll, N.Y.: Orbis Books, 1990), 73; Wolfgang Roth and Rosemary Ruether, *The Liberating Bond: Covenants, Biblical and Contemporary* (New York: Friendship Press, 1978); Philip Keane, *Christian Ethics and Imagination* (New York: Paulist Press, 1984); Margaret A. Farley, *Personal Commitments: Beginning, Keeping, Changing* (San Francisco: Harper and Row, 1986); National Conference of Catholic Bishops, *Economic Justice for All: Catholic Social Teaching and the U.S. Economy* (Washington, D.C.: United States Catholic Conference, 1986).

2. Herman E. Daly and John B. Cobb Jr., *For the Common Good: Redirecting the Economy toward Community, the Environment, and a Sustainable Future* (Boston: Beacon Press, 1989); Douglas Sturm, *Solidarity and Suffering: Toward a Politics of Relationality* (Albany: State University of New York Press, 1998). See particularly his treatment of democracy as expression of the common good (147) and his proposal of a "relational economy" as an alternative beyond a strictly market economy that is directed by the public or common good as its criterion (154). William F. May, *Testing the Medical Covenant: Active Euthanasia and Healthcare Reform* (Grand Rapids, Mich.: Eerdmans, 1996); Ronald F. Thiemann, *Religion in Public Life: A Dilemma for Democracy* (Washington, D.C.: Georgetown University Press, 1996); Robert Bellah et al., *The Good Society* (New York: Alfred A. Knopf, 1991). A recent Catholic collection on the common good is James Donahue and M. Theresa Moser, R.S.C.J., eds., *Religion, Ethics, and the Common Good* (Mystic, Conn.: Twenty-Third Publications, 1996).

3. Thiemann, *Religion in Public Life*, 102.

4. Ibid., 105. He includes Jean Bethke Elshtain, William Galston, Michael Perry, Nancy Rosenbaum, Jeffrey Stout, Charles Taylor, Michael Walzer, and the later John Rawls.

5. As Thiemann elaborates, Susan Moller Okin, *Justice, Gender, and the Family* (New York: Basic Books, 1989), has documented Aristotle's exclusion of farmers, artisans, merchants, and women from the active life of the polis. Jean Bethke Elshtain, *Women and War* (New York: Basic Books, 1987), traces the role of recurrent hostility toward a common enemy in achieving solidarity from Machiavelli to the Gulf War.

6. Thiemann, *Religion in Public Life*, 109. Michael Novak, *Free Persons and the Common Good* (Lanham, N.Y.: Madison Books, 1989), xi. Novak seeks to marry two traditions—the common good ethic of his own Catholic tradition with the legacies of liberal society. Liberal society's elevation of freedom with justice insists on "the right of individuals to define the good for themselves" and "an unplanned and uncovered social order." He believes that the common good tradition needs these liberal discoveries. The balance Novak seeks would tilt harder toward individual liberties, and Thiemann would lean more toward communal solidarity. To capture the diverse approaches to the common good tradition by democratic capitalists and democratic socialists, the reader should pair Novak's apology for capitalism with Gary J. Dorrien, *Reconstructing the Common Good: Theology and the Social Order* (Maryknoll, N.Y.: Orbis Books, 1990), which is a defense of democratic socialism.

7. Robert Bellah et al., *Habits of the Heart: Individualism and Commitment in American Life* (Berkeley: University of California Press, 1985); Bellah et al., *The Good Society*. Michael Novak distinguishes communitarians of the left (Michael Sandel, Robert Bellah, Michael Walzer, and Benjamin Barber) from communitarians on the right (Robert Nisbet, William Shambra, Peter Berger, and Richard John Neuhaus). Michael Novak, *Free Persons and the Common Good* (Lanham, N.Y.: Madison Books, 1989), x.

8. Edward O. Laumann et al., *The Social Organization of Sexuality* (Chicago: University of Chicago Press, 1994); "Unmarried Couples Top Four Million for First Time," *Louisville Courier-Journal*, 27 July 1998, A2.

9. Michael Walzer speaks of "Four Mobilities" that we prize—geographical, social, marital, and political. Walzer, "The Communitarian Critique of Liberalism," *Political Theory* 18, no. 1 (February 1990): 12.

10. Edward Farley, *Deep Symbols: Their Postmodern Effacement and Reclamation* (Valley Forge, Pa.: Trinity Press International, 1996), 3.

11. E. J. Dionne Jr., ed., *Community Works: The Revival of Civil Society in America* (Washington, D.C.: Brookings Institution Press, 1998).

12. Peter Berger and Richard John Neuhaus addressed this issue in the 1970s using the term "mediating structures." Peter L. Berger and Richard John Neuhaus, *To Empower People: The Role of Mediating Structures in Public Policy* (Washington, D.C.: American Enterprise Institute for Public Policy Research, 1977).

1. The Currency of Covenant

1. E. Farley, *Deep Symbols*, 2.

2. Ibid., 3.

3. H. Richard Niebuhr, *Faith on Earth* (New Haven, Conn.: Yale University Press, 1989), 48.

4. Daniel Elazar, *Covenant and Policy in Biblical Israel*, vol. 1 of *The Covenant Tradition in Politics* (New Brunswick, N.J.: Transaction Publishers, 1995), 53.

5. H. Richard Niebuhr, "The Idea of Covenant and American Democracy," *Church History* 23 (1954): 126–35.

6. Ibid., 130.

7. Ibid., 132–33.

8. Robert N. Bellah, *The Broken Covenant: American Civil Religion in Time of Trial* (New York: Seabury Press, 1975).

9. Rosemary Ruether, *Gaia and God: An Ecofeminist Theology of Earth Healing* (San Francisco: HarperSanFrancisco, 1992), 217.

10. E. Farley, *Deep Symbols*, 3.

11. Margaret A. Farley, *Personal Commitments: Beginning, Keeping, and Changing* (San Francisco: Harper and Row, 1986), 111.

12. George E. Mendenhall, *Law and Covenant in Israel and the Ancient Near East* (Pittsburgh: Biblical Colloquium, 1955).

13. Ina Caro, *The Road from the Past and Traveling through History in France* (San Diego: Harcourt Brace, 1994), 270.

14. Ada María Isasi-Díaz, "Solidarity: Love of Neighbor in the 1980s," in *Lift Every Voice*, ed. Susan Brooks Thistlethwaite and Mary Potter Engel (San Francisco: HarperSanFrancisco, 1990). In "Mujerista Theology: A Challenge to Traditional Theology," in *Introduction to Christian Theology*, ed. Roger A. Badham (Louisville, Ky.: Westminster John Knox Press, 1998), 251 n. 12, she credits Georgene Wilson, O.S.F., as the source of the word "kin-dom."

15. Carol S. Robb with Carl J. Casebolt, "Introduction," in *Covenant for a New Creation*, ed. Carol S. Robb and Carl J. Casebolt (Maryknoll, N.Y.: Orbis, 1991), 11.

16. Rebecca S. Chopp, *Saving Work: Feminist Practices of Theological Education* (Louisville, Ky.: Westminster/John Knox Press, 1995), 67.

17. M. Farley, *Personal Commitments*, 129–30.

18. William Johnson Everett, *God's Federal Republic: Reconstructing Our Governing Symbol* (Mahwah, N.J.: Paulist Press, 1988), 105–6; Charles McCoy, "Creation and Covenant," in *Covenant for a New Creation*, ed. Robb and Casebolt, 214.

19. Daniel Elazar, *Covenant and Polity in Biblical Israel*, 2.

20. Leo G. Perdue, "The Household, Old Testament Theology, and Contemporary Hermeneutics," in *Families in Ancient Israel*, ed. Leo G. Perdue et al. (Louisville, Ky.: Westminster John Knox Press, 1997), 225–26.

21. Carol Meyers, "The Family in Early Israel," in *Families in Ancient Israel*, ed. Leo G. Perdue et al. (Louisville, Ky.: Westminster John Knox Press, 1997), 34.

22. Elizabeth Bounds, "Conflicting Harmonies: Michael Walzer's Vision of Community," *Journal of Religious Ethics* 22, no. 2 (fall 1994): 368. In *Boundaries: Psychological Man in Revolution* (New York: Vintage Books, 1970), 37–38, 43–44, 51, Robert Jay Lifton distinguishes between selves and communities that are "closed off" in rigid identities and those that are protean or emptied out, that is, so flexible that they lack fixed identities and boundaries.

23. Major J. Jones, *Christian Ethics for Black Theology: The Politics of Liberation* (Nashville: Abingdon Press, 1974), 41–50; Tyler Roberts, "Michael Walzer and the Critical Connections," *Journal of Religious Ethics* 22, no. 2 (fall 1994): 341, 343, 351.

24. Joseph L. Allen, *Love and Conflict: A Covenantal Model of Christian Ethics* (Nashville: Abingdon Press, 1984), 131–49; M. Farley, *Personal Commitments*, 128–

29; Thomas Ogletree, *Hospitality to the Stranger* (Philadelphia: Fortress Press, 1985); Darrell J. Fasching, *Narrative Theology after Auschwitz: From Alienation to Ethics* (Minneapolis: Fortress Press, 1992), 1–4, 16, 27, 67, 85, 192–93; Paula M. Cooey, *Family, Freedom, and Faith: Building Community Today* (Louisville, Ky.: Westminster John Knox Press, 1996), 59.

25. S. Dean McBride Jr., "Polity of the Covenant People: The Book of Deuteronomy," *Interpretation* 16, no. 3 (July 1987): 243.

26. Michael Walzer, "The Idea of Holy War in Ancient Israel," *Journal of Religious Ethics* 20, no. 2 (fall 1992): 225–26.

27. John T. Pawlikowski, "Christology, Anti-Semitism, and Christian-Jewish Bonding," in *Reconstructing Christian Theology*, ed. Rebecca Chopp and Mark Lewis Taylor (Minneapolis: Fortress Press, 1994), 245–68.

28. Jean François Lyotard, *The Postmodern Condition: A Report on Knowledge*, trans. Geoff Bennington and Brian Massumi (Minneapolis: University of Minnesota Press, 1984), 6.

29. Alasdair MacIntyre, *After Virtue* (Notre Dame, Ind.: University of Notre Dame Press, 1981), and *Whose Justice? Whose Rationality?* (Notre Dame, Ind.: University of Notre Dame Press, 1988).

30. Glen Stassen, "Michael Walzer's Situated Justice," *Journal of Religious Ethics* 22, no. 2 (fall 1994): 381; Michael Walzer, *Thick and Thin: Moral Argument at Home and Abroad* (Notre Dame, Ind.: University of Notre Dame Press, 1994), 8.

31. Darrell J. Fasching, *The Ethical Challenge of Auschwitz and Hiroshima: Apocalypse or Utopia?* (Albany: State University of New York Press, 1993), 3, 181, 182; David Hollenbach, *Justice, Peace, and Human Rights: American Catholic Social Ethics in a Pluralistic World* (New York: Crossroad, 1988), 123; Glen H. Stassen, *Just Peacemaking: Transforming Initiatives for Justice and Peace* (Louisville, Ky.: Westminster/ John Knox Press, 1992), 158–59.

32. Michael Walzer, *Interpretation and Social Criticism* (Cambridge: Harvard University Press, 1987).

33. Bounds, "Conflicting Harmonies," 357, 367; Tyler Roberts, "Michael Walzer and the Critical Connections," *Journal of Religious Ethics* 22, no. 2 (fall 1994): 343.

34. Robb with Casebolt, "Introduction," 11.

35. M. Farley, *Personal Commitments*, 132–33.

36. Robb with Casebolt, "Introduction"; Carol S. Robb, "A Covenant for Life," *Chimes* 43, no. 2 (summer 1998): 14–17; Wesley Granburg-Michaelson, "Covenant and Creation," in *Liberating Life: Contemporary Approaches to Ecological Theology*, ed. Charles Birch et al. (Maryknoll, N.Y.: Orbis Books, 1998), 27–36; George Kehm, "The New Story: Redemption as Fulfillment of Creation," in *After Nature's Revolt*, ed. Dieter T. Hessel (Minneapolis: Fortress Press, 1992), 89–106; Holmes Rolston III, "Environmental Ethics: Some Challenges for Christians," *Annual of the Society of Christian Ethics* (1993): 163–88; William Everett, "Biblical Bases for Modern Politics," *Bangalore Theological Forum* 23, no. 3 (September 1993): 13; Everett, *God's Federal Republic*, 103–6; Jürgen Moltmann, "Reconciliation with Nature," *Word and World* 11, no. 2 (spring 1991): 117–123; Ruether, *Gaia and God*, 207–14; James A.

Nash, "Biotic Rights and Human Ecological Responsibilities," *Annual of the Society of Christian Ethics* (1993): 148–49, 162; James A. Nash, *Loving Nature: Ecological Integrity and Christian Responsibility* (Nashville: Abingdon Press, 1991).

37. Charles Taylor, "Cross-Purposes: The Liberal-Communitarian Debate," in *Liberalism and the Moral Life*, ed. Nancy L. Rosenblum (Cambridge: Harvard University Press, 1989), 169–70.

38. Timothy P. Jackson, "Liberalism and Agape: The Priority of Charity to Democracy and Philosophy," *Annual of the Society of Christian Ethics* (1993): 47–72.

39. E. Farley, *Deep Symbols*, 44–45.

40. William F. May, *Testing the Medical Covenant: Active Euthanasia and Health-care Reform* (Grand Rapids, Mich.: Eerdmans, 1996), 53.

41. Immanuel Levinas, *Totality and Infinity: An Essay on Exteriority*, trans. Alphonso Lingis (Pittsburgh: Duquesne University Press, 1966), esp. pages 34, 38, 80, 173, 213, 295; Ogletree, *Hospitality to the Stranger*; Edward Farley, *Good and Evil: Interpreting a Human Condition* (Minneapolis: Fortress Press, 1990), 33–46; Wendy Farley, *Tragic Vision and Divine Compassion: A Contemporary Theodicy* (Louisville, Ky.: Westminster/John Knox Press, 1990); W. Farley, *Eros for the Other: Retaining Truth in a Pluralistic World* (University Park: Pennsylvania State University Press, 1996). For further explanation of Levinas, see Colin Davis, *Levinas: An Introduction* (Notre Dame, Ind.: University of Notre Dame Press, 1996), esp. pages 38–54.

42. E. Farley, *Good and Evil*, 33, 42–43.

43. John D. Caputo, ed., *Deconstruction in a Nutshell: A Conversation with Jacques Derrida* (New York: Fordham University Press, 1997), chap. 4. Caputo's conversation quotes extensively from Derrida and provides extended commentary. The specific comments on his Jewishness are found on pages 114 and 171.

44. William F. May, *The Physician's Covenant: Images of the Healer in Medical Ethics* (Philadelphia: Westminster Press, 1983).

2. The Commonality of the Common Good

1. Aristotle, *Ethics*, trans. J. A. K. Thompson and Hugh Tredennick (New York: Penguin Books, 1976), book 1, 64.

2. James B. Nelson, *Moral Nexus: Ethics of Christian Identity and Community* (Philadelphia: Westminster Press, 1971), 119.

3. Thomas Vernor Smith, *The Ethics of Compromise and the Art of Containment* (Boston: Starr King Press, 1956), 54.

4. Susan Moller Okin, *Justice, Gender, and the Family* (New York: Basic Books, 1989).

5. Sallie McFague, *Supernatural Christians* (Minneapolis: Fortress Press, 1997), 152–53.

6. John Rawls, *A Theory of Justice* (Cambridge: Harvard University Press, 1971), 246.

7. Herman E. Daly and John B. Cobb Jr., *For the Common Good* (Boston: Beacon Press, 1989), 172. Amitai Etzioni defines community more formally and less

normatively in *The New Golden Rule: Community and Morality in a Democratic Society* (New York: Basic Books, 1996), 127. For him, community can be defined by precisely two characteristics: "First, a web of affect-laden relationships among a group of individuals, relationships that often crisscross and reinforce one another (rather than merely one-on-one or chainlike individual relationships), and second, a measure of commitment to a set of shared values, norms, and meanings, and a shared history and identity—in short, to a particular culture." He has described community generally, but his definition could cover the Ku Klux Klan as easily as a Buddhist or Christian monastery. Daly and Cobb load their definition with the kind of ethical content that staves off the oppressions of tyrannical communities as well as diffusion of communities with no discernible identity.

8. H. Richard Niebuhr, *The Responsible Self: An Essay in Christian Moral Philosophy* (New York: Harper and Row, 1963), 79–89.

9. See Jean Bethke Elshtain, *Women and War* (New York: Basic Books, 1987).

10. Michael Walzer, *Thick and Thin: Moral Arguments at Home and Abroad* (Notre Dame, Ind.: University of Notre Dame Press, 1994), 96–100.

11. Catharine A. MacKinnon, *Only Words* (Cambridge: Harvard University Press, 1993), 39.

12. Ibid., 101.

13. Ibid., 98, 107.

14. Paula M. Cooey, *Family, Freedom, and Faith: Building Community Today* (Louisville, Ky.: Westminster/John Knox Press, 1993), 75.

15. Neva R. Goodwin, "Introduction—Global Commons: Site of Peril, Source of Hope," *World Development* 19 (January 1991): 1–15 as summarized in *A Survey of Ecological Economics*, ed. Rajaram Krishnan, Jonathan M. Harris, and Neva R. Goodwin (Washington, D.C.: Island Press, 1995), 323.

16. Ibid., 324.

17. Edwin M. Hartman, *Organizational Ethics and the Good Life* (New York: Oxford University Press, 1996).

18. John Rawls, *Political Liberalism* (New York: Columbia University Press, 1993).

19. Hartman, *Organizational Ethics and the Good Life*, 75.

20. Ibid., 4, 172.

21. Ibid., 68, 178.

22. Albert O. Hirschman, *Exit, Voice, and Loyalty: Responses to Decline in Firms, Organizations, and States* (Cambridge: Harvard University Press, 1970).

23. Hartman, *Organizational Ethics*, 9.

24. United States Catholic Bishops, *Economic Justice for All: Catholic Social Teaching and the U.S. Economy* (Washington, D.C.: National Conference of Catholic Bishops, 1986), par. 79. This definition is an appropriate expression of the Catholic tradition, but James Donahue observes that the Catholic tradition has "no universal interpretation of the exact meaning of the common good." James Donahue and M. Theresa Moser, R.S.C.J., eds., *Religion, Ethics, and the Common Good* (Mystic, Conn.: Twenty-Third Publications, 1996), x.

25. Maura A. Ryan, "Particular Sorrows, Common Challenges: Specialized Infertility Treatment and the Common Good," *Annual of the Society of Christian Ethics* (1994): 201.

26. David Hollenbach, S.J., "Liberalism, Communitarianism, and the Bishops' Pastoral Letter on the Economy," *Annual of the Society of Christian Ethics* (1987): 19–40.

27. United States Catholic Bishops, *Economic Justice for All*, par. 36, 66, 71, 77.

28. Ibid., par. 80, 85.

29. Ibid., par. 88.

30. Ibid., par. 111.

31. Ibid., par. 115, 124.

32. Warren Copeland, *Economic Justice* (Nashville: Abingdon Press, 1988), 137.

33. Karen Lebacqz, *Six Theories of Justice* (Minneapolis: Augsburg Publishing House, 1986), 81.

34. Copeland, *Economic Justice*, 145, 146, 238.

35. Anne E. Patrick, *Liberating Conscience: Feminist Explorations in Catholic Moral Theology* (New York: Continuum, 1996), chap. 4, 7.

36. Cooey, *Family, Freedom, and Faith*, 67.

37. Ibid., 67.

38. Ibid., 43, 67.

39. Ibid., 74.

40. Ibid., 6.

41. Daniel Elazar, *Covenant and Polity in Biblical Israel*, vol. 1 of *The Covenant Tradition in Politics* (New Brunswick, N.J.: Transaction Publishers, 1995), 64.

42. Cooey, *Family, Freedom, and Faith*, 72, 73.

43. S. Dean McBride Jr., "Polity of the Covenant People: The Book of Deuteronomy," *Interpretation* 16, no. 3 (July 1987): 237, 243.

44. Ibid., 237.

45. Ibid., 243.

46. E. Farley, *Good and Evil*, 41.

47. Max L. Stackhouse, *Creeds, Society, and Human Rights: A Study in Three Cultures* (Grand Rapids, Mich.: Eerdmans, 1984), 33, 34, 102, 192, 256.

48. Elazar, *Covenant and Polity in Biblical Israel*, 35, 42, 84, 85.

49. James M. Gustafson, *Ethics from a Theocentric Perspective*, vol. 1 of *Theology and Ethics* (Chicago: University of Chicago Press, 1981), 292–93.

50. McFague, *Supernatural Christians*, 152, 169.

51. Miriam Schulman, "Affirmative Action or Negative Action," *Issues in Ethics* 7, no. 6 (summer/fall 1996): 2–4.

3. Homing In on Family Values

1. John Witte Jr., *From Sacrament to Contract: Marriage, Religion, and Law in the Western Tradition*, The Family, Religion, and Culture (Louisville, Ky.: Westminster John Knox Press, 1997), 217–18.

2. "Perspectives," *Newsweek,* 29 June 1998, 19.

3. Witte, *From Sacrament to Contract,* 10.

4. Wendell Berry, *A Continuous Harmony: Essays Cultural and Agricultural* (New York: Harcourt Brace Jovanovich, 1972), 162.

5. Barbara Vobejda, "Decline of Traditional Families Has Slowed, Census Reports," *Lexington Herald Leader* 28 May 1998, A3.

6. Don S. Browning et al., *From Culture Wars to Common Ground: Religion and the American Family Debate* (Louisville, Ky.: Westminster John Knox Press, 1997), 106.

7. Witte, *From Sacrament to Contract,* 214–15.

8. Ted Peters, *For the Love of Children: Genetic Technology and the Future of the Family,* The Family, Religion, and Culture (Louisville, Ky.: Westminster John Knox Press, 1996), 4.

9. Mary Potter Engel, "Evil, Sin, and Violation of the Vulnerable," from *Lift Every Voice: Constructing Christian Theologies from the Underside,* ed. Susan Brooks Thistlethwaite and Mary Potter Engel (San Francisco: HarperSanFrancisco, 1990), 152–53.

10. Mary Stewart Van Leeuwen et al., *After Eden: Facing the Challenge of Gender Reconciliation* (Grand Rapids, Mich.: Eerdmans, 1993), 514.

11. Anne E. Patrick, *Liberating Conscience: Feminist Explorations in Catholic Moral Theology* (New York: Continuum, 1996), 155.

12. E. Farley, *Good and Evil,* 41–42.

13. Rebecca S. Chopp, *Saving Work: Feminist Practices of Theological Education* (Louisville, Ky.: Westminster/John Knox Press, 1995), 56.

14. Department of Justice, Bureau of Investigation, "Uniform Crime Reports for the United States" (Washington, D.C.: GPO, 1996), 24.

15. "Are We Really Living in a Rape Culture?" in *Transforming a Rape Culture,* ed. Emilie Buchwald, Pamela Fletcher, and Martha Roth (Minneapolis: Milkweed Editions, 1993), 8.

16. Information from Lexington Rape Crisis Center of Central Kentucky brochure

17. "Are We Really Living in a Rape Culture?"

18. Laurel Fingler, "Teenagers in Survey Condone Forced Sex," *Ms.,* February 1981, 23.

19. Karen Lebacqz, "Appropriate Vulnerability," in *Sexuality and the Sacred: Sources for Theological Reflection,* ed. James B. Nelson and Sandra P. Longfellow (Louisville, Ky.: Westminster/John Knox Press, 1994), 260.

20. Lewis Smedes, "Respect for Covenant," in *From Christ to the World: Introductory Readings in Christian Ethics,* ed. Wayne G. Boulton, Thomas D. Kennedy, and Allen Verhey (Grand Rapids, Mich.: Eerdmans, 1994), 351.

21. John B. Cobb Jr., *Matters of Life and Death* (Louisville, Ky.: Westminster/John Knox Press, 1991).

22. James B. Nelson, *Embodiment: An Approach to Sexuality and Christian Theology* (New York: Pilgrim Press, 1978): 358.

23. Philip W. Turner III, excerpt from "Limited Engagements," in *From Christ to the World*, ed. Wayne G. Boulton, Thomas D. Kennedy, and Allen Verhey (Grand Rapids, Mich.: Eerdmans, 1994), 360.

24. Nelson, *Embodiment*, 258–61.

25. Marvin M. Ellison, *Erotic Justice: A Liberating Ethic of Sexuality* (Louisville, Ky.: Westminster John Knox Press, 1996), 4.

26. Ibid., 120.

27. Ibid., 78.

28. Ibid., 86.

29. James Luther Adams, *The Prophethood of All Believers* (Boston: Beacon Press, 1986), 30.

30. Ellison, *Erotic Justice*, 77, 106.

31. John Leland and Mark Miller, "Can Gays Convert?" *Newsweek*, 17 August 1998, 51.

32. Max L. Stackhouse, *Covenant and Commitments: Faith, Family, and Economic Life*, The Family, Religion, and Culture (Louisville, Ky.: Westminster John Knox Press, 1997), 14, 17, 28.

33. Paula M. Cooey, *Family, Freedom, and Faith: Building Community Today* (Louisville, Ky.: Westminster/John Knox Press, 1993).

34. William Johnson Everett, *Blessed Be the Bond: Christian Perspectives on Marriage and the Family* (Philadelphia: Fortress Press, 1985), 101–4.

35. Don S. Browning et al., *From Culture Wars to Common Ground: Religion and the American Family Debate*, The Family, Religion, and Culture (Louisville, Ky.: Westminster John Knox Press, 1997), 287.

36. Everett, *Blessed Be the Bond*, 94–101.

37. H. Richard Niebuhr, *Faith on Earth* (New Haven, Conn.: Yale University Press, 1989), 52, 56.

38. Peters, *For the Love of Children*, 120. Peters requests both, "no babies without sex" and "no sex without babies."

39. Peters, 174, about Cahill.

40. Stackhouse, *Covenant and Commitments*, 22.

41. Bonnie Miller-McLemore, *Also a Mother: Work and Family as a Theological Dilemma* (Nashville: Abingdon Press, 1994), 92. The same point about the sharing of "mothering" is made in Browning, *From Culture Wars to Common Ground*, 356, and Peters, *For the Love of Children*.

42. Patricia Cohen, "Daddy Dearest: Do You Really Matter?" *New York Times* 11 July 1998, A11.

43. Sonya Ross, "Rule Change Gives Poor, Working Couples Medicaid," *Louisville Courier-Journal*, 5 August 1998, A3.

44. Kurt Vonnegut Jr., "Playboy Interview," in *Slapstick or Lonesome No More! A Novel* (New York: Delacorte Press, 1976); Kurt Vonnegut Jr., *Wampeters, Foma, and Granfalloons* (New York: Dell Publishing, 1974), 248; a speech by Kurt Vonnegut Jr., Lexington, Ky., 1 November 1993, sponsored by Midway College.

45. "A Day in the Life of America's Children," *Peaceways* (April 1996).

46. Eileen W. Lindner, "Ecumenical and Interdenominational: Private and Public Approaches to Family Issues," in *Faith Traditions and the Family*, ed. Phyllis D. Airhart and Margaret Lamberts Bendroth (Louisville, Ky.: Westminster John Knox Press, 1996), 163; Lisa Sowle Cahill, "Sex, Gender, and the Common Good: Family," in *Religion, Ethics, and the Common Good*, ed. James Donahue and M. Theresa Moser, R.S.C.J. (Mystic, Conn.: Twenty-Third Publications, 1996), 145.

47. Daphne J. Anderson and Terence R. Anderson, "United Church of Canada: Kingdom Symbol or Lifetime Choice?" in *Faith Traditions and the Family*, ed. Phyllis D. Airhart and Margaret Lamberts Bendroth (Louisville, Ky.: Westminster John Knox Press, 1996), 126–42.

48. William P. DeVeaux, "African Methodist Episcopal: Nurturing a Sense of 'Somebodyness,'" in *Faith Traditions and the Family*, ed. Phyllis D. Airhart and Margaret Lamberts Bendroth (Louisville, Ky.: Westminster John Knox Press, 1996).

49. Cooey, *Family, Freedom, and Faith*, 5, 101.

50. Ibid., 40.

51. Peters, *For the Love of Children*, 112–14. The differentiation process is what distinguishes one individual from another, and it is called the primitive streak. The process begins, according to Peters, "when the inner embryonic mass becomes surrounded by an outer or epiblastic form" (p. 114).

52. Thomas A. Shannon and Allen B. Wolter, O.F.M., "Reflections on the Moral Status of the Pre-Embryo," in *Bioethics: Basic Writings on the Key Ethical Questions That Surround the Major, Modern Biological Possibilities and Problems*, 4th ed., ed. Thomas A. Shannon (Mahwah, N.J.: Paulist Press, 1993).

53. William Werpehowski, "The Pathos and Promise of Christian Ethics: A Study of the Abortion Debate," *Horizons* 12, no. 2 (1985): 295.

54. Beverly Wildung Harrison, *Our Right to Choose: Toward a New Ethic of Abortion* (Boston: Beacon Press, 1983), 255, 256.

55. Marjorie Reiley Maguire, "Personhood, Covenant, and Abortion," *Annual of the Society of Christian Ethics* (1983): 117–45.

56. Peters, *For the Love of Children*, 55, 110–16.

57. Bellah et al., *The Good Society*.

58. Jürgen Habermas, "Moral Consciousness and Communicative Action," in *Discourse Ethics: Notes on a Program of Philosophical Justification*, trans. Christian Lenhardt and Sherry Weber Nicholsen (Cambridge: MIT Press, 1990), 86; Seyla Benhabib, *Situating the Self: Gender, Community, and Postmodernism in a Contemporary Ethics* (New York: Routledge, 1992), 29. Benhabib attaches these names to the principles found in Habermas.

59. Susan Moller Okin, *Justice, Gender, and the Family* (New York: Basic Books, 1989), 18–19; Bonnie J. Miller-McLemore, *Also a Mother: Work and Family as a Theological Dilemma* (Nashville: Abingdon Press, 1994), especially chap. 7.

60. *Lumen Gentium* (no. 11) from Vatican II and *Familiaris Consortio* (no. 12) from John Paul II are her specific citations. Cahill, "Sex, Gender, and the Common Good: Family," 162; Thomas A. Shannon, "Response to Lisa Sowle Cahill's "Sex, Gender, and the Common Good: Family," in *Religion, Ethics, and the Common Good*,

eds. James Donahue and M. Theresa Moser, R.S.C.J. (Mystic, Conn.: Twenty-Third Publications, 1996), 171; Stackhouse, *Covenant and Commitments*, 87.

4.   Covenants of Work, Family, and Welfare

1. Wendell Berry, *A Continuous Harmony: Essays Cultural and Agricultural* (New York: Harcourt Brace Jovanovich, 1972), 160–61.

2. Ibid., 164.

3. Advisory Committee on Social Witness Policy of the General Assembly Council, *God's Work in Our Hands: Employment, Community, and Christian Vocation* (Louisville, Ky.: The Office of the General Assembly, Presbyterian Church [USA], 1995), 10–11.

4. United States Catholic Bishops, *Economic Justice for All*, par. 71.

5. Rosemary J. Brown, "Sweatshop and Child Labor: Exploding the Myths," and "Where in the World Are All the Children Working?" *Co-Op America Quarterly*, no. 42 (summer 1997): 16–17; information from National Labor Committee brochure—"The People's Right to Know Campaign: A Call for Corporate Disclosure."

6. Scott Adams, *The Dilbert Principle: A Cubicle's View of Bosses, Meetings, Management Fads, and Other Workplace Afflictions* (New York: HarperBusiness, 1996).

7. Rebecca Goodell, "National Business Ethics Survey Findings," *Ethics Journal* (fall/winter 1994): 1, 3, 5.

8. Anne Wilson Schaef and Diane Fassel, *The Addictive Organization: Why We Overwork, Cover Up, Pick Up the Pieces, Please the Boss, and Perpetuate Sick Organizations* (San Francisco: Harper and Row, 1988).

9. Advisory Committee on Social Witness Policy, "God's Work in Our Hands," 10–15.

10. William F. May, "On Slaying the Dragon: The American Myth," in *From Christ to the World: Introductory Readings in Christian Ethics*, ed. Wayne G. Boulton, Thomas D. Kennedy, and Allen Verhey (Grand Rapids, Mich.: Eerdmans, 1994); William F. May, "Moral Leadership in the Corporate Setting," in *Profits and Professions: Essays in Business and Professional Ethics*, ed. Wade L. Robison et al. (Clifton, N.J.: Humana Press, 1983); Charles McCoy, *Management of Values* (Boston: Pittman, 1985), 223–24; Douglas Sturm, *Community and Alienation: Essays on Process Thought and Public Life* (Notre Dame, Ind.: University of Notre Dame Press, 1988), 112–13; Max L. Stackhouse, *Public Theology and Political Economy* (Grand Rapids, Mich.: Eerdmans, 1987), 24–26, 127, 135; Eric Mount Jr., *Professional Ethics in Context: Institutions, Images, and Empathy* (Louisville, Ky.: Westminster/John Knox Press, 1990), 62–69; Laura L. Nash, *Good Intentions Aside: A Manager's Guide to Resolving Ethical Problems* (Boston: Harvard Business School Press, 1991), 20–22, 98, 101, 110, 121.

11. Stewart W. Herman, "The Modern Business Corporation and an Ethic of Trust," *Journal of Religious Ethics* 20, no. 1 (spring 1992): 111–48.

12. Ken Estey, "A Case Study in Covenantal Business Ethics: Employee Man-

agement Participation Programs" (paper presented at the Thirty-Ninth Annual Meeting of the Society of Christian Ethics, Atlanta, Ga., 9 January 1998).

13. John C. Raines and Donna C. Day-Lower, *Modern Work and Human Meaning* (Philadelphia: Westminster Press, 1986), 52.

14. Information from National Labor Committee brochure—"The People's Right to Know Campaign: A Call for Corporate Disclosure."

15. Joseph Allen, *Love and Conflict: A Covenantal Model of Christian Ethics* (Nashville: Abingdon Press, 1984), chap. 5.

16. Sandra G. Boodman, "Stress Hormones Are High in Working Mothers, Study Finds," *Louisville Courier-Journal*, 31 August 1997, H1; David Coburn, "Will We Ever Close the Gap?" *Charlotte Observer*, 1 September 1997, 10D.

17. Coburn, "Will We Ever Close the Gap?" 10D–11D.

18. Maggie Jackson, "Study: Family Life Low on Employer's List," *USA Today*, 15 July 1998, 4B.

19. Coburn, "Will We Ever Close the Gap?" 10D.

20. Ibid.

21. Ibid., 10D–11D.

22. Joseph B. White and Carol Hymowitz, "Glass-Ceiling Breakers Have Many Traits in Common," *Louisville Courier-Journal*, 16 February 1997, E1.

23. Arlie R. Hochschild, *Time Bind: When Work Becomes Home and Home Becomes Work* (New York: Metropolitan Books, 1997); Arlie R. Hochschild, *Second Shift: Working Parents and the Revolution at Home* (New York: Viking, 1989).

24. Ellen Goodman, "A Nation of Workaholics," *Louisville Courier-Journal*, 3 June 1997, A7.

25. Susan Moller Okin, *Justice, Gender, and the Family* (New York: Basic Books, 1989).

26. S. Adams, *The Dilbert Principle*, chap. 26.

27. *Marriage in America: A Report to the Nation* (New York: Council on Families in America of the Institute for American Values, 1995). The Browning team that produced the Family, Religion, and Culture series also advocates the combined sixty-hour week. Don S. Browning et al., *From Culture Wars to Common Ground: Religion and the American Family Debate* (Louisville, Ky.: Westminster John Knox Press, 1997), 25, 177, 327–28.

28. Marsha Weinstein, "A Women-Led Agenda," *Louisville Courier-Journal*, 25 April 1997, 11A.

29. Fian Fact Sheet, "Welfare by Corporations Is Corporate Welfare," http://www.foodfirst.org/corpwell.htm.

30. "Not Old against Young, But Rich against Poor," *Economist*, 11 January 1997, 24; John Heilemann, "The GOP's War on the Poor," *Louisville Courier-Journal*, 31 October 1995, 9A; "Facts about Wealth and Poverty in the World," *Peaceways* (August 1998): 5; Ellen Goodman, "Checking Up on the CEOs' Paycheck," *The Courier-Journal* (Louisville, Ky.), April 16, 1999, A9.

31. Warren R. Copeland, *And the Poor Get Welfare* (Nashville: Abingdon Press, 1994); Frederick Edward Glennon, "Toward a Welfare Ethic: A Theological-

Ethical Critique of Poverty Policy in the United States" (Ph.D diss., Emory University, 1990); Frederick Edward Glennon, "Renewing the Welfare Covenant: Welfare Reform and Responsible Poverty Policy," in *Living Responsibly in Community*, ed. Glennon et al. (Lanham, Md.: University Press of America, 1997).

32. Robert Reich, *Tales of a New America* (New York: Times Books, 1987).

33. Copeland, *And the Poor Get Welfare*, 142.

34. Max L. Stackhouse, *Covenant and Commitments: Faith, Family, and Economic Life* (Louisville, Ky.: Westminster John Knox Press, 1997), 53–57.

35. Ronald F. Thiemann, *Religion in Public Life: A Dilemma for Democracy* (Washington, D.C.: Georgetown University Press, 1996), 109.

36. William F. May, *The Physician's Covenant: Images of the Healer in Medical Ethics* (Philadelphia: Westminster Press, 1983).

37. E. J. Dionne Jr., ed., *Community Works: The Revival of Civil Society in America* (Washington, D.C.: Brookings Institution Press, 1998), 3.

38. Stackhouse, *Covenant and Commitments*, 108.

39. John Wall, "The New Middle Ground in the Family Debate: A Report on the 1994 Conference of the Religion, Culture, and Family Project," *Criterion* 33 (autumn 1994): 25.

40. Paula M. Cooey, *Family, Freedom, and Faith: Building Community Today* (Louisville, Ky.: Westminster/John Knox Press, 1993), 93, 95 ff., 100, 116.

41. Bellah et al., *The Good Society*, 255–87.

42. Pamela D. Couture, "Rethinking Private and Public Patriarchy," in *Religion, Feminism, and the Family*, ed. Anne Carr and Mary Stewart Van Leeuwen (Louisville, Ky.: Westminster John Knox Press, 1996), 267–72.

5.   Global Community, Covenant, and the Common Good

1. Pope John XXIII, "Pacem in Terris," in *Proclaiming Justice and Peace: Papal Documents from Rerum Novarum through Centesimus Annus*, ed. Michael Walsh and Brian Davies (Mystic, Conn.: Twenty-Third Publications, 1991), par. 132.

2. Herman E. Daly and John B. Cobb Jr., *For the Common Good* (Boston: Beacon Press, 1989), 177.

3. Michael Walzer, *Thick and Thin: Moral Arguments at Home and Abroad* (Notre Dame, Ind.: University of Notre Dame Press, 1994), 81–82.

4. Daly and Cobb, *For the Common Good*, 177.

5. Jean Raspail, *The Camp of the Saints* (Petoskey, Mich.: Social Contract Press, 1995).

6. Matthew Connelly and Paul Kennedy, "Must It Be the Rest against the West?" *Atlantic Monthly*, December 1994, 69, 76.

7. Ibid., 76.

8. Daly and Cobb, *For the Common Good*, 172.

9. William Drozdiak, "French, Germans Nudging EU in Different Directions," *Washington Post*, 6 January 1995, A25.

10. Arthur Schlesinger Jr., "Three Steps to Tame Tribalism and Unify Europe," *International Herald Tribune*, 17 June 1994, 6.

11. Eric Gorham, "Disintegrating Theories of Integration," *Soundings* 77, no. 1–2 (spring/summer 1994): 191.

12. Giles Merritt, "European Community: Look Outward to the World," *International Herald Tribune*, 20 July 1998, 4.

13. Schlesinger, "Three Steps to Tame Tribalism and Unify Europe," 6.

14. Merritt, "European Community: Look Outward to the World,"4.

15. Gustavo Gutiérrez, *A Theology of Liberation*, trans. Sister Caridad Inda and John Eagleson (Maryknoll, N.Y.: Orbis Books, 1991); Richard Axtell, "Nicaragua, the World Bank, and Our Blue Jeans: A Case Study in the Ethics of Development" (paper presented at the Southeastern Commission for the Study of Religion, Macon, Ga., 15 March 1997).

16. Samir Amin, *Eurocentrism*, trans. Russell Moore (New York: Monthly Review Press, 1989), 84, 87, 89, 107.

17. Ibid., 139, 152.

18. Christopher Layton, *Europe and the Global Crisis: A First Exploration of Europe's Potential Contribution to World Order* (London: International Institute for Environment and Development and Federal Trust for Education and Research, 1986), 70.

19. H. Richard Niebuhr, *The Responsible Self* (New York: Harper and Row, 1963), 87.

20. Jürgen Habermas, "Moral Consciousness and Communicative Action," in *Discourse Ethics: Notes on a Program of Philosophical Justification*, trans. Christian Lenhardt and Sherry Weber Nicholsen (Cambridge: MIT Press, 1990), 86; Seyla Benhabib, *Situating the Self: Gender, Community, and Postmodernism in a Contemporary Ethics* (New York: Routledge, 1992), 29.

21. Reich, *Tales of a New America*.

22. John B. Cobb Jr., "For the Sake of the World," *The Spire* 16, no. 1 (winter 1994): 19–21.

23. Al Gore, *Earth in the Balance: Ecology and the Human Spirit* (New York: Penguin, 1993), 269.

24. Fasching, *The Ethical Challenge of Auschwitz and Hiroshima*, 179.

25. Ibid., 192.

26. Ibid., 144–45.

27. Glen Stassen, "Michael Walzer's Situated Justice," *Journal of Religious Ethics* 22, no. 2 (fall 1994): 381; Heiner Bielefeldt, "Muslim Voices in the Human Rights Debate," *Human Rights Quarterly* 17, no. 4 (1995): 587–617; Goran Hyden, "The Challenges of Domesticating Rights in Africa," in *Human Rights and Governance in Africa*, ed. Ronald Cohen, Goran Hyden, and Winston P. Nagan (Gainesville: University Press of Florida, 1993), 256–80; Amartya Sen, "Universal Truths: Human Rights and the Westernizing Illusion," *Harvard International Review* 20, no. 3 (1998): 40–43. My Centre colleague, Nayef Samhat, guided me to these sources concerning a range of religions.

28. Alasdair MacIntyre, *After Virtue: A Study in Moral Theory* (Notre Dame, Ind.: University of Notre Dame Press, 1981), 69.

29. Walzer, "The Divided Self."

30. Douglas Sturm, "Human Rights and Political Responsibility: A Religious Inquiry," *Criterion* 26, no. 1 (winter 1989): 7; Douglas Sturm, *Solidarity and Suffering: Toward a Politics of Relationality* (Albany: State University of New York Press, 1998), chap 2.

31. Carlos Fuentes, "500 Years Later" (address at Transylvania University, Lexington, Ky., 4 November 1991), is the source of the claim about every Latin American baby.

32. Ronnie D. Lipschutz, "Reconstructing World Politics: The Emergence of Global Civil Society," *Millennium: Journal of International Studies* 21, no. 3 (1992): 389–420; Paul Wapner, *Environmental Activism and World Civic Politics* (Albany: State University of New York Press, 1996).

33. Andrew Linklater, "The Question of the Next Stage in International Relations Theory: A Critical-Theoretical Point of View," *Millennium: Journal of International Studies* 21, no.1 (1992): 77–98.

34. Nayef H. Samhat, "International Regimes as Political Community," *Millennium: Journal of International Studies* 26, no. 2 (1997): 349–78.

35. Habermas, *Discourse Ethics*; Benhabib, *Situating the Self.*

36. Walzer, *Thick and Thin*, 8.

6.   Covenantal Virtue for the Common Good

1. May, *Testing the Medical Covenant*, 56.

2. Bellah et al., *The Good Society*, 4.

3. Amitai Etzioni, *The New Golden Rule: Community and Morality in a Democratic Society* (New York: Basic Books, 1996), 241, 244.

4. Wendell Berry, *A Continuous Harmony: Essays Cultural and Agricultural* (New York: Harcourt Brace Jovanovich, 1972), 157.

5. Ibid., 152, 165.

6. Niebuhr, *The Responsible Self*, 118.

7. Berry, *A Continuous Harmony*, 159.

8. Peter C. Hodgson, *Winds of the Spirit: A Constructive Christian Theology* (Louisville, Ky.: Westminster/John Knox Press, 1994), 204–8.

9. Fasching, *Narrative Theology after Auschwitz*, 6, 15–16, 73, 123, 126, 187–88.

10. Leo Rosten, *The Joys of Yiddish* (New York: Pocket Books, 1968).

11. Anne E. Patrick, *Liberating Conscience: Feminist Explorations in Catholic Moral Theology* (New York: Continuum, 1996), 105, 116.

12. "Perspectives," *Newsweek*, 9 May 1994, 19.

13. Walter Lowe, "Militarism, Evil, and the Reign of God," in *Reconstructing Christian Theology*, ed. Rebecca S. Chopp and Mark Lewis Taylor (Minneapolis: Fortress Press, 1994), 200.

14. E. J. Dionne Jr., ed., *Community Works: The Revival of Civil Society in America* (Washington, D.C.: Brookings Institution Press, 1998), 28.

15. Martin Luther King Jr., "Letter from a Birmingham Jail," in *Why We Can't Wait* (New York: Penguin Books, 1963), 86.

16. Russell Watson, Joseph Contreras, and Joshua Hammer, "Black Power!" *Newsweek*, 9 May 1994, 34, 39.

17. Jim Wallis reports this statement made by Nelson Mandela in *The Soul of Politics: Beyond "Religious Right" and "Secular Left"* (San Diego: Harcourt Brace, 1995), 280.

18. Ibid., 278.

19. Paul W. Taylor, "The Ethics of Respect for Nature," in *Environmental Philosophy: From Animal Rights to Radical Ecology*, ed. Michael E. Zimmerman et al. (Englewood Cliffs, N.J.: Prentice-Hall, 1993), 71.

20. Wendell Berry, *Remembering* (San Francisco: North Point Press, 1988).

21. James M. Gustafson, *Can Ethics Be Christian?* (Chicago: University of Chicago Press, 1975), 110.

22. E. Farley, *Deep Symbols*, 106.

23. Martin Luther King Jr., "A Tough Mind and a Tender Heart," in *Strength to Love* (Philadelphia: Fortress Press, 1963), 16.

24. André Brink, "The End of Separateness," *Newsweek*, 9 May 1994, 39.

25. E. Farley, *Deep Symbols*, 49.

26. H. Richard Niebuhr in collaboration with Daniel Day Williams and James M. Gustafson, *The Purpose of the Church and Its Ministry: Reflections on the Aims of Theological Education* (New York: Harper and Brothers, 1956), 35.

27. Wendy Farley, *Eros for the Other: Retaining Truth in a Pluralistic World* (University Park: Pennsylvania State University Press, 1996), 76–78.

28. Elie Wiesel, *The Town beyond the Wall*, trans. Stephen Becker (New York: Schocken Books, 1964), 118.

29. Nel Noddings, *Caring* (Berkeley: University of California Press, 1984), 30.

30. Richard Zaner, *Ethics and the Clinical Encounter* (Englewood Cliffs, N.J.: Prentice-Hall, 1988), 318.

31. Wendy Farley, *Tragic Vision and Divine Compassion: A Contemporary Theodicy* (Louisville, Ky.: Westminster/John Knox Press, 1990).

32. Ibid., 81, 87.

33. Ibid., 81.

34. Anne E. Patrick, *Liberating Conscience*, 78, 86.

35. Wendell Berry, commencement address at Centre College, Danville, Ky., June 1978.

36. May, *Testing the Medical Covenant*, 74, 80.

37. Bill Bradley, "America's Challenge: Revitalizing Our National Community," in *Community Works*, ed. E. J. Dionne Jr. (Washington, D.C.: Brookings Institution Press, 1998), 113.

38. Ibid., 107.

39. William F. May, *A Catalogue of Sins: A Contemporary Examination of Chris-*

tian Conscience (New York: Holt, Rinehart, and Winston, 1967), 79. May's fourth chapter, "The Sin against the Brother: Envy," offers a most insightful discussion of envy in general and of its being a sin of the eyes in particular.

40. Judith Rich Harris, *The Nurture Assumption: Why Children Turn Out the Way They Do; Parents Matter Less Than You Think and Peers Matter More* (New York: Free Press, 1998), 39.

41. Timothy P. Jackson, "Liberalism and Agape: The Priority of Charity to Democracy and Philosophy," *Annual of the Society of Christian Ethics* (1993): 47–72; James E. Gilman, "Compassion and Public Covenant: Christian Faith in Public Life," *Journal of Church and State* 36 (autumn 1994): 747–71.

42. Eric Mount Jr., *Professional Ethics in Context: Institutions, Images, and Empathy* (Louisville, Ky.: Westminster/John Knox Press, 1990), 101; Laird Harrison, "Playing the Aging Game: Through the Eyes of the Elderly," *Duke Alumni Magazine* 78, no. 1 (October–November 1991): 37–39.

43. Nelle Morton, *The Journey Is Home* (Boston: Beacon Press, 1985), 202–10.

44. Ronald F. Thiemann, *Religion in Public Life: A Dilemma for Democracy* (Washington, D.C.: Georgetown University Press, 1996), 95.

45. Bradley, "America's Challenge," 110.

46. Clifford Christians et al., *Good News: Social Ethics and the Press* (New York: Oxford University Press, 1993), 110, 116.

47. Jackson, "Liberalism and Agape," 72.

48. Max L. Stackhouse, *Covenant and Commitments: Faith, Family, and Economic Life* (Louisville, Ky.: Westminster John Knox Press, 1997), 22.

49. Ibid., 7, 22, 165 n. 20.

INDEX

Gustafson, James, 49, 113
Gutiérrez, Gustavo, 116
Gutman, Amy, 22

Haas, Ernst, 129
Habermas, Jürgen, 77, 119, 130, 136, 153
Harrington, Michael, 100
Harris, Judith Rich, 157
Harrison, Beverly Wildung, 75
Hartman, Edwin M., 39–42, 83
Hauerwas, Stanley, 2, 125
health care, 5, 50, 148, 150; and common good, 32–33; health care, poverty, and welfare, 84, 96, 105; systems, 35
Hebraic tradition, 1, 15, 19, 21, 25, 61, 145. *See also* Israel
Herman, Stewart, 85–86
heterosexism, 45–46, 55, 63, 65, 84
hierarchy, 10, 13–15, 31, 34, 44, 49, 78
Hinduism, 31, 49, 117
Hirschman, Albert, 39, 44
Hochschild, Arlie, 90
Hodgson, Peter, 136
Hollenbach, David, 18, 42
Holocaust, 17–18, 136–37
home–work bind, 87–94
homosexuality, 4, 45, 55–57, 64–67, 69, 155
hope, 7–8, 137–44
hospitality to strangers, 16, 18, 26, 47, 81, 124, 159; faith as, 135–36
human rights, 67, 109, 117, 130; Catholic bishops' statement on, 43; as core value for global community, 18, 51, 123–28; opposition to universal human rights claim, 125; various understandings of, 123, 125

idealism, 128
identity, 2, 7; as community requirement, 33–34, 46, 50, 68; covenant and new identity, 132; deep symbols and, 4, 9; European, 109, 114–15;

home and work identities, 84, 91, 94; Israelite, 48, 57, 81; problems of closed or narrow identity, 15–16, 25–26, 34, 119, 123, 159, 163 n. 22
idolatry, 12–13, 24, 29, 50, 67, 119, 140, 143
image of God, 16, 42, 45, 57, 67, 97, 120
immigration, 110–11, 113–14
inclusion. *See* exclusion
individualism: in Canadian and U.S. constitutions, 35; contrast of covenant and common traditions to liberal individualism, 1–3; "The Triumphant Individual" as morality tale, 98–99, 101; tie to contractualism, 49; types of American individualism, 11, 23–24, 31
individuality, respect for, 33–34, 46, 68, 84, 112, 126. *See also* difference
inheritance myth, 70
institutions: attention to, 76, 105; bureaucracy institutions, 105; covenants and, 28; democratic, 106; families as, 65, 76; global, 39, 129, 131; institutional cultures, 40–41, 83, 91, 92; institutionalization as danger, 91; institutional racism, 50; institutional vice and virtue, 50, 83, 133, 135; intermediate, 100; law as institution, 132; marriage as institution, 52; professions and schools as, 103; social institutions as third human reality, 49
integration, in Europe, 107–12, 114, 118, 128
interdependence, 42, 44, 45, 158. *See also* solidarity
interhuman, the, 25–26, 57
intermediate institutions, 100, 106–7. *See also* civil society
International Monetary Fund, 116, 120–21
Isasi-Díaz, Ada María, 14
Islam, 18, 19, 31, 117, 121, 124; in Europe, 109, 113–14